The Life and
the Adventures of
a Haunted Convict

The Life and the adventures

of a Haunted convict

Or the inmate of a gloomy prison

With the mysteries and miseries

of the New York House of Reffuge

and Auburn Prison unmasked
With the rules and regulations of
Auburn prison from — 1840 — up
to the present time — and the different
modes of punishments

The Life and
the Adventures of a
Haunted Convict

Edited and with an Introduction
by Caleb Smith
Foreword by David W. Blight
and Robert B. Stepto

RANDOM HOUSE

NEW YORK

Published in the United States by Random House, an imprint and division
of Penguin Random House LLC, New York.

RANDOM HOUSE and the HOUSE colophon are registered trademarks
of Penguin Random House LLC.

LIBRARY OF CONGRESS CATALOGING-IN-PUBLICATION DATA
Reed, Austin, 1823?–
The life and the adventures of a haunted convict / by Austin Reed; edited by
Caleb Smith; with a foreword by David W. Blight and Robert B. Stepto.
pages cm
ISBN 978-0-8129-9709-5
eBook ISBN 978-0-8129-9710-1
1. Reed, Austin, 1823?– 2. African American prisoners—New York (State)—
Biography. 3. African Americans—Biography. 4. Reformatories—New
York (State)—History—19th century. 5. Prisons—New York (State)—
History—19th century. 6. United States—Social conditions—
19th century. 7. United States—Race relations—History—
19th century. I. Smith, Caleb, 1977– II. Title.
HV9468.R44A3 2016
365'.34—dc23
[B]
2015017693

Printed in the United States of America on acid-free paper

randomhousebooks.com

2 4 6 8 9 7 5 3 1

First Edition

Book design by Victoria Wong

Foreword

by David W. Blight and Robert B. Stepto

R eading *The Life and the Adventures of a Haunted Convict* today, in our era of mass incarceration and militarized policing, we immediately feel the force of Austin Reed's protest against the horrors of New York's House of Refuge and the Auburn State Prison. However, like the best of memoirs, this fascinating book has no one single task. Composed when the author was in his mid-thirties, it attempts to make sense of his life since his early childhood. Reed was not born into slavery, but as we get to know him in his pages we are well aware that he is a young African American, attempting to find his way in the antebellum United States. Like many of his contemporaries— enslaved, fugitive, and free—the story Reed had to tell was one of harsh oppression and grinding exploitation. It was also the story of the development of his own mind. Carefully authenticated by Caleb Smith and a team of researchers from Yale University and elsewhere, Reed's book can now be placed in the great literary tradition that has rendered black life and experience from the first-person point of view. By 1858, when Reed concluded his account, the tradition already included a rich variety of slave narratives, poems, sermons, speeches, and works of fiction—but there was nothing quite like this sustained treatment of African American life inside the prison system that was just taking its modern shape.

As Reed's memoir circles back, again and again, to Rochester, New York, we are especially intrigued to consider him alongside another African American writer who has been central to our own scholarship on the tradition. Frederick Douglass escaped from slavery in the South and, in time, took up residence in Reed's home city. In a trilogy of autobiographical works, Douglass offered some of the most memorable castigations of American slavery ever written. "Such is the constitution of the human mind," he wrote in 1855, "that when pressed to extremes, it often avails itself of the most opposite methods. Extremes meet in mind as in matter." Looking back on his experience as a slave child on a Maryland plantation, Douglass remembered a world of stark opposites, all but unalterable extremes he had to learn to navigate and survive. The plantation South of his childhood was a place of beauty and evil, of decadence and production, both his playground and his "prison." (Douglass's rendering of slavery is full of prison metaphors.) As he became more aware of his predicament, he tried desperately to protect his body from destruction and to preserve his mind from disintegration.

Douglass famously told the story of his rise from bondage into freedom. Reed's story moves in the opposite direction, describing his fall from a tenuous liberty into the isolation and torment of incarceration. In this way, *The Life and the Adventures of a Haunted Convict* provokes us to reconsider nineteenth-century African American literature and, indeed, the long arc of American history. Reading Austin Reed in the twenty-first century, we see how the formal abolition of Southern slavery may not have secured the liberty that Douglass risked everything to obtain for himself and many thousands more. Even before the Civil War, the free North was already building the penal system that now imprisons nearly a million African Americans. A century and a half after emancipation, one in three black men will spend time under confinement in America's prisons and jails. Reed came of age inside some of the earliest institutions of penal captivity, and he had his own ideas about freedom, which seemed always to be receding beyond his grasp. In the meantime, he did his best to hold on to the elements of a life—physical safety, a basic education, and a sense of belonging.

Two of Douglass's insights have special resonance as we study

Reed's pages. First, thinking in part about his own childhood, Douglass declares that all slaves are orphans. Douglass never knew the true identity of his father, although it was likely one of his first two owners, and after the age of six he never again saw his mother, Harriet Bailey. Douglass spent much of his life trying to establish a durable identity and a sustainable set of relationships. Reed's history of incarceration, too, is a story about being orphaned from his home and his race. We note that Reed begins not at the House of Refuge but rather at the deathbed of his father, who is gasping his last breaths and giving his last fatherly advice. From this passage forward, the memoir tells of Reed's search for family. Revealingly, Reed almost always capitalizes the word *Home*.

Reed introduces us to a number of men who have been paternal figures or reminded him of his own father. One is Nathaniel Hart, or "Mr. Heart," a superintendent of the House of Refuge, whose farewell address is praised by Reed because it offers the "very parting words of my beloved father." Hart is replaced by Samuel S. Wood, who arranges for Reed's education in reading and writing. Later in the memoir, Reed recites a poem he learned thanks to Mr. Wood. Quite significantly, it is an antislavery poem. Mr. Wood, the man most responsible for Reed's literacy in his early years, is the abolitionist father figure in the memoir. At one point, Reed temporarily escapes from the reformatory, and he is taken into the home of a Mr. McCollough, the father of another Refuge boy. When the authorities come for Reed, McCollough confronts them. Reed is captured and reincarcerated in the end, but for an unforgettable moment McCollough becomes a protective father figure, a man standing up for Reed and against the reformatory.

Reed remembers Hart, Wood, and McCollough with fondness, for he had not always been treated so kindly by the men who had custody of him. Indeed, he had suffered many of the hardships that modern readers might associate with slavery. His first crime, we learn, is an act of vengeance, prompted by the indignity of being "tied up like a slave" and whipped. Many more whippings will occur in Reed's future, including the especially brutal beating he receives from Mr. Terry, the Presbyterian minister who takes over the House of Refuge after Samuel Wood's departure. With the Reverend Mr. Terry we are reminded of those moments in slave narratives when men of the cloth are depicted as particularly harsh, even vicious, slaveholders. As it turns out, the House of Refuge is hardly a refuge. Like the names of the slave ships that Robert Hayden invokes in his poem "Middle Passage"—names like *Mercy*, *Adventure*, and *Amistad*—House of Refuge is a "bright ironical name."

All of the father figures Reed mentions are white men. His mother is apparently alive in Rochester, but the women who take young Reed in and feed him are the Irish mothers of New York. Mrs. Flinn stands out in that regard. She is the mother of Mike Flinn, who joins Reed and Jack Kimbell in Reed's first attempt to escape the House of Refuge. Mike and Jack are Reed's tutors as well as his accomplices in the escape; arguably, they become the brothers in his life after Reed's family is, for him, demolished. When Reed is jailed with a young Scotch girl from Canada, Fanny Miller, he finds a sister in the world of incarceration. The two young inmates read together, and Reed sings for Fanny, noting that he used to sing the same song with his own sister. These orphans are in search of love and friendship they can convert into notions of Home.

During his early years at Auburn State Prison, there comes a day when Reed breaks the rule against inmates sharing food with each other. He is caught and whipped, but the punishment doesn't stop there: He is dragged off to the prison's dungeon and put in stocks. What date does Reed remember that horrible day to be? The Fourth of July. And here we see a second connection to Douglass: a shared critique of the promises of American liberty and justice. In his great speech of 1852, Douglass asked, "What to the Slave Is the Fourth of July?" What the occasion demanded, said Douglass, was "scorching irony . . . withering sarcasm, and stern rebuke." The Fourth of July, to an African American in bondage, represented "gross injustice and cruelty": "To him," Douglass declared, "your celebration is a sham;

your boasted liberty, an unholy license; your national greatness, swelling vanity; . . . your shouts of liberty and equality, hollow mockery." Douglass had his address, the rhetorical masterpiece in an unparalleled career as an orator, printed and widely distributed. Could Reed have known about it? If so, he probably would have appreciated the biblical language and the Old Testament arguments, and he surely would have thrilled to Douglass's glorious attack against American hypocrisy. He may have summoned the memory of Douglass's words as he clenched his fists and teeth to face his next punishment. What, to the haunted convict, is the Fourth of July?

Despite his hardships, Reed was able to fashion himself as a playful and powerful writer. It is nothing short of marvelous to observe how he gains an author's ownership of the scenes of brutal whippings by inventing new, even dear, names for the lash; he refers to the implement of his punishment as "little kittens," "the darling little puss," and "them little fellows." Moreover, Reed can reflect on the broad shape of his entire narrative. A great example is his careful attention to the significance of possessing a Bible at key moments in his life. It begins when his mother gives him a "pocket bible" that contains a prayer she wrote. Later, shortly after the Fourth of July episode, Reed loses control and tears up a Bible in his prison cell. The tatters, he declares, represent the "mother's prayers and father's blessings beaten from me." When remorse sets in, Reed asks himself how he could have torn up *that* book: "that humble old monitor that learnt you A, B, C." These responses tell us much about what Reed has lost and what all his songs, poems, and stories might provide in helping him survive in his world.

Finding consolation and a resource of resistance in the written word, Austin Reed was not alone. Looking at what other African Americans produced in just the same decade, we find William Wells Brown's *Clotel* (1853), Solomon Northup's *Twelve Years a Slave* (1853), Frederick Douglass's *My Bondage and My Freedom* (1855), Harriet Wilson's *Our Nig* (1859), and the beginnings of Harriet Jacobs's *Incidents in the Life of a Slave Girl* (published in 1861). Now, at last, Austin Reed's *The Life and the Adventures of a Haunted Convict* (1858) joins these great works in the canon of classic African American literature, and we can rejoice at how it enriches a tradition that continues to grow and evolve. It is ever so important that *The Life and the Adventures of a Haunted Convict* is finally available to a wide reading public. It may forever change our understanding of antebellum America and the emerging institutions—well conceived or not—that became the foundations for the modern nation.

Contents

List of Illustrations

Editor's Introduction

"The Life and the Adventures of a Haunted Convict" surfaced at a Rochester, New York, estate sale a few years ago, a mystery out of the deeper American past. The manuscript appeared to have been finished in 1858. In a bound journal and two hand-sewn gatherings of loose paper, it gave a first-person account of a young black man's life as an indentured servant, a juvenile delinquent, and a prisoner in New York State. The author, calling himself "Rob Reed," composed in a steady, clear script. His spelling and grammar were irregular, but he was an accomplished reader and a gifted storyteller. In some places, his work followed the conventions of nineteenth-century popular literature. Elsewhere, in passages of fierce lamentation and lyricism, a more distinctive style emerged. Whoever he was, Reed seemed to be writing for an audience, pacing his adventures with a novelist's sense of plot and connecting his personal struggles to the public conflicts of the antebellum years. From a position just beyond the boundaries of Southern slavery, he described the rise of the new penal system that would capture so many thousands of black men and women in later years. The "Life and Adventures" was a haunting discovery—testimony from a painful history, prophecy of a violent future.

At first, almost nothing was known about Rob Reed or his manuscript. Could it be a draft of a sensational novel? A long-form criminal confession, taken down by a lawyer or a minister? Although the original sellers declined to say how they had acquired the text or where it had been kept, the rare book dealers who brought it to light believed that it was an autobiography. Using city directories and census records, they identified a handful of Reeds, people of color from Rochester who might have been related to the author—but their research came up against several dead ends. How did you pin down the 150-year-old history of a person who thought of himself as a fugitive and a vagabond, who lived in poverty and segregation, who spent most of his years locked up for petty crimes? The most important questions were still unanswered.

In 2009, when curators at Yale University's Beinecke Rare Book Library learned about the discovery of this manuscript, they asked David Blight, Robert Stepto, and me to take a look. I had been writing about the cultural history of America's prison system for a decade, but I had never seen anything quite like this before. I started working with archivists and researchers to find out anything we could about the document and its author. We searched through some of New York State's prison records, but there was no sure sign of any Rob or Robert Reed whose life conformed to the story we had read. Could the name be a pseudonym—and if so, how might we uncover the historical identity behind it? Genealogical databases and newspapers gave us no clearer answers. We turned to New York City's House of Refuge, the nation's first juvenile reformatory, which had stood on the Bowery in lower Manhattan in the 1830s. The author of the "Life and Adventures" remembered being sent there as a child. The Refuge kept good records, and they are well preserved in the New York State Archives in Albany. We found the case histories of some of the inmates mentioned in the manuscript. There was no Robert Reed, but there was a file for another boy named Reed, and it helped us to open up the mystery.

We recognized the handwriting as soon as we saw it. The key documents were two 1895 letters to the superintendent, sent by a former inmate who was trying to recover the details of his time in the Refuge, more than a half century earlier. The correspondent mentioned giving "a History of my life" and asked about the circumstances of his trial and confinement. He still knew his inmate number, 1221, and was able to provide the names of the men who had served as superintendent, assistant superintendent, and schoolteacher during his sentence. "I was the first colord boy that was bound out after the old Reffuge burnt down," he wrote. These were the memories—of the identity the institution had given him, of the officials who had watched over him, of a fire set by Refuge boys—which he hoped might lead to his file. "Will you please to do me the kindness as to look over some of your old record books and See if you can find my name in any of them[?]" he asked. "My name is Austin Reed."[1]

The reformatory staff had kept Austin Reed's file, including a brief account of the crime for which he had been confined. The case history identified Reed as a "boy of color" from Rochester. His father was dead, and his mother supported the family by taking in washing. Unlike many children in the reformatory, Reed had not been arrested for a crime of poverty; he was not a thief or a vagrant. "This bright looking little negro says that he never stole any thing," the superintendent noted, "but a Mr. Whitmore in Rochester whipped some boys— + they were determined to set his house on fire." These boys were not after money or bread. They resented being whipped, and setting a fire was their way of getting even. Some of them were sent to jail. Reed was given a few lashes, then released—but he had been initiated into crime and punishment. Within a year, he was making trouble again. Bound out to work as an indentured servant on the Ladd farm in the village of Avon Springs, he tried to burn the farmer's house to the ground. Local officials took him into custody, and the Livingston County court sentenced him to a term at the Refuge. He arrived in New York City in September 1833. According to the case file, he was ten years old.

The official record describes inmate number 1221 as an intractable, unruly boy. The superintendent's notes refer to Reed as "a very unpromising child" (June 1835), "very dishonest" (November 1835), and "a deep knowing impudent brazen faced boy" (October

1836). The entry for March 1837 is a single phrase—"a most notorious liar." Austin Reed, it appears, carried on an unceasing rebellion against the masters and wardens who tried to govern his conduct. Early in life, he had become familiar with the hard facts of poverty, servitude, and punishment, but he had also developed a deep knowledge about games of power, a feeling for words and images. He knew that the whip, in nineteenth-century America, was not only a weapon but also an emblem of slavery. He understood that fire was a symbol of insurrection. "Will tell an untruth and stick to equal to any boy we know of," the superintendent observed. By the time he was a teenager, the young man who would come to write his memoir under the name Rob Reed had already distinguished himself by his commitment to his own version of a story.

All those years later, in 1895, Refuge officials apparently responded to Reed's request, sending a copy of the file to the address he provided, 70 Frankfort Street, Rochester. "Dear Sir," Reed wrote back, "I am ever so much oblige to you for the trouble you put your self to in looking over the record." Speaking of trouble, he went on: "if you only knew the troubles and trials I have been through since I left the old reffuge it would make your heart bleed." After leaving the reformatory in 1839, Reed spent most of the next twenty years in New York's penal institutions, mainly at the world-famous Auburn State Prison. He became the object of some of nineteenth-century America's most elaborate experiments in the punishment of crime and the management of human character. He became a victim, though not technically an innocent one, of exotic tortures and grinding cruelty. Thousands of people were locked up in similar institutions. Their crimes, like his, were written in the ledgers. Their bodies, like his, were counted and inspected. Their lives and prospects were appraised by the authorities. But very few would write their own stories—in the small corpus of American prison literature that was published before the Civil War, there was nothing with such literary power and no other memoir by a self-identified black writer who could suggest such profound connections between the penal system and plantation slavery. Reed was in his mid-thirties in 1858, when he brought his story to a close. It was, as he said, a "history" of troubles and trials, but it was also an act of protest, a book to light a fire.[2]

Apprenticeship

A PRISON RECORD gives a terse verbal sketch of Austin Reed in 1859, just after he completed his book: "5' plus 5½ inches in height. Mulatto. Breasts covered with scars. Scar from burn on left arm. Scar on left side of back." Reed was never a slave, but he lived through the era of moral and political crisis before the Civil War. When he saw a white man grip a lash, when he was put to work all day without a rest or a wage, he saw slavery encroaching, only half-disguised. In the century and a half since Reed wrote his story, Americans have grown accustomed to thinking about slavery as the South's peculiar institution, abolished in the crucible of the Civil War. By the 1850s, some Northerners had already accepted the idea of a nation split between freedom and slavery. They defined their progress against the backwardness of the slaveholding South. But Reed would learn that the landscape of liberty and captivity was not divided up so neatly. Even as they were outlawing slavery, the Northern states were inventing new instruments of unfree labor, new sites of confinement, and new patterns of inequality. Reed was caught up in these snares, and he struggled hard against them. He carried the evidence on his body, in the marks of the whip and the flame.

As Reed composed his narrative, he told three stories about living and laboring within New York's interlocking systems of legal captivity. The first was about his brief time as an indentured servant or "apprentice" on the Ladd farm in Avon Springs. The second was about the House of Refuge, where he worked in the workshops and received a basic education. The third was about his many years as an inmate at Auburn, the birthplace of New York's "congregate system" of prison discipline, which was adopted in institutions around the country in the antebellum years. Telling these three stories, drawing from the education he received in the Refuge but also from his own promiscuous reading, Reed played with various genres and styles. He began in the mode of the confession. He would draw from popular traditions like the rogue's tale and the sensational exposé. Outlaw ballads and temperance sermons would intermingle in his pages, and he would copy a few passages from published works of fiction. Reed described his own vulnerability, his fall into dependency under various keepers, anticipating a future in which emancipation from slavery, for people like him, would not ensure the fullness of freedom. But in writing, taking up different forms and turning them to his own designs, he also achieved a kind of mastery.

Because Reed was under state control so often and for so long, there exists another version of his life story, one that can be pieced together from archival sources—the House of Refuge files, prison ledgers, newspapers, census documents—and compared to the narrative he composed. The similarities between these two accounts are substantial, but the differences are significant, too. Reed was born in upstate New York, probably between 1823 and 1825. He was the descendant of Africans, Europeans, and freeborn people of color from the northeastern United States; nineteenth-century record keepers referred to his family as "mulatto" or just "colored." His father, Burrell Reed, was an early settler of the region who moved to Rochester and set up shop as a barber. His mother, Maria, was a literate and devoutly religious woman, originally from Massachusetts, many years younger than her husband. Austin had two brothers, Edward and Charles, and at least one sister, whose name has not been recovered. The Reeds joined a small, close circle of middle-class people of color who protected each other against racist attacks and, over time, would establish one of North America's great centers of black intellectual and political culture.[3]

In the 1820s, Rochester was still a small settlement, but it was growing quickly, gaining a reputation for commerce, evangelical revival, and social reform. The city was also known as a sanctuary for fugitives on their way to Canada. A Rochester grocer and preacher named Austin Steward, who had been born into slavery in New York State, would help to lead the abolitionist movement on both sides of the northern border, eventually publishing a narrative of his life, *Twenty-Two Years a Slave, and Forty Years a Freeman* (1857). Steward was a temperance man and an outspoken antiracist who built up his business and supported his friends in the face of vicious, sometimes criminal hostility. The Reed family maintained close ties to him. When Steward organized Rochester's first black congregation, the African Methodist Episcopal Church, Burrell Reed pledged twenty-five dollars, one of the largest commitments from any single patron. Austin Reed and his siblings probably attended Steward's Sabbath school for children of color. It is possible that Burrell and Maria Reed named their son in honor of this friend and patron.[4]

Reed's earliest memories were not of hardship. In 1827 his father bought a new house on Hunter Street, on the outskirts of the city, and Reed could recall a secure life whose privileges, taken for granted by many white families, were rare and precious to people of color in his time. The "Life and Adventures" tells how, before Reed leaves for Avon Springs, his mother sends him to spend one last night in his bedroom upstairs. For a child of color in the 1820s to have a bed in a two-story house was an exceptional sign of material security. But Reed's life was disrupted when he was still very young. His father, Burrell, died on February 4, 1828, having prepared no will, and the family was left in debt. Maria drew up an inventory of their property—furniture, clothes, a long list of barber's tools—for their creditors. With support from Austin Steward and others, she was able to keep the house, where she stayed through the Civil War, but she was forced into the humblest kinds of labor, doing laundry and piecework to get by. According to a local newspaper, she died of starvation and cold in 1865, at the age of seventy. Her body was found "lifeless and frozen stiff," and her children were "scattered over the world."[5]

Unlike most other nineteenth-century autobiographers, includ-

The African Methodist Episcopal Church in Rochester,
New York. Austin Reed's father, Burrell Reed, pledged a gift
of $25 toward establishing Rochester's first African Ameri-
can church, an effort organized by Austin Steward in 1827.

ing the authors of the best-known slave narratives, Reed does not
open his story with the circumstances of his birth; he starts, instead,
with the news of his father's passing. It is as if he is tracing his origins
to the scene of a disappearance, as if his life begins with the trauma
of losing a figure of moral authority and economic self-determination.
When, on later occasions, Reed is able to make his way back from
New York or Auburn to his hometown, he is conscious that his father's grave is waiting for him there. "Where may I go that I may
shun that voice? It comes a pealing upon my ear like a heavy clap of
thunder, and the voice of my father is haunting me tonight, and his

advice and prayer seems to prick my very heart." From the beginning, Reed calls himself a haunted convict. It is a phrase with several meanings, but one of them is that the memory of his father is his ghostly conscience and companion.

Reed's first stories are of wandering, without direction, after his father's death. He describes falling into mischief with his friends in Rochester, disobeying his mother, committing little acts of defiance that hint at original sin: "We jump over into a man's orchard and cut down several of his fruit trees and made our way for the city." Reed's early chapters echo the language and imagery of many other convict autobiographies. Since colonial times, enterprising American printers had been peddling execution sermons and gallows speeches, turning the news of crime into a vibrant, lucrative popular culture. The earliest published confessions reduced the rich complexity of autobiography to the crude form of didactic allegory. Some crime narratives were attributed to black authors, but they were usually written, or heavily edited, by the white ministers and lawyers who ran the penal system. Pamphlets like *Sketches of the Life of Joseph Mountain, A Negro* (1790) and *"Black Jacob," A Monument of Grace* (1842) found wide audiences. The rules of the genre required the authors to justify the powers that condemned them. Speaking from a jail cell or addressing the public from the scaffold, with a noose around their throats, they were expected to describe the circumstances of their childhoods, tell about their first temptations, and take responsibility for their crimes. They were supposed to accept their punishment and warn readers to obey the law.[6]

"I soon broke through the restraints of my mother and fell a victim to vice and crime," Reed writes, following the conventions. The genre had its limits, but it also provided a rare opening into the public sphere of the printed word. Migrant workers, servants, and other people who would normally have been excluded from the world of letters found, in crime literature, a place where their stories might be told, and they began to exercise more and more control over the telling. By the 1850s, when Reed wrote his book, the criminal autobiography was becoming something other than propaganda for the penal system. There were convicts who used sensational narratives to indulge readers' curiosities about transgression or to glorify the brotherhood of thieves. Some appealed to the public's sympathy, and a few justified themselves as martyrs, condemned by a corrupt, oppressive legal system.

Reed seems to have read his share of popular crime literature. He draws from its repertoire of terms and predictable scenes, and he sensationalizes some of the details of his story. Verses from crime ballads are woven into his prose. One of the sources of his alias, Rob Reed, may have been Sir Walter Scott's popular outlaw romance, *Rob Roy* (1817), which was widely reprinted in the United States. In recounting the crime for which he would be sent to the Refuge, though, Reed keeps fairly close to facts that can be reconstructed from other records. When he was about eight or ten, his mother bound him out to work for the Ladds, a prominent family in nearby Avon Springs. "My mother had firmly made up her mind that I should be sent from a city life and live a country life," Reed recalls. Widowed a few years earlier, Maria Reed was struggling to support her children alone, and she may have felt that there were too many troubles, too many temptations, in Rochester.

Still, it was a painful thing to break up the family. In his book, Reed remembers his brother and sister trying to keep him at home. They don't trust the white farmer who comes to claim him. "Who knows," his brother asks, "but what he is goin' into the hands of some slave holder?" This is a serious question. There were still some recognized forms of slavery in New York in the 1820s. Even when full emancipation was granted by law in 1827, the illegal trade in kidnapped African Americans continued. Another free black man from upstate, Solomon Northup, would document the harrowing experience of his capture in his autobiography, *Twelve Years a Slave* (1853). The Reed children knew that their freedom was precarious.[7]

Reed's description of "Mr. Lad" as an "old man" with grown daughters suggests that he is probably the wealthy patriarch Herman Ladd, who built his mansion in East Avon in about 1806. The Ladds were not slave traders, but Reed was being taken from home against his will, and his legal status as an apprentice left him with very few rights or liberties. Indenture, a form of temporary servitude, was still a common labor arrangement in the early nineteenth century. Masters agreed to provide food, shelter, and a practical education: for boys, ordinarily, training in manual labor and a rudimentary knowledge of reading and arithmetic; for girls, the skills of housekeeping. Some families were able to negotiate valuable apprenticeships for their boys or places in comfortable homes for their girls. The rest—illegitimate children, orphans, and the sons and daughters of widows like Maria Reed—accepted harsher conditions.

Historians have documented stark racial inequalities in nineteenth-century indenture contracts. After slavery was abolished in Northern states, the technically voluntary, contractual system of indentured servitude was adapted to serve a similar function. Black servants could expect to serve as menial laborers, with few prospects

The Ladd house in Avon, Livingston County, New York. The house was built in about 1806 and is still standing today. Austin Reed was indentured to the Ladd family and remembered their "lordly mansion" and farm. He was convicted of arson against the family's property in 1833.

of acquiring a craft or advancing in their studies. Authorities in New York noted that parents who had endured slavery often refused to indenture their children, "under the apprehension, that they may be treated as they themselves have been while slaves." It was well known that masters disciplined their apprentices with lashes and rods. Harriet Wilson's *Our Nig* (1859), now considered the first novel published by an African American woman, depicted the heroine's terrifying experience as a servant on a farm in New England, reminding readers in that self-righteous region "that slavery's shadows fall even there." There were reports of escapes and insubordination, and arson against a master's property was such a common offense that the official journal of the New York State Lunatic Asylum in the nineteenth century discussed "incendiarism from homesickness" as a condition likely to afflict child servants who had been sent away from their families.[8]

By his own account, the new servant at the Ladd farm was an unwilling laborer. In the memoir, Reed refuses to perform his assigned tasks. He has trouble eating, and he drifts around the property, dejected. In these passages, Reed's writing takes on a nostalgic, almost bluesy feel, as he refashions the sentiments of popular literature in vernacular cadences: "Home still kept hanging on my mind." After a few unhappy days, "Mr. Lad" decides to punish the apprentice for his idleness. Reed describes being dragged off to the barn, his hands fastened behind his back with a halter, his back beaten and cut with a black whip. His blood rises at the memory of being "tied up like a slave and thrash by the rough hand of a farmer who had no business nor no right nor authority to lay a hand on me." Reed feels that his father's death has exposed him to this mortification, leaving him unprotected and dependent. As soon as his hands are untied, he runs away.

Back in Rochester, Reed finds his family slipping into poverty and falling apart. His mother is becoming hopeless and sickly, quarreling with her children. His sister is in a rage. Hearing what he has been through at Avon Springs, she encourages him to "take the life of that infernal villain that had the boldness to horse whip you." From this point forward, Reed associates crime with a feminized passion, as if the provocation to break the law tempted him to betray his father's memory and to surrender his own identity as a boy on the way to manhood. The revenge plot that he attributes to his sister has the trappings of sensational crime fiction—cross-dressing, gunfire, screams of bloody murder, dramas of arrest and escape. There are touches of romance in the tale. But Reed concludes the episode with his attempt to burn Ladd's property, the crime for which he was in fact arraigned, tried, and convicted by a Livingston County jury in 1833. Reed may have dreamed up some embellishments. He took his crucial images, the whip and the flame, from life.[9]

Refuge

"IN THE COURSE of time I was tried and sentence to the New York House of Refuge until I was one and twenty." Reed's second story of captivity begins when he arrives at America's first juvenile reformatory. The Refuge was like a self-contained city for the sons and daughters of the poor—a school but also a prison, a church but also a factory. The surviving pamphlets and popular journalism attest to the nineteenth-century public's appetite for information about the controversial experiment. Was the Refuge in the business of nurturing children or of punishing them? What were the inmates like? Could they be saved? Reed plays the guide to its obscure passageways: "Reader, go with me while I take you by the hand and conduct you through every department of the House of Refuge that stood in the Bowery in 1833, and give you a description." Perhaps influenced by Charles Dickens or by the popular travel writing of his contemporaries, Reed's writing begins to change. He stops breaking his text into numbered chapters. He becomes more preoccupied with repetitions—schedules, daily rituals—than with events. He measures time not in years but in regimes, overseen by a series of superintendents. One is a stern but humane guardian, a keeper with a heart. Another is a vindictive monster. Looking back from his cell in a state prison, Reed remembers the education he received and the friendships he made, but in the end he depicts the Refuge mainly as a house of bondage, ruled with the whip.[10]

New York's House of Refuge was chartered in 1824 and opened on New Year's Day, 1825. The original structure was a decommissioned armory. Soon the inmates were conscripted into the work of expanding the facilities. There were boys' and girls' cellblocks, called "dormitories," and proto-industrial factories, called "workshops." There was a dining hall, an exercise yard, a classroom, and a stage for plays. The new Refuge was one of the monuments of a large-scale reform movement that was changing how New York handled crime and deviancy, but it was never really secure; the inmates always seemed to be raising hell or running away. During a riot in 1830, a boy named Charles Peterson badly wounded an assistant keeper, David Terry, with a razor. Reed came to the Refuge three years later, but he included the story of Terry's injury by allowing

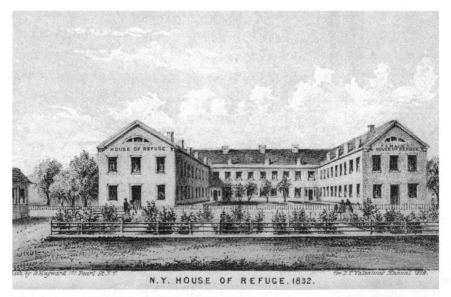

N.Y. HOUSE OF REFUGE, 1832.

The first juvenile reformatory in the United States, the House of Refuge, stood on the Bowery in New York City from 1825 until it was destroyed by fire in 1839. Austin Reed was confined there from 1833 to 1839.

another inmate to recount it. (Peterson becomes "Petterson," and the razor becomes a knife.) Reed did get to know William Burris, William McCullough, and other boys who escaped from the reformatory in the late 1830s. He remembered and recorded their names.

The Refuge was operated by the Society for the Reformation of Juvenile Delinquents (formerly the Society for the Prevention of Pauperism), a group of elite reformers who were in the grips of a moral panic. In the early nineteenth century, New York City was becoming a capital of manufacturing and trade. African Americans, escaped or expelled from Southern states, came north in search of new lives. European immigrants arrived in waves, thousands of Irish Catholics among them. The metropolis was taking on its modern character as the scene of the creolized beauty and the motley cosmopolitanism that would be described so vividly by Reed's contemporaries, Walt Whitman, Herman Melville, and Edgar Allan Poe—but in the masses of impoverished laborers and their families, the ruling classes saw the faces of vice and crime. Gangs seemed to be massing in the alleyways. Pickpockets lurked along the boulevards.

Well-connected reformers tried to shore up the social order by founding new institutions. They organized charities for the destitute and temperance clubs to keep men out of the taverns. Evangelical churches and tract societies set out to convert wayward souls. Conceived in this era of anxiety and change, the House of Refuge was funded, in part, through sin taxes on the licenses granted to taverns and theaters. Its mission was to turn the children of the disorderly populations into obedient laborers, teaching them the habits of industry and submission "by which," as the society's board of managers put it, "they may earn an honest living, and become, from degraded outcasts, useful and reputable citizens of this Republic." In most cases, the inmates were bound out as apprentices after an indenturing committee determined that they were ready for work.[11]

As the society abandoned its hopes of preventing poverty and turned to the more modest task of reformation, it helped to invent a new category of person in American society, the juvenile delinquent, who was no longer an innocent child but not yet a hardened criminal. Juvenile delinquents went to the reformatory because they still had a chance at rehabilitation. Some Refuge children were judged to be living in unsafe homes. Some were vagrants, swept up by officials as they hung around the playhouses and the docks. Some had been convicted of minor offenses. The society was a private corporation, but it was closely tied to the state, and the reformatory received many girls and boys, including Reed, directly from the courts. Nearly half of the inmates were Irish children, who were treated as aliens but not as unredeemables. There was a strong demand for Irish servants on farms and ships. "A discerning public seek for children who have been disciplined at the Refuge," the society's president, Stephen Allen, wrote with satisfaction in 1834.[12]

The case of a "boy of color" like Reed was more delicate. In its early years, the Refuge housed all its boys, black and white, in the same dormitory, worked them in the same shops, and fed them in the same hall, but the lines of race were already being drawn. Just a few months before Reed was sent down from Livingston County, in 1833, the British journalist and abolitionist Edward Abdy had visited the Refuge. Officials welcomed him, gave him a tour, and showed him essays on anatomy written by two inmates. Abdy was impressed, but he had one reservation: "It was painful to observe the studied manner in which the white and colored children were separated and distinguished from each other, as if moral improvement could be promoted in either by encouraging pride and inflicting humiliation." The Refuge was teaching its inmates the American codes of racial identity—pride for the white children, humiliation for the rest. Reed documents the casual racism of the contractors and the guards, who call him a "darkie" and a "nig." He had been locked up for a year and a half in December 1834, when the society took steps to formalize segregation at the Refuge. The managers secured funding from New York's Manumission Society, and a separate dormitory for up to 126 children of color opened in 1835.[13]

Reed, then about twelve years old, was classified as "colored" in the superintendent's files; it is likely that he was moved to the segregated dormitory. The "Life and Adventures" makes no mention of the new system, though, and by the author's own account he continued to work in integrated workshops and classrooms. Reed seems to have felt a sense of solidarity with the sons of immigrants. "Yes, me brave Irish boys," he writes, mimicking their brogue and the phrasing of their ballads, "me loves you till the day that I am laid cold under the sod, and I would let the last drop of this dark blood run and drain from these black veins of mine to rescue you from the hands of a full blooded Yankee." When Reed escapes, in the company of a few friends, Irish families take the boys in and try to protect them from the merciless "Hayse" (New York's legendary high constable Jacob Hays), who drags them back into confinement. This escapade may be one of Reed's inventions, but it speaks to the social realities of nineteenth-century New York. At a time when the Refuge was hardening the lines of segregation, Reed was writing about a cross-racial alliance between Irish immigrants and black Americans, based on their common circumstances and a shared suspicion of police and prisons.[14]

Juveniles—girls up to the age of eighteen and boys up to twenty-one—often arrived at the Refuge under "indefinite" sentences; they could be released only at the discretion of the society's managers, who held extraordinary power over their futures. Refuge boys might be bound out to farms in faraway counties or on long voyages at sea, and many lost touch with their parents. The legitimation for these policies came from the common-law doctrine of *parens patriae*, or the state's authority to take custody of orphaned and neglected children. From time to time, families tried to recover their sons and daughters, but the courts routinely rejected their petitions. In the view of the judges, the Refuge was more like an orphanage or a school than a penal institution. Because it was conducting its business under the auspices of moral instruction, not of imprisonment, delinquents in the reformatory had fewer habeas corpus rights, a weaker claim to relief, than adults charged with crimes. This was one of the paradoxes of juvenile reformation: by portraying its system as an effort to save children, rather than to punish them, the society tightened its hold on the bodies and souls entrusted to its care. It was a long journey from Rochester to New York City in the 1830s. Reed says that it took him five days, in the custody of state officials. There is no sign that he had a visit from his family during his six years in the Refuge. When he recalls his homesickness, Reed is telling his own story, but he is also writing against a policy that broke families apart.[15]

As long as they remained in the Refuge, inmates worked seven or eight hours a day, resting only on Sundays. The exploitation of their labor was justified as a kind of character building; according to the reformatory's original *Rules and Regulations* (1825), "the introduction of labor into the House of Refuge, will be regarded principally with reference to the moral benefits, and not merely to the profits, to be derived from it." From the start, though, the society hired out the boys and girls to private contractors, who set up manufacturing in the shops. The inmates made shoes, rope mats, brooms, and other simple commodities. Refuge boys and girls received no pay; the money went to the society. Reed recalls going to work in the furniture shop, putting together wicker chairs. It was the beginning of a long career in penal servitude.[16]

Part of each day was devoted to what the authorities called "moral instruction." Protestant services and Sabbath school made up a regimen that seemed, to some Catholic families, like an exercise in compulsory heresy. The inmates read the Bible and memorized their favorite verses; Reed's prose absorbed several parables from Scripture and some of the thunder of evangelical preaching. His religious education, like his labor, was supposed to prepare him for a sober, well-regulated life. The society blamed the miseries of poverty on the viciousness of the poor. According to the reformers, crime expressed a depraved appetite for luxury and sex. To guard against temptation, they laid down a doctrine of manly self-control. It was probably in the reformatory that Reed heard his first temperance sermons, discourses on sobriety that smuggled in darkly entertaining anecdotes of brawling and seduction. Reed would try his hand at the genre later in his memoir. "What is it that has caused so many orphans and widows to go a mourning through our streets? What is it that has caused many a weeping mother and sister to visit their unfortunate son shut up in a gloomy prison?" The answer, according to the temperance societies, was not the inequities of the industrializing economy or an unjust legal system. It was the wicked demon, alcohol.[17]

The Refuge provided a common school education, dividing the inmates into classes, ranked first through ninth. The teacher worked with the most advanced students, who instructed novices in the basics of reading, writing, and arithmetic. Reed remembers studying his letters under the guidance of an inmate he calls Jack Kimbell: "every spare minute that Jack could get, he would run to me with his little pointer in his hand and show me which was A, and which was B, and by the space of nine months I was sitting at the head of the ninth class every night, reading and studying pieces from *The English Reader*." The *Reader* was both a textbook and a moral primer; its selection of poems, dialogues, and histories taught students the basics of grammar and style while introducing them to such principles as temperance and opposition to slavery. Early patrons of the Refuge also donated a small library of books. Reed's favorite teacher, Albert Williams, reported in 1834 that the 484 volumes were "a rich source of instruction." A member of the society provided a copy of Daniel Defoe's *Robinson Crusoe* (1719), and Reed mentions reading the story of the shipwrecked sailor who spends so many years in solitude. Seeming not to know, or not to acknowledge, that Defoe's work was fiction, Reed thinks of Crusoe as a wanderer, "leaving the happy Home of his youth and childhood under the cover of darkness to become a marine of the sea." Home still keeps hanging on his mind.[18]

In the classrooms and throughout the reformatory, the staff imposed a harsh discipline. Infractions of the rules might be punished with a diet of bread and water, of unsalted gruel, or of bitter tea; with solitary confinement, fetters, and handcuffs; or with the notorious "cat of nine tails." Reed anticipates that the public will want to hear about the lash and the origins of its name: "Reader, these cats are made out of cat gut with a small knot made at the ends of them and wound around with a small wire, then rubbed well with shoe maker's wax and attach to a piece of rattan that has a pretty good spring to it, so as when the officer strikes, it leaves a deep cut in the back, causing the tender skin to burst while the blood flows freely down the back from the cuts it leaves, leaving the back entirely striped with red." Reed's prose is richly layered, mixing information and lamentation. His sentence begins with the design of the whip, but it ends with the victim's bleeding flesh; it starts as a description and finishes as an appeal to the tender heart.

During the first half of the nineteenth century, the lash became an icon of cruelty. Sailors protested the inhumanity of flogging at sea. Prison reformers worried over the use of corporal punishment in the penitentiaries, which were supposed to be places of moral rehabilitation. Most of all, abolitionists used the image of the whip to stigmatize the brutalities of slavery. In her memoir, *Incidents in the Life of a Slave Girl* (1861), Harriet Jacobs wrote of her brother, William, "He did not mind the smart of the whip, but he did not like the *idea* of being whipped." It was the idea of being handled without respect; whip scars were signs of degradation. The same controversy troubled the Refuge. The institution's first superintendent, Joseph Curtis, was pushed out of his job because he was not severe enough with his punishments. "Gentlemen, I am not a slave-driver," he said to his bosses in the society. The reformers who founded the Refuge were mostly antislavery men, and Curtis's words reminded them of their commitment to gentle ways. The managers were not moved. As they searched for Curtis's replacement, they sought the advice of the toughest jailer in America, Elam Lynds. The head keeper at Auburn and later at Sing Sing, Lynds was legendary as a defender of severe punishments. He told the society to find a man who was not afraid to use the whip on juveniles. Curtis's successors in the office of superintendent were Nathaniel Hart, David Terry, and Samuel Wood. All of them, even Reed's fatherly "Mr. Heart," kept the cat ready to hand.[19]

When Reed describes the vicious whippings in the reformatory, he is joining others who attacked the Refuge as a scene of racism, exploitation, and violent cruelty against boys and girls; he is drawing from a lexicon that reformers had used to expose the contradictions between the society's humane promises and its dehumanizing realities. A vivid example appeared in 1848, when Elijah Devoe published *The Refuge System, or Prison Discipline Applied to Juvenile Delinquents*. Devoe was a former officer who had quarreled with his superintendent over the management of discipline, and for several months he kept a secret diary on the job. When the society fired him, he went public, denouncing the Refuge as a modern-day dungeon where children were locked up and brutalized. "The House of Refuge is, and from the beginning to the present time has been, to all intents and purposes, a prison. The discipline and treatment have been physical and mechanical, rather than moral and intellectual. And the 'bloody cat' has been a familiar instrument in the hands of the keeper during the whole history of the institution." Devoe had a grudge against his bosses, but his fiery polemic was one of the few inside accounts not written by an apologist.[20]

To defend the Refuge—to protect its funding and its special legal status—the society operated a sophisticated publicity campaign. In annual reports, newspaper articles, pamphlets, and broadsides, the managers described the progress of their experiment in reform. They documented their expenses and the payments they received; they counted the number of boys and girls in their custody, the number bound out and released. Because their legitimacy depended, in part, on their promise to turn wayward children into productive citizens, they also collected letters from former inmates who had moved on to respectable lives. These writings were handpicked and edited, if not fabricated, by Refuge officials. Critics and historians have read them with suspicion. "We are often told of the contentedness of the children in the Refuge," Devoe warned, "but we must not forget that these assertions do not proceed from them."[21]

While Reed was doing his time at the reformatory and, later, in a state prison, men and women who had escaped from slavery were beginning to write firsthand accounts of Southern plantations; testimonies of endurance and resistance like *The Life of William Grimes, the Runaway Slave* (1825) and *Narrative of the Life of Frederick Douglass, an American Slave* (1845) helped to establish a tradition of African American autobiography. Meanwhile ex-convicts were revealing the secrets of Northern penitentiaries; one of the most scandalous, *The Memoirs of the Celebrated and Beautiful Mrs. Ann Carson*, appeared in two editions in the 1830s. (In Reed's era, memoir was understood to be a flexible genre, sometimes mixing facts with fiction and sensationalism.) And there were records of lives passed in asylums and aboard ships. But no one had published the truth about the Refuge from the inmates' point of view. The children had left a record of actions—traces of resistance and escape—but they had not been given a chance to speak for themselves. Inside the workshops, where a rule of silence was supposed to keep the boys' minds on their labor, they communicated through a system of gestures and signals. "I began to learn the winks, the motion of the fingers, the shake of the head," Reed writes, remembering his education in the codes of subversion. But no one had translated this secret knowledge for the world at large. Half the story had never been told.[22]

Reed took up the task. It is difficult to say exactly when he began writing—perhaps as early as 1846 or 1847—but the politics of his attack on the Refuge are clear enough. His homesick reveries were testimony against the disputed legal doctrine that gave the society its claim to custody over so many children, and his protest against the cat became an indictment of one controversial official in particular. David Terry, the longtime Refuge officer who had been slashed by Charles Peterson's razor back in 1830, was appointed superintendent in 1838. Over the next few years, he was caught up in a public feud between the society and Governor William H. Seward over the management of the Refuge. Reed's memoir takes a side; it celebrates Seward as a great humanitarian, and it depicts Terry as a sadist and a hypocrite, a former Presbyterian minister who introduces a reign of terror: "The old chap would sway seventy or eighty on a boy's back, and then fall down upon his knees and ask heaven to pardon him for all the blood he had drew from those little innocent boys' backs."[23]

In his opening chapters, set in Rochester and Avon Springs, Reed offers something like a confession of the misdeeds that led to his detention. When he comes to describe the Refuge, though, he turns the tables on the justice system, dramatizing the cruelties of constables and keepers. The society advertised the Refuge as a place where delinquents would be reborn as "reputable citizens." As Reed sees it, the opposite is true: the reformatory locks up "innocent boys," and Terry abuses them so severely that the ones who survive become hardened criminals, destined for the prison or the gallows. In later passages, Reed emphasizes how many Refuge boys end up in state prison. Along the way, he remembers countless acts of noncompliance and mutual consolation among the inmates—how they protect each other against Terry's punishments and care for each other's wounds, how they pass secrets and hatch schemes to escape. They never conform to the mechanical discipline or the moral orthodoxy handed down by the society.

In May 1839 the House of Refuge burned, probably as a result of arson—"set on fire by some rude hands of some of the inmates," as Reed puts it. He had been in the reformatory for six years. "Mr. Heart" had seen to it that he received an education, but Nathaniel Hart had moved on to a new job elsewhere. Some of the inmates had become like a second family to Reed, but they were beginning to disperse. One, a French boy named Nicholas Miller, was indentured to a farmer in New Jersey. Another, Henry Strongman, was bound out as a servant aboard the whale ship *Helvetia*, which sailed from Hudson, New York, for a three-year cruise of the South Pacific.

After the fire, the Refuge itself moved to a new, larger facility at Twenty-third Street and the East River. Embarrassed but unyielding, David Terry stayed on as the superintendent.

A month later, in June, the society secured an apprenticeship for Austin Reed with Abraham Haring, a farmer in Rockland County, New York. The text of the indenture agreement was boilerplate, yet its administrative jargon worked a subtle kind of magic: the Refuge inmate, imprisoned and stripped of most civil rights, appeared as a responsible, voluntary legal actor, signing up for servitude "of his own free will." Thus his bondage was established a matter of contract, not of slavery. Reed's signature on the document is probably the earliest surviving example of his handwriting. The arrangement was scheduled to last four years and nine months, expiring on Reed's twenty-first birthday, and it was designed to re-create, more or less, the circumstances of his first indenture to Ladd in Avon Springs. It ended the same way, too. Reed's consent to indentured servitude was a fiction, and by January 1840, according to the official record, the sixteen-year-old servant had "left his master." With that remark, the superintendent closed his file.[24]

Interlude

REED HAD EXPERIENCED more, at the Refuge, than beatings and deprivations. He remembers plotting escapes and playing cards for money, and in one curious passage he describes being cast in an "Indian play" for the Refuge stage. The splendid costume gives him some delight: "I was dress in a little red gown coming down to my knees and a pair of buck skin leggings on with little bell buttons attach to them, and my face painted red and black. A large scalping knife stuck in my belt." The audience for this piece of entertainment, in Reed's telling, is a group of visitors from Philadelphia, probably reformers interested in juvenile delinquency. Reed gives them a good show, playing the painted savage who murders a mother and child. The Society for the Reformation of Juvenile Delinquents likcd to say that its mission was to teach wayward boys and girls the habits of hard work and obedience. In his tough years at the reformatory, Reed had learned other lessons as well: how to trust his friends; how to protect himself against abuse; and how to perform, when he had to, for the white authorities who had the power to hurt him or to do him some good.[25]

When Austin Reed left the Refuge and walked away from his indenture in Rockland County, he was on his own, without a master or a superintendent, for the first time in six years. He was still a teenager, and he was still very poor. His treatment of this phase in his "Life and Adventures" forms a kind of interlude. Reed is leaving the Refuge, but he is not quite free. He is trying to get home but struggling to find the means. He will end up in Auburn, the reader knows, but he has not yet committed the first of his adult crimes. The timeline of the "Life and Adventures" departs substantially from the official record—a few months of actual liberty are stretched to three years—and I have been unable to corroborate the stories Reed tells here by comparisons to other sources. A few of the names Reed introduces do refer to historical persons and places, and more evidence may be discovered, in time. For now, these episodes might be seen as chapters from a novella or a romance, dropped into the middle of a narrative whose other sections seem more closely autobiographical. Set mostly outside the closed worlds of the reformatory and the prison, the interlude features Reed's sophisticated reflections on his relationships with certain white benefactors. He is still learning to play scripted roles for them, to present himself to their curious eyes, and to persuade them to give him what he needs.

Reed's own letters to the superintendent acknowledge that he was bound out as a servant after the 1839 fire, but in the "Life and Adventures" he invents another story about leaving the Refuge. Reed and Henry Strongman are falsely accused of hiding a gold watch from the superintendent's eyes. Their accuser is another inmate, "Thom King." Thomas King was a real person, a boy of color from New York City, raised by a single mother. According to his case file, he was a former indentured servant who ran with the "gang of Bowery thieves," served time at Blackwell's Island, and entered the Refuge in May 1833, a few months ahead of Reed. King died in custody less than a year later, on May 2, 1834. The official cause of his death was "typhus fever," and he was buried in a coffin donated by the local almshouse.[26]

The Thom King who appears in Reed's story is a racist caricature, speaking in the dialect of the minstrel stage and seeming to embody the vices that the Refuge staff attributed to Reed himself: the unredeemable blackness, the lack of intellectual promise, and, most of all, the lying. King snitches on Reed and Strongman and stands by, complicit, as David Terry bloodies their backs. It is the worst beating that either of them has ever received. Soon afterward, when King is killed in an accident, Reed and Strongman visit him in the hospital ward to tell him that he is going to hell for his lies— "Yes, King, our blood will haunt you till the day of judgment"—and to watch him die. Then Reed makes his escape, along with Strongman and Nicholas Miller, into a life that has not been plotted by the authorities at the Refuge. The same fallen plank that kills King becomes their bridge over the reformatory walls.

Reed and his companions set out toward their uncertain futures, and they have an occasion, right away, to tell their story. It is a cold spring day. The three fugitives are at a steamboat landing, hoping to catch a ride north, but they have no money for the passage. Reed decides to ask for the captain's charity: "I rose upon my feet and told him that we was three boys who had just made our escape from the House of Refuge, and that we wanted to be carried back to the land of our nativities. I then pulled off my shirt and showed the captain my back." To any reader of antebellum slave narratives and abolitionist novels, it is a familiar scene. The fugitive on his way north, with only his wounds for currency, testifies to the cruelties he has endured. The cuts from Terry's whip are still raw, a terrible sight. "Poor boys," the captain says. "I feel sorry for you all." In the white man who spirits the boys out of the city, Reed offers a model for how the testimony of his miseries might be received. "The reader may sympathize with us and imagine what a sad condition we was in, two of us with our backs sore and raw with the cats, and the back of our shirts stained and gored with blood." In the interlude of his time at large, Reed is reflecting on race and performance, including literary performance, in nineteenth-century America.

When the boat lands at "Harvest Straw" (Haverstraw, a small town on the Hudson, not far from the Haring farm), Reed finds work and board at the American Hotel. He tends bar, a job that gives him a chance to rehearse some of the temperance rhetoric he learned at the Refuge. Serving tourists and the local elites, Reed finds himself called on to give more performances—not only to display his dark, lacerated skin, which they view as a bizarre curiosity, but also to recite some poetry. He flirts with the idea of singing a crime ballad, but he settles on a piece by William Cowper, whose works were anthologized in the textbook Reed had studied in the reformatory, *The English Reader*, and cited by African American writers of the period including Frederick Douglass, Harriet Jacobs, and William Wells Brown. "The Morning Dream" envisions a goddess or angel who crosses an ocean to liberate an enslaved race: "She sung of the slave's broken chain, wherever her glory appeared." Hearing Reed recite these lines, the ladies and gentlemen of Haverstraw are overcome with feeling. Their hands go right to their pockets; they give Reed gold and cash, and they offer to help his boss, Esquire Johnson, to pay for his further education. Reed knows that he has given his listeners just what they were hoping for: "Thinking that the piece which I had spoken was enough for that day, I turned and left those delicate little creatures to themselves." He has figured out how to operate within a complex economy of racial feeling, and he has seen how much literature might be worth to him in polite Northern circles that oppose slavery but still indulge in a sentimental racism.

In Reed's telling, the American closes its doors at the end of the tourist season, and he hires himself out as a private servant to a couple of gamblers, who take him around New York State. He sees the underworld and starts carrying a loaded pistol. Arrested for shooting a black man late one night, he spends some time in jail. And then, at last, the fugitive makes it back to Rochester. Approaching home, he pauses at the doorstep, not quite ready to knock. His narration shifts from the simple past to the present tense, rendering, as if in real time, the anxious movements of his thoughts: "Some other family may be living here." Reed's sense of anticipation seems laced with dread. He looks at an old tree in the yard and remembers that he used to sit with his sister in the shade of its branches, singing a ballad. The words "we soon must part" echo in his mind. The song that comes back to him, "The Watchman," by the Irish poet Thomas Moore, is not about reunion; it is about saying goodbye. Even as Reed walks into the home he has been missing for six years and seven months—he gives the precise figure himself—he feels that he can never really return to the childhood that was interrupted by his father's death. "I am now under the roof of my mother's cottage, ready to close my eyes in sleep, and must bid the reader a good night, while I lay a dreaming of the sufferings and cruelties which I have gone through, and preparing myself one day or another to be a harden convict and the inmate of a gloomy prison." Home is only a way station, a place to rest for a little while, between the Refuge and the prison.

Prison

As he sets the scene for the drama of his first adult felony, Reed describes walking the streets around his mother's house, seeing how much the neighborhood has changed since he was sent away. There are new hotels and taverns, and he takes a job at one of them. He passes by "Houses of infame," where young women loiter in the doorways, and meets a hustler in fine clothes, traveling under a fake name. Reed's hometown has become a city of strangers—and Reed himself is a person in transition. In some passages, he poses as a hardened criminal. In others, he becomes childlike again, a naïve

New York's Auburn State Prison, the birthplace of the "congregate" or "silent" system of prison discipline, has been in operation since it opened in 1816. Austin Reed was sentenced to his first term in Auburn in 1840.

boy, caught up in the schemes of con men, wicked women, and corrupt lawyers. Beneath Reed's moral language of guilt and innocence, under his melodramatic tale of how he was drawn in and betrayed, lie the tough conditions of the author's life in 1840. Reed was a young man of color, raised mostly in a reformatory, returning to a family that had fallen into poverty in a segregated city. He was unwilling to work under the threat of the whip as a master's apprentice, and his time in the Refuge had taught him to view the law as a code that protected the propertied classes and oppressed the poor. He turned to stealing, and before long he was hauled off to his third scene of captivity, the state prison.

The official records indicate that Reed served two years at Auburn for his first offense, and he was released in May 1842, but he had been on the outside for just seven months when he was convicted of a second larceny. He would serve three more sentences at Auburn for stealing before he wrote his memoir: December 1842 to January 1848; December 1848 to April 1853; March 1854 to July 1858. The author of the "Life and Adventures" had spent more of his life locked up than at large. Like many of the boys and men he would describe, he had become a creature of the penal system, caught in a pattern of recidivism and reincarceration. Unruly, unbroken, Reed had been beaten with the cat; confined to an unlighted dungeon on a diet of bread and water; and strapped into the "showering bath," a device for dumping water over the head of an immobilized prisoner to simulate drowning (and a forerunner of today's waterboarding). Living almost exclusively in the company of boys and men, he had seen some of them die from sickness and abuse. During one of his brief periods outside, in January 1848, he signed a quitclaim deed to sell his share of ownership in his family's house on Hunter Street. Reed was unmoored, adrift. The prison was more familiar to him than any other home.[27]

The authorities in Reed's time, as in ours, saw crime in terms of personal responsibility. It was the roads of vice and insubordination, they said, that led to the prison's gates. Reed never denied that he had rebelled against authority at every turn, and he admitted that he had broken the law. But he also understood that the reformatory and the prison had made him who he was. "In that day when I shall stand before God," he writes,

> I'll show him my back where the tyrant has printed it with the cats, and will point him to a dark and a gloomy dungeon where I've laid my head many a cold night, without a bed or a blanket, and some days not a morsel of bread to eat, and I will point him to the showering bath and tell him of the water that has been showered on my head. I will show him the tyrants that has tortured and tormented me during my confinement within the gloomy walls of a prison. Those who might have done me a heap of good turned to be my destroyers, and took away all of the good principles and reasons to which I was endowed with, and the high and noble mind which God had given to me have all been destroyed by hard usage and a heavy club. The very prayers which my mother printed upon my lips have all been wash away beneath the waters of a showering bath.

Recollecting his prison years, Reed collapses his second, third, and fourth terms at Auburn into a single, unbroken sentence. He seems less and less interested in telling stories from outside the walls. He is writing a prison memoir now, reckoning with the ways the institution has transformed him. His vision of an appearance before a divine judge is also an appeal to his audience, an invitation to recognize the injustice of his suffering. The penal system put Reed down as an unredeemable criminal, but he expected some clemency in the eyes of God and in the hearts of his readers.

Erected in 1816, New York's Auburn State Prison was one of nineteenth-century America's most famous and most copied institutions. It was a product of the same long, slow revolution in punishment that produced the House of Refuge. In the late eighteenth century, on both sides of the Atlantic, traditional public spectacles—hanging, branding, burning, and the stocks—had fallen out of favor. The scaffold was shaken by rioting mobs. There were Christian protests against cruelty, and there was the liberal argument, coming out of the Enlightenment's political theories, that even criminals who broke the social contract still retained some human rights. By the early 1800s, influential philanthropic societies were ready to benefit from state investments in new punishments. Wounding and killing offenders in the town square, they argued, was an ugly, wasteful ceremony, out of place in the modern world; governments should make use of convicts' labor and, if possible, bring about their rehabilitation. The penitentiary was born.[28]

Some of the leading penal reformers in the early United States were Pennsylvania Quakers. Their abhorrence of violence guided their search for alternatives to the gallows, and their faith in the soul's inner light shaped what came to be known as the "separate system" of penitentiary discipline, placing every inmate in a solitary cell. Meanwhile, officials in New York began to fashion their own methods of discipline. Invented at Auburn, the "silent" or "congregate" system, featuring solitary confinement by night and group labor by day, would become the model for most other states in the nineteenth century. The Pennsylvania system embodied, in stone, a whole theory of the redeemable soul. The New York system was not

Inmates under the "Auburn system" slept in solitary cells but were assembled for congregate labor, meals, and religious services in the daytime hours.

dreamed up by ministers or philosophers; it was worked out by the keepers and guards who managed daily operations. Pennsylvania reformers talked about saving convicts through kindness. New York officials regarded such notions as softhearted, bookish fantasies. Their job, as they understood it, was to break the inmate's spirit and put him to work. Auburn was not a college or a chapel. It was a machine.[29]

Beyond maintaining the internal security of the prison, the New York system's central aim was to extract labor with ruthless efficiency. The inmates slept in solitary cells, but they came together, eight hours a day, six days a week, in the workshops. Private contractors, looking to profit from cheap prison labor, supplied the raw materials and instructions. Reed describes these men as cynical, lazy schemers who "lay heavy and tedious burdens upon the convicts' shoulders to do, but they themselves won't so much as dirty their little fingers." The prison staff enforced discipline, and almost no one was exempt from duties in the shops. With its policy of penal servitude, the New York system did not just reorganize prison discipline. It changed the status of convicts in the eyes of authorities. They weren't lost souls to be reclaimed. They were usable bodies, stripped of legal rights, condemned to work without the prospect of gain—bound laborers under state control.

Auburn would go through many reforms after the 1820s, but penal servitude would remain in place. By the time of the Civil War, it had become so essential to punishment in the United States that the epoch-making Thirteenth Amendment to the Constitution, abolishing slavery, made an exception for the criminal justice system: "Neither slavery nor involuntary servitude, *except as a punishment for crime* whereof the party shall have been duly convicted, shall exist within the United States, or any place subject to their jurisdiction." In the post-Reconstruction South, convict leasing and state prison farms put thousands of emancipated African Americans and their children and grandchildren back in chains. In New York, inmates worked in manufacturing and mines—but the nineteenth and twentieth centuries would bring stark racial inequalities to Northern penal systems, too. When Reed arrived at Auburn in 1840, there were 629 inmates in the prison, and sixty-two of them, less than 10 percent, were black. Today more than half of New York's prisoners are black, and only about a quarter of the incarcerated population is white. The sprawling prison farms and factories of the twenty-first century are, in significant ways, the descendants of a system that was invented at Auburn.[30]

In the nineteenth century, a hidden gallery allowed Auburn's officers and visitors to pass through, unseen, and observe the shops in action. Every year thousands of tourists paid the twenty-five-cent admission fee to watch the inmates working in eerie quiet, dressed in the iconic striped uniforms that Reed calls the "robes of disgrace." Talking was forbidden. So were hand signals, winks, and the exchange of glances. The standard-bearer of Auburn's "silent system" was Elam Lynds, who was appointed head keeper in 1825. Lynds and his assistant, John Cray, were both war veterans, and they treated their inmates like soldiers. Marching them in lockstep, enlisting them in building and maintenance projects, meeting every infraction with a quick, harsh punishment—these tactics for governing a large mass of men brought the culture of the barracks into the prison. Other institutions put symbols of justice above their gates. Auburn had "Copper John," a soldier with a musket. Reed sees the figurine as the emblem of a brutal regime. It sets him dreaming of a fiery apocalypse: "you will melt away like wax before the burning blaze."

Reed presents himself as a hot-tempered, rebellious young man—"my bosom was burning with madness and my eye a flashing like fire"—and the prison records bear him out. The staff at Auburn kept a daily account of the punishments they imposed on the inmates. Only an incomplete version has survived, but it is a nightmarish document, and Austin Reed's name is all over it. Between April 1843 and May 1845, a span of just over two years, Reed was whipped on at least twenty-three different occasions—three stripes for slighting his work in the shop; five for "trying to make a disturbance among the convicts"; four for encouraging another inmate to burn a bunch of cane; five for "using profane language in the chapel during service." In February 1845 Reed was confined to the prison's dungeon on a diet of bread and water for "obtaining ivory from the cutlery shop under false pretences." In June 1843 he was punished in the showering bath for "showing temper" in front of the keeper. In August 1843 he was given twelve lashes "for going into the shop on Sunday without permission and burning 2 setts of matting and caning tools and lying and insolence, and threatening to cut his throat." It goes on and on. Reed continued to endure a harsh discipline, and he kept up a fierce resistance, filling the halls with his curses and kindling blazes when he got the chance.[31]

In the contest to establish America's new standard in punishment, New York won its victory because its system was more efficient. Pennsylvania inmates were condemned to solitary confinement at all times, so their labor was piecework, and complicated engineering and plumbing systems were necessary to provide sufficient water and ventilation to the isolation cells. New York's cells were smaller and less expensive. The quarters collected from tourists helped to offset costs. The new industrial economy, built on factories, required group labor, and the income from the contract system allowed the prison to be more or less self-sustaining. From the beginning, though, Auburn was suspected of being a house of cruelty. The Pennsylvania system got by with far less corporal punishment. The New York system was known for the whip, and its critics seized on the emblem of tyranny. The tireless reformer Dorothea Dix, who visited Auburn and Sing Sing in the early 1840s, acknowledged "the horrible abuses, and the bloody atrocities, which at times, within a few years have blackened the annals of the prisons." At the center of the scandal was "that compound instrument of torture, jeeringly called by officials 'the cat.'" The revolution in punishment was incomplete. The penitentiaries had not abolished torture. They had hidden it behind stone walls. One way to attack the silent system was to expose the bloody facts.[32]

It was not only the elite members of the charitable societies who wrote against the inhumanity of prison conditions. Ex-convicts joined the pamphlet war, publishing such exposés as *Narrative of the Imprisonment of John Maroney in the Prisons of New-York and Auburn* (1832), Levi Burr's *A Voice from Sing Sing* (1833), and James Brice's *Secrets of the Mount-Pleasant State Prison, Revealed and Exposed* (1839). At least one Auburn inmate, Isaac E. Clark, was working on his memoirs, essays, and poetry while he was incarcerated alongside Reed in 1858; Clark published his book, *A Voice from the Prison*, the following year. New York's early prison literature drew on long-established literary traditions like the captivity narrative and new ones like the urban "Mysteries and Miseries" genre, promising a

"The-Cat-o'-Nine-Tails." An officer administers stripes to an immobilized prisoner while a keeper looks on. According to Auburn's Ledger of Punishments, Austin Reed was whipped on many occasions for violating prison rules.

glimpse inside the gothic territory of the cellblocks. These authors were interested less in confessing their crimes than in shining a light on prison conditions. "What I have here related, I have seen with my own eyes, and proved by woful experience," Horace Lane wrote in *Five Years in State's Prison* (1835). Lane found that his intimate knowledge of exclusion and shame had, curiously, given him a special kind of power in the eyes of the public. He was able to reveal truths and satisfy curiosities that prison officials could never touch. Even if his writing would not win him the love of his contemporaries, Lane admitted, he expected that it would earn him a little money. It worked. Lane became a minor celebrity. His book went through multiple editions, and in 1836 he published a follow-up, *The Question, What Did You Do to Get There? Answered.*[33]

Like Horace Lane, Reed probably hoped that he could collect some money from the sale of his book, but he also took an interest in the ongoing debate over prison policies. He was locked up for the first time in May 1840, and his memoir includes bleak recollections from that era in Auburn's history.

Reader, those was the dark and gloomy days when gross darkness hovered over the prison, and the prisoners sat in one total darkness of ignorance and heathenism. Those was the dark days when no prisoner was allowed to write a letter to his friends or to make one single mark with a pencil, and though the Honorable Wm. H. Seward was chief justice of the state, yet he in all of his power couldn't grant the prisoner the privilege of writing one kind word Home to his friends, though they laid at the point of death. Those was the dark and lonesome days when the convict had no library books to read, nothing but his bible and tract, and if he wanted to kill time during the long summer days, he must take his bible or tract from his shelf and wear away the long and lonesome hours that came a hanging on him like a heavy weight by reading them. The convict had no slate and pencil to kill time with, nor did he dare to have a knife in his possession to whittle time away. Ah, Reader, those was the dark and cruel days when young Plume was stripped stark naked and laid across the bench with his hands tied to the floor, and received such a severe punishment with the cats that he expired a few days after. Them was the days when the prisoners' backs was cut and lacerated with the cats till the blood came running down their backs. Many was the nights that the prisoners returned to their cells with their backs cut and hacked up with the cats, and cursing and damning their makers and uttering hard and horrible oaths.

Documenting the cruelties of Auburn in its unreformed years, Reed remembers the loneliness and the tedium of the silent system, the deprivation of reading and writing, and the cruelty of the cat, yet the passage is much more than a catalogue of institutional problems. There is a kind of poetry to be heard in a phrase like "uttering hard and horrible oaths," with its martial, parade ground rhythms. Reed creates complex patterns as he returns to and modifies a line—"the dark and gloomy days," "the dark and lonesome days," "the dark and cruel days"—like a motif in a symphony. He is telling his readers how he became a convict, a person whose life is so structured by repetition that the slightest variation is rich with meaning, but he is showing that he has also become a writer. He does not submit to the demands of confessional genres or play sensational journalism's rule-governed games of exposure. He masters these forms and keeps moving, fugitivelike, between and beyond them.

The market for prison literature was created, in part, by the controversies that surrounded institutions like Auburn. Even while New York officials carried on their campaign against Pennsylvania, they were internally divided between hard-liners like Lynds and reformers like his successor, Gershom Powers, who promoted the ideal of rehabilitation. In time, the reformers won a series of modest victories. Over Lynds's objection, prison chaplains were appointed, and lessons were offered to inmates who could not read. Tract societies distributed Bibles and evangelical literature to the cells, and state officials, encouraged by Governor Seward, installed prison libraries. Eventually, inmates were permitted to send and receive private letters. Lynds had overseen the construction and management of Sing Sing, then returned for a second tenure as keeper of Auburn, but his power was diminishing. In 1839, after two inmates died on his watch, he was persuaded to step down. Lynds did go on to serve another term at Sing Sing, but within a few years the prison chaplain was able to get him fired—a sure sign that the politics of penitentiary discipline had shifted. A new philanthropic society, the New York Prison Association, was founded in 1844. Three years later, after an inmate named Charles Plumb (Reed's "young Plume") was beaten to death at Auburn, the New York legislature abolished the use of the whip in the state's penitentiaries, favoring alternative punishments like the showering bath, which could break an unruly spirit without leaving unsightly scars on the body. The reformers were on the rise.[34]

The conflict over prison reform took shape, to some degree, along political party lines. Lynds and his defenders were Jacksonian Democrats. The new reformers tended to be aligned with the Whig Party and, later, with the Republicans. They found their champion in Seward, who held the office of governor from 1838 to 1842. Seward had started out as a lawyer in the town of Auburn, and for the rest of his career he remained interested in prison reform. While he moved on to the governor's office in Albany and, eventually, to a Senate seat and the secretary of state's office under Abraham Lincoln in Washington, he entrusted the cause to his friends in the region, men like Horace Cook, an attorney and long-term Cayuga County treasurer, and Benoni I. Ives, a Methodist minister who became the Auburn chaplain in 1856. These local officials seem to have been Reed's personal connections to the party politics of reform.

Tucked inside Reed's manuscript is a small scrap of wrapping paper. On one side are written a few sentences that may have been intended as a kind of preface to the book he was writing: "The adventure of our story was born of humble parents in the city of Rochester and lost his father at the early age of six let us trace him up from that period untill he became the vagavond and the fugtive of a dark and a gloomy prison the bright rays of the sun was just glittering through the window when the voice of a female call'd him to come and witness the death of his dying father." On the other side of the scrap is a note to Ives, which seems to have been jotted down in pencil, in a hurry: "Mr ives this is the beging of the first chapter of my book—please not lose it." At least one prison official knew that Reed was working on a narrative and was willing to help. The little scrap was not lost, and it has remained with the rest of Reed's text for a century and a half.

Within his memoir, too, Reed appears to make some concessions, taking pains to acknowledge the men who have improved Auburn. By the time Reed arrived, Lynds was gone, and the post of head keeper had gone to Robert Cook—a "venerable gentleman," Reed calls him, "whose gray hairs I honor and respect to this very

The adventure of our story was borne of humble parents in the city of Rochester and lost his father at the early age of six let us trace him up from that period untill he became the vagavond and the fugitive of a dark and a gloomy prison mindain when the bright rays of the sun was just glittering through the witness the death of his dying father

Mr Ives this is the leging of the first chapter of my book — please not lose it

Scraps of paper kept with Reed's manuscript, including his note to "Mr. Ives."

day." Reed makes his peace with religion, taking a special interest in the idea of an angry God who might bring his tormentors to a day of reckoning; pasted into the back cover of his journal is a fiery passage from the Book of Lamentations. Reed joins the Whig reformers in preaching against such vices as gambling, masturbation, and the reading of novels. He has kind words for the prison chaplain, the state-appointed inspectors, and even Parsons and Hewson, the contractors who employed him in the cabinet shop. He sings the praises of the "great" Seward, "who is fighting against the world of enemies every day for the promotion and benefit of his country." Had Reed really experienced a moral reformation under the tutelage of these men, or was he giving his benefactors the performance he thought they would want to see? In either case, Seward's political allies in the reform movement had consoled Reed during his most miserable days, and their policies had made it possible for him to keep working on his story while he was doing time.[35]

Reed seems to have taken his discharge from Auburn in 1858 as

CHAP. III.

Jeremiah bewaileth his calamities.

I *AM* the man *that* hath seen affliction by the rod of his wrath.

2 He hath led me, and brought *me into* darkness, but not *into* light.

3 Surely against me is he turned; he turneth his hand *against me* all the day.

4 My flesh and my skin hath he made old; he hath broken my bones.

5 He hath builded against me, and compassed *me* with gall and travail.

6 He hath set me in dark places, as *they that be* dead of old.

7 He hath hedged me about, that I cannot get out: he hath made my chain heavy.

8 Also when I cry and shout, he shutteth out my prayer.

9 He hath enclosed my ways with hewn stone, he hath made my paths crooked.

10 He *was* unto me as *a* bear lying in wait, *and as* a lion in secret places.

11 He hath turned aside my ways, and pulled me in pieces: he hath made me desolate.

12 He hath bent his bow, and set me as a mark for the arrow.

13 He hath caused the arrows of his quiver to enter into my reins.

14 I was a derision to all my people; *and their* song all the day.

15 He hath filled me with bitterness, he hath made me drunken with wormwood.

16 He hath also broken my teeth with gravelstones, he hath covered me with ashes.

17 And thou hast removed my soul far off from peace: I forgat prosperity.

18 And I said, My strength and my hope is perished from the LORD:

19 Remembering mine affliction and my misery, the wormwood and the gall.

20 My soul hath *them* still in remembrance, and is humbled in me.

21 This I recall to my mind, therefore have I hope.

22 *It is of* the LORD's mercies that we are not consumed, because his compassions fail not.

23 *They are* new every morning: great *is* thy faithfulness.

24 The LORD *is* my portion, saith my soul; therefore will I hope in him.

25 The LORD *is* good unto them that wait for him, to the soul *that* seeketh him.

26 *It is* good that *a man* shou d both hope and quietly wait for the salvation of the LORD.

27 *It is* good for a man that he bear the yoke in his youth.

28 He sitteth alone, and keepeth silence, because he hath borne *it* upon him.

29 He putteth his mouth in the dust; if so be there may be hope.

30 He giveth *his* cheek to him that smiteth him: he is filled full with reproach.

31 For the LORD will not cast off for ever:

32 But though he cause grief, yet will he have compassion according to the multitude of his mercies.

33 For he doth not afflict willingly, nor grieve the children of men.

34 To crush under his feet all the prisoners of the earth,

35 To turn aside the right of a man before the face of the Most High,

36 To subvert a man in his cause, the LORD approveth not.

37 ¶ Who *is* he *that* saith, and it cometh to pass, *when* the LORD commandeth *it* not?

38 Out of the mouth of the Most High proceedeth not evil and good?

39 Wherefore doth a living man complain, a man for the punishment of his sins?

40 Let us search and try our ways, and turn again to the LORD.

41 Let us lift up our heart with *our* hands unto God in the heavens.

42 We have transgressed and have rebelled: thou hast not pardoned.

43 Thou hast covered with anger, and persecuted us: thou hast slain, thou hast not pitied.

44 Thou hast covered thyself with a cloud, that *our* prayer should not pass through.

45 Thou hast made us *as* the off-scouring and refuse in the midst of the people.

46 All our enemies have opened their mouths against us.

47 Fear and a snare is come upon us, desolation and destruction.

48 Mine eye runneth down with rivers of water for the destruction of the daughter of my people.

49 Mine eye trickleth down, and ceaseth not, without any intermission,

50 Till the LORD look down, and behold from heaven.

51 Mine eye affecteth my heart because of all the daughters of my city.

52 Mine enemies chased me sore, like a bird, without cause.

53 They have cut off my life in the dungeon, and cast a stone upon me.

54 Waters flowed over my head; *then* I said, I am cut off.

55 ¶ I called upon thy name, O LORD, out of the low dungeon.

56 Thou hast heard my voice: hide not thine ear at my breathing, at my cry.

57 Thou drewest near in the day *that* I called upon thee: thou saidst, Fear not.

58 O LORD, thou hast pleaded the causes of my soul; thou hast redeemed my life.

59 O LORD, thou hast seen my wrong: judge thou my cause.

60 Thou hast seen all their vengeance *and* all their imaginations against me.

61 Thou hast heard their reproach, O LORD, *and* all their imaginations against me;

62 The lips of those that rose up against me, and their device against me all the day.

63 Behold their sitting down, and their rising up; I *am* their music.

64 ¶ Render unto them a recompence, O LORD, according to the work of their hands.

65 Give them sorrow of heart, thy curse unto them.

66 Persecute and destroy them in anger from under the heavens of the LORD.

Inside back cover of Reed's manuscript, with pasted excerpt from Lamentations.

First draft of title page from Reed's manuscript. The original title was "The Life and Adventures of Rob Reed."

a chance to prepare his manuscript for publication. At that time, he had a different title in mind: "The Life and Adventures of Rob Reed: His fifteen years imprisonment, with the mysteries and miseries of Auburn Prison, with the rules and regulations of the prison unmasked. The troubles and sorrows of the prisoner, from the time he enters the prison until he is discharged." The figure, fifteen years, would appear to count the period from 1840, when Reed was first sent to Auburn, until his release in the summer of 1858, minus the three short years when he was outside, between terms. But Reed was not able to get the book into print before he was arrested for another larceny. He returned to prison in November 1858, and he had to change his title. He wrote the new one, "The Life and the Adventures of a Haunted Convict," on a sheet of rough-grained wrapping paper, which he glued to the inside cover of his bound journal, over the original title page. It was probably the end of 1858, perhaps early the following year. Reed's revision of the phrase "until he is released" to "up to the present time" is a bleak sign that the manuscript was finished inside Auburn.

Probably written in pieces, perhaps carried in and out of the prison as a work in progress, "The Life and the Adventures of a Haunted Convict" can be connected to the two kinds of prison literature that took shape in antebellum New York State. There are the passages of exposé, revealing the operations of the prison and the grotesque punishments, and then there are the chronicles of reform, telling how a rising generation of officials lifted the prison out of its "dark and cruel days," into a more enlightened era. Reed had learned, though, that well-intentioned reforms could lead to awful consequences. On December 2, 1858, just a few weeks after Reed returned to the prison, an African American inmate named Samuel Moore (or More) died after a session in the showering bath. The inmates rioted in protest. Newspapers and magazines played up the gruesome story. After an investigation, prison inspectors exonerated the officers who had killed Moore, but they resolved to end the use of the showering bath at Auburn. The device, introduced as a humane substitute for the whip, was now condemned as a new kind of torture.

The public could easily have concluded that Moore had been treated with special cruelty because of his race. An illustration of his death, published in *Harper's*, was like many other images of black suffering that circulated in the media in the 1850s, but with a new modification: the primitive brutality of slavery's whips and chains had been replaced by a distinctly modern piece of machinery. Reed knew from experience that the showering bath could kill an inmate or drive him insane. The thought of it, he wrote, "makes me shiver and ache." With or without the scandal of Samuel Moore's death,

"The Negro Convict, More, Showered to Death"
The scandal provoked a prison riot and an investigation into the use of the showering bath at Auburn.

the men who ran Auburn might have decided that Reed's memoir, with its cursing inmates and its fiery visions, was too incendiary to do them any good.

Release

REED WROTE HIS book for the public. He used the conventions he had learned from popular literary genres, addressing himself to the imaginary stranger he called, simply, "Reader," and he took up the contentious questions of penal history and prison reform. At the same time, though, his project was a private labor of recovery. Reed saw the prison as a dehumanizing institution that had nearly destroyed his mind and erased his identity. To shore himself up against oblivion, he went about reconstructing his life from memory and, when he could, from the surviving records. (His memoir tells how he visited the Refuge in New York during one of his periods of liberty, hoping to see his file, and as late as 1895 he was sending his letter from Rochester, still searching for it.) Like many other writers, Reed found that the task of telling his story involved not only recollection but also reinvention. More than any of his contemporaries, he wrote the kind of prison literature that would flourish in the twentieth century. With the intensities of its first-person voice and its deep insights into American racial violence, his book bears comparison to *The Autobiography of Malcolm X* (1965) and George Jackson's *Soledad Brother* (1970).

When Reed finished his manuscript, he was once again a person in transition. In May 1859, the records tell us, Austin Reed and forty-nine other prisoners were transferred from Auburn to Clinton State Prison at Dannemora, in the northeastern corner of New York State. It was the officers at Clinton who recorded Reed's physical description, lingering over his scars and burns. What they saw disturbed them. One member of the board of inspectors proposed that they ask their colleagues at Auburn to investigate Reed's treatment there. The motion was laid aside, presumably for political reasons, but it shows that Reed was in bad shape, and it suggests that someone at Clinton took an interest in his welfare. While Reed served out his time, he was given permission to begin seeking a pardon. In September 1860, he wrote to Theodore Medad Pomeroy, a well-known Auburn attorney and antislavery Republican who would be elected to the U.S. Congress during the Civil War. Two years later, in 1862, Reed sought the help of J. D. Kingsland, a contractor at Clinton, for the same purpose. Reed was released from prison in May 1863, and

Pardon of Austin Reed, signed by New York governor Samuel J. Tilden in 1876.

he kept up his effort to secure the pardon that, he hoped, would restore his citizenship rights. It was a long time coming, but Reed's petition was finally granted by Governor Samuel Tilden on August 26, 1876. The pardon is the last sure sign of Austin Reed's name in the public records before his 1895 letter to the superintendent of the Refuge.[36]

Where did he go? It is plausible that he had become the "Robert Reed" who is listed in an 1863 city directory for Rochester, a boarder at a temperance hotel, working as an artificial leg maker. The Civil War was shattering the bodies of soldiers with terrible efficiency, and a local businessman named Douglas Bly was making a fortune by selling prosthetics to disabled veterans. Trained in furniture making at the Refuge, long accustomed to laboring in the cabinetry shops at Auburn, Reed may have adopted the name he had given himself in his memoir and tried to earn an honest wage in Bly's factory. If so, he didn't last long. On January 30, 1864, "Robert Reed" was convicted of larceny after felony and sent to Auburn for a term of three years and three months; prison records refer to him as "Robert Reed alias Austin Reed." In 1866 he was once again discharged. His mother had died during his term, and the war had ended—and, in this changed world, Reed seems almost to have disappeared.[37]

Maybe he continued to live as Robert Reed. There are so many men by that name that no single one of them can easily be tracked down in the archives. Maybe he drifted westward or north into Canada, or maybe he changed his name yet again. His book is full of men who travel under pseudonyms and call each other by nicknames. His 1895 letters, signed "Austin Reed," briefly sketch his life after prison, including a battlefield conversion to Christianity. Some of the details that Reed provides in the letters are contradicted by prison records and census data. Given the dates of his confinement, for example, it is unlikely that he ever made it to a Civil War battlefield, though he surely heard many stories of the war from veterans in Rochester and elsewhere. His references to "goin all over the union and telling sinners the troubles and trials that I Have been through and How I came to be a christian" and "Having . . . a collection made up for me" indicate that he may have followed an itinerant career as a preacher or a lecturer, perhaps on the temperance circuit. As his book demonstrates, he certainly knew how to deliver an exhortation. "I am Now given a History of my life," he writes to the superintendent. Does he mean that he is planning to revise and expand his "Life and Adventures," which concludes in 1858? Did he still even have the manuscript in his possession in 1895, or did he have a new autobiography in mind? The last few decades of Reed's life are still mostly a mystery, at least for now.

What has endured, almost miraculously, is Reed's book, a memoir of hard times, sometimes awful in its details, rendered with a haunting eloquence. Even in its bleakest sections, the "Life and Adventures" is more than an exercise in the popular conventions of confession or sensationalism. It is a work of subtlety and complexity, seeming to anticipate its readers' expectations, only to exceed them. It has its own peculiar, sometimes gorgeous style. The memoir comes out of anger, and it is tempered by regret, but it is written with a delight in the pleasures of phrasemaking; it wanders into the expanses opened up by storytelling, the consolations of memory, and the liberties of invention. It slides from sentimentality into gallows humor. The author, a self-styled "fugitive," plays the role of the survivor, the preacher, and the prophet. In the unlikeliest places, he seems to sing.

Editor's Note on the Text

From time to time, as I worked on "The Life and the Adventures of a Haunted Convict," I made my way across Yale's campus to visit the Beinecke Rare Book Library and look at Austin Reed's original manuscript. The 304-page holograph (handwritten) document is made up of one bound quarto notebook (the paper folded into quarters) and two sewn gatherings of folio sheets (folded in half, lengthwise). The notebook was a fairly inexpensive object, available from shops in Rochester and many other American cities by the 1840s; common sailors kept their journals in similar blank books. When Reed had filled the last page, he continued his story on loose paper. One sheet bears the embossed stamp of Carson's Mill in Dalton, Massachusetts, the Berkshires-based company that made Herman Melville's favorite writing paper. (Melville visited the factory while he was drafting *Moby-Dick* and later described it as a deathly place, comparing the workers to prisoners and slaves.) The logo, a wreath of flax leaves, signals that Carson's still made its paper from linen and other textiles, and chemical testing on fibers from Reed's journal detects none of the wood pulp that would prevail in the later nineteenth century. Paper was not a commodity that Reed could take for granted, and he used it sparingly. He did not break his prose into regular sentences or paragraphs—sometimes marking pauses, instead, with dots or dashes of varying lengths—and his writing ran into the margins. Every inch of free space seems to have been valuable to him.[1]

The ink from Reed's pen tests positive for iron, which helps to confirm a date in the mid-nineteenth century. The handwriting reveals even more. We can be confident that Reed wrote his story himself because certain aspects of his hand are consistent, across his life; from the first known example, the signature on his 1839 indenture agreement, through "The Life and Adventures" in 1858, to his letters to the House of Refuge in 1895, Reed used "business script," a plain, unadorned style, easily learned and easily read, that was taught in American common schools well into the nineteenth century. Today those of us who still write by hand tend, perhaps unconsciously, to imitate mechanical or digital print, but in Reed's era very few novice writers would have learned to model their manuscripts on the format of printed books. A boy trained in the Lancastrian method at a reformatory, as Reed was, would have been unlikely to adopt regularized spelling, capitalization, punctuation, or paragraph breaks. Fancier techniques were more commonly taught to girls, for whom an elegant hand was seen as a mark of cultured refinement, rather than a practical business skill.[2]

Reed's script thus tells the trained paleographer something about the quality of his education, acquired mostly inside penal institutions. But readers of the "Life and Adventures" will encounter an author who is also an artist. He organizes his memoir with a literary design in mind—it is a narrative, not a diary—and his unorthodox grammar and irregular spelling create some fascinating effects. Now and then he breaks one word, *icicle*, into two, *ice sickel;* blends the meanings of two words like *hunted* and *haunted;* or creates a phrase like *scoalding tears*, which might express either the heat of sorrow (*scalding*) or the sharpness of a parent's rebuke (*scolding*). There are historical clues and literary pleasures to be found in what might look, at first, like simple errors.

Even professional scholars have a tough time, though, reading hundreds of pages of unedited, irregularly punctuated prose. Preparing this Random House edition, I attempted to preserve Reed's own style and characteristic phrasing while also respecting his im-

Reed's manuscript, page 22. The author describes the reading lessons he received at the House of Refuge.

plicit intention to publish his text. Inevitably, this meant making some changes, and I confess that it was a difficult task, raising hard questions about language and power. My hope was that the "Life and Adventures" would reach a broad audience and provoke readers to think seriously about race and criminal punishment in the United States—that it would become an event in our own time, not an antiquarian curiosity—but I knew that there was a long history of well-meaning reformers imposing their own designs on writings by inmates and fugitives. I had studied a prisoner-poet called Harry Hawser, whose verses were used to defend Pennsylvania's "solitary system" against its critics in the 1840s, and I had written about how a white editor, Lydia Maria Child, suppressed important parts of Harriet Jacobs's slave narrative to soften the author's abolitionist message. Researching New York's early prison literature, I learned about Jacob Hodges, a nineteenth-century inmate who became the subject of a short biography, "*Black Jacob,*" meant to prove that Auburn could redeem even a "homeless, friendless African sailor." After Hodges's death and burial, his black neighbors in upstate New York demanded that his grave be opened; they seem to have suspected that his body had been stolen for dissection, just as his life story was being turned into propaganda.[3]

Editors, like everyone else, work within unequal economies of resources and status, and some readers may feel that I've done a kind of violence to Reed's text by regularizing the spelling and inserting modern punctuation. I thought seriously about leaving it alone, trying to publish a raw transcription, rather than an edited version. In the end, though, I decided that there were stronger arguments in favor of making (and taking responsibility for) some light, careful edits. After all, there really is no way to print a piece of writing without changing it. Compare the photograph of a manuscript page to a transcription of the same, and you can see, right away, how much has been lost. This passage brings the matters of literacy and authority to the surface:

> evry spare minute that Jack could get he would run to me with his little pointer in his hand and show me wich was A. and wich was B. and by the space of nine months - I was siting at the head of the ninth class evry night reading and studying peices frem the english reader—I had now made such an improvement in reading and writing by the help of Jack Kimbell and little mike Flinn that work aside of me. that it gave mr Wood a great encouragement.

one year rooll'd away and I found myself the master of a pen and the reader of a book - and a conquor of arithmetic - them was the days when I would chalange old england or america to throw down any histoy before me - and let me read it through just once and I was the boy that would stand before any historian that ever stood between england and america and argure with him on the subject of wich I had been reading. I had such a greedy apitite for Reading that I was call'd up before mr. Williams the school teacher one day and laid across the stool where I got fifteen cutts with the ratan - for having more then one book in my desk - [. . .]

Even a direct transcription gives the reader only the false promise of completeness and fidelity. An imperfect copy of a unique artifact, the transcription can never communicate the texture of the paper or the shapes of the handwriting, the smudges or the fading of the ink. The Beinecke has made page scans of Reed's entire manuscript freely available through its website, and readers should look at them. (Researchers may see the original in the library.) The digital images may not give you a sense of the paper's smooth feel or the antique smell of the sheep's leather binding, but they will disclose some aspects of the document that could never have been reproduced in any transcription or edited version.[4]

More compelling still, in deciding how to prepare the text, were the strong indications in the manuscript that Reed himself intended it for publication. If the author had found the means to get his manuscript into print during his own lifetime, it would have gone through the ordinary processes of regularization, punctuation, and paragraphing. In other words, Reed, like virtually all authors in his time and country, would have been edited before he was published. The manuscripts of Jacobs's *Incidents*, Hawser's poetry, and Hodges's confession have been lost or destroyed. Normally, the scholarly editor's business is to review the surviving printed editions, attempting to recover authors' intentions long after their manuscripts have disappeared. Working on Reed's memoir presented the opposite challenge: how to honor both the author's choices on the page and his implicit intention to reach a "Reader" through print.[5]

Trying to strike that balance, I applied the following principles silently throughout the text:

1. Follow the author's own edits, as indicated in the manuscript—-i.e., delete words that have been struck through and incorporate words that have been inserted in the margins.
2. To make the text more easily legible to modern readers, add punctuation, including periods, question marks, commas, quotation marks, and apostrophes; and add paragraph breaks and section breaks, attempting where possible to follow the long dashes or other cues Reed sometimes uses to indicate a shift in topic or scene. My section breaks are indicated with a [——]. Reed's own section breaks are unmarked.
3. Regularize spelling, except in passages of dialogue where Reed uses shifts in dialect and register for literary effect. Where Reed seems to invent a word (e.g., *scoalding* or *doneful*), preserve it and explain the decision with a note.
4. Where Reed varies the spelling of a proper name (e.g., *Orsband* and *Osborne*), edit for internal consistency. Because Reed seems to play with the allegorical resonance of names (e.g., *Mr. Heart* and *Mr. Lad*), do not change them to match the names of historical persons (e.g., *Hart* and *Ladd*).
5. Verb tenses: Reed indicates the past tense in a variety of ways, including —*'d*, —*d*, or —*ed*. Except in passages of verse, where the variations are used for metrical effects, modernize all of these (in most cases, to —*ed*). Otherwise, do not change the tense of any verb.
6. Where appropriate, correct usage by substituting *than* for *then* as well as homophones—e.g., *their* for *there*; *good bye* for *good buy*; *whole* for *hole*; *right* for *rite*; *bear* for *bare*; *tales* for *tails*; *know* for *no*; *presence* for *presents*; *meet* for *meat*.

7. Regularize capitalization of nouns and at beginnings of sentences, with one exception: Whereas Reed's capitalization in the manuscript is otherwise inconsistent, he almost always capitalizes the words *House* and *Home*. This effect, which gives special weight and meaning to two key terms, has been retained.

Beyond applying these general principles, I made some other emendations—deleting repeated words, supplying a few missing words—and listed them in Appendix C. The passage transcribed above, from page 22 of Reed's manuscript, appears this way in the edited text:

> . . . every spare minute that Jack could get, he would run to me with his little pointer in his hand and show me which was A, and which was B, and by the space of nine months I was sitting at the head of the ninth class every night, reading and studying pieces from *The English Reader.*
>
> I had now made such an improvement in reading and writing by the help of Jack Kimbell and little Mike Flinn that work aside of me, that it gave Mr. Wood a great encouragement. One year rolled away and I found myself the master of a pen and the reader of a book, and a conqueror of arithmetic. Them was the days when I would challenge old England or America to throw down any history before me and let me read it through just once, and I was the boy that would stand before any historian that ever stood between England and America and argue with him on the subject of which I had been reading. I had such a greedy appetite for reading that I was called up before Mr. Williams the school teacher one day and laid across the stool, where I got fifteen cuts with the rattan for having more than one book in my desk.

Some editors would have made fewer changes; others might have made more. What comes through, I hope, is not only the vernacular voice of a speaker who identifies with the poor and the dispossessed, against the educated and refined "big bugs" of high society, but also the powerful, surprising literary effects created by the gifted, self-conscious writer of this uniquely terrifying, mysterious, and beautiful book.

The Life and the Adventures of a Haunted Convict

Or The Inmate of a Gloomy Prison
With the Mysteries and Miseries
of the New York House of Refuge
and Auburn Prison Unmasked;
With the Rules and Regulations of
Auburn Prison from 1840 up
to the Present Time, and the Different
Modes of Punishments

Chapter I

THE BRIGHT SUN was just a shining into the window of my father cottage when I was called by the voice of a female to come and take the last look of my dying father. I was then at the age of six. After taking the last look of the dying man, I turned from the dying scene, leaving the angel of death to finish the last and awful work: but oh, who could describe the feelings of my boyish heart, when I saw my father laid cold and lifeless in the coffin? Then, that was the hour when all the fond recollection of my dying father came rushing in my mind. His last look, his last dying advice, i.e., his last prayer and his last blessing, that I might be kept from all the snares and temptations of the world, and that I might grow up and become a useful man, that I might be a help meet to my mother when she should be bowing down beneath the weight of old age.

How often in my boyish days, when the bright sun was just about to sink beneath the mountain tops, and the night hawks a hovering over my head, have I stolen away from the cottage and from the side of my mother, and gone and sat for hours at the grave of my beloved father, all unnoticed to him, and there wept like an infant. How fresh does the dying scene yet impress upon my memory, although my father has now been dead for nearly twenty years, and in yonder's old grave yard in the city of Rochester lies the cold remains of my father, moldering away to dust.[1] While the feet of the traveler has trampled o'er his grave, unmind of who the slumber is that lies beneath his feet, the cold winter winds are howling and playing o'er his grave, yet there he lays, unmindful of those northern blasts that comes whistling o'er his tomb.

Chapter II

No sooner had the cold clods covered the remains of my father before I forgot his last blessing and dying prayer with all of his advice. I soon broke through the restraints of my mother and fell a victim to vice and crime.

'Twas a beautiful summer's morning that my mother put fifty cents into my hand and bade me to go to the grocery and get her four pounds of sugar. I took the fifty cents and went off to the bank and got it change all into coppers. I then steered my way behind an old barn where a lot of boys was pitching pennies. I fell into the game with them and soon found that they both was pitching against me. I left their company, and being the winner of three cents I then went to the grocery and bought the sugar and returned home.

As I entered the door my mother ask me if I had been making that sugar. She order me to be seated in one corner of the room and not to leave the House again during the day. While she went out to the well to draw a pail of water, I slip out of the back door and made my way to the city, a loitering round the street until night overtook me. I then steered my way for Home.

The dim light of a candle was burning in the House. I crept softly under the window, and there I laid a listening and shivering with fear of an awful punishment the moment I entered the room. As I laid there under the window, I could hear my mother talking to my brothers and sisters[2] in the following manner—

"That boy will surely be the cause of bringing my gray hairs with sorrow down to the grave."

As she said them words, I rose and went to the door, and giving a genteel rap, my mother bade me enter. I opened the door and went in and saw the scoalding tears come a rushing down my mother cheeks. She order me off to bed, where I turned in and slept away the gloomy hours of the night. It was a long time after breakfast before I arose and went down stairs.

There sat my mother with her needle and thread, all alone, while my brothers and sister were gone off to school. My mother now took me into the bedroom, and with all the affection and the tears of a mother she talk to me in the following manner—

"My son, I see since your father has been dead that you are beginning to cause me a great deal of trouble. Remember that if you follow the paths of sin that you will surely come to some bad and awful end." With these and many other words of instruction did my mother try to bring up before my mind and to implant the truths of religion in my heart. She then gave me a severe whipping and sent me off to school.

On my way to school I met several boys who ask me to join their company that day, that they was goin' to have some fun. I stuff my book into my pocket and joined their company—but alas that day's fun proved the dearest fun to me than ever I witness before in my life, for we were no sooner together before we jump over into a man's orchard and cut down several of his fruit trees and made our way for the city. It was three days afterwards before my mother found it out. The farmer came up to my mother's House and informed her all about the deed. My mother bursted out in a full flood of tears and predicted that if I went on in this way, regardless of my father's dying advice, that I would one day or another become the felon of a cell, and that it would be better for me if I was laying in my grave aside of my father. As she uttered those sacred words and the name of my father, the prayers, the blessing, and the advice of my dying father all sprung up afresh into my mind.

My mother told the farmer that I should be punished right on the spot for the deed, that she wouldn't allow her children to destroy other folks' property if she knew it. As she said these words, she took a rawhide from the mantelpiece and ordered me to strip off my coat. I jump for the ax that stood behind the door and, raising it at my mother's head, told her if she struck me one blow with that rawhide that I would sliver her brains out on the floor. The old farmer arose to take the ax from my hand, to which I threw it at him with all my might, which left a deep cut in his leg. I then ran out the door and went into the city and was gone from Home three days.

Chapter III

'Twas a wet drizzly day in the month of July as I was strolling the street, and had been gone from Home three days, that the heavy hand of a constable was laid upon me to restore me back to my mother. As I went along through the streets, I was stared at by every one that went along. Shivering with the wet and cold and pinched with hunger, I soon gain the threshold of my mother's cottage door, covered with rags and dirt. There sat a rich old farmer in the House who lived out to Avon Springs, ready to take me away. Oh how I wept, how I cried, how I beg my mother not to let me be separated away from her. With what fair and faithful promises did I make to my mother for the time to come, if she would only let me stay with her at Home. My promises, my tears availed me nothing. My mother had firmly made up her mind that I should be sent from a city life and live a country life.

After striking a bargain with the old country hound, the day was appointed to which I was to start for the country. My mother wash me and gave me something to eat and then took a bed cord and made my hands and feet fast to keep me in custody until Mr. Lad (for that was the farmer's name) came after me.[3] At night my mother unloosed me and sent me off up stairs to bed, taking good care to lock the door to keep me safe. The next morning before my mother was up my youngest sister came up stairs and told me that the farmer would be after me that day at ten o'clock, and that mother had got my Sunday clothes ready for me to put on. She advise me not to stir a step with him, for if I did I should never see my Home nor her again.

The tears came from my sister eyes as she said those words to me. The call of my mother soon brought her from my bed side, telling her to make haste and get the House cleaned up, for she expected Mr. Lad along very soon. My mother then called me up and wash me from head to foot, put a new suite of clothes on me which I use to wear Sundays. While my mother was getting me ready, I casted my eyes out of the window and saw a splendid carriage driving up to the door.

"Wonder who is there!" exclaimed my sister in an angry tone.

"Why, it Mr. Lad and his daughter," said my mother with a smile.

The horses was made fast at the fence and the carriage flung open, while my mother stood ready to take the hand of a beautiful country female to help her from the carriage. There me and my sister stood in the door, both bathe in tears. The country girl made a low bow to my sister, to which she got an ugly sour look for her compliment.

My mother then took me into the bedroom, and kneeling down she implored the blessing of the almighty to go with me and be with me, to protect me and to be the guide of my youth. She then arose, a putting a pocket bible into my hand, beg me to read it and to take it as the man of my counsel, and that if I obeyed it precepts, it would do me good in after life.

There me and my sister stood, hand in hand, bathe in tears of grief and sorrow. My mother then imprinted a kiss on my cheek and told Mr. Lad that I was now all ready to start.

As the old man and his daughter arose, my sister told me not to stir from the House one step, that she would protect me. By this time my elder brother came in and, seeing me and my sister bathe in tears, could not bear to witness the scene of separation and the grief and sorrow between me and my sister.

"Are you goin' to take my brother away?" exclaimed my sister.

"Yes," said the countryman.

"By whose authority?" said my brother.

"We will give you to understand," said my sister, "that he is not a goin' with you."

"Who knows," said my brother, "but what he is goin' into the hands of some slave holder?"

"Not at all!" exclaimed the country girl. "His work will be easy and light, and at the end of every three months he may return Home."

My mother all this time during the conversation stood on the floor with one hand up to her face, not knowing what to say.

"I suppose, mother," said my sister, "that you think it hard to see your children arising up and interfering in your business."

"I do," said my mother. "The city will surely spoil that boy if he stays Home."

"Unless that man can prove before me by good and substantial witnesses that he is no slave holder," said my brother, "he can't go one step with him."

"I think it proper," said my sister, "that we should know where he is goin' and into whose hands he is goin' into, and I think my mother has taken a very improper course in this matter, and I think it my duty as a sister to interfere into this matter, before our brother is torn from his Home."

"Well," said Mr. Lad, "I live out to Avon Springs, and it is getting quite late in the day, and I have twenty miles to go. I would like to have the boy, for he looks like a smart boy." The old man whispered something into my mother ear and drove off without me.

Early the next morning, the tramp of horses and the rattling of a carriage was heard at the door. Peeping out of the window, I saw Mr. Lad and his daughter standing at the gate. He had a new pair of shoes into his hand, while his daughter held a new cap in her left hand. He had bought those things for me for inducement, to get me to go Home with him.

As he entered the door, he said that he was in a hurry and ask me if I had made up my mind to go Home with him. I told him that I would let him know in a few minutes. I then left him and called my sister out of doors and talk the matter over with her, to which she consented I should go, providing that I should be sent Home every three months. The bargain being struck, the old farmer drove off with his prize, and I soon found myself seated under the roof of a lordly mansion at Avon Springs.

Chapter IV

'TWAS IN THE year of 1833 that my troubles commenced. I now found myself under the roof of a new Home at Avon Springs. With a sad and a heavy heart I went out under the wood shed, and seating myself on a pile of wood, I began to repent that ever I had left the Home of my nativity, while ten thousand thoughts came pouring into my breast, with fond recollections of those brothers and sisters at Home, of the advice of my dying father, the tears which my sister shed before I left my Home, the prayer which my mother had offered up the day before I left. After pondering over those things with deep feelings, I drew the little pocket bible which my mother had given me before I left Home from my pocket, and there I saw the handwriting of my mother, and the little prayer which she had wrote there for me to learn. After reading a few of its contents I closed the little book, and have never open it from that day to this, but still my mother's handwriting still stands against me—the prayer, the tears, the griefs and her sorrows.

After closing the book and looking around me, I arose and strolled around by the barns, and so around by the kitchen door, to which the servant girl ask me if I wouldn't come in and sit down with her and eat some breakfast, to which I replied that I was not hungry. She then ask me if I wouldn't go out under the wood shed and bring her in some wood. After I had fetch in the wood, she sat a chair by the stove for me to sit on. She then began to talk to me in the most feelingest manner than ever I heard from the mouth of a female before in my life. She ask me where my mother lived, how many brothers and sisters I had, if my father was yet alive, and as she mention the name of my father, she broke the golden pitcher, and the silver cord was loose, and I bursted out in a full flood of tears and went out of doors to seek some place where I might give vent to my feelings.

How sad and gloomy the country did look to me, although it was a stately mansion where I was to live. I had not been inside of the House during the day and had not eaten anything all that day. The day wore away slowly, and the curtains of evening soon threw her dark mantle over the earth. I went out into the barn, and covering myself over with hay, I soon fell fast asleep and did not awake until I was aroused by the hand of a female. She then took me by the hand and led me down stairs and so on into the House, and sat some breakfast before me, of which I did not touch.

While I was sitting in the kitchen, Mr. Lad two daughters came in, and one of them pick me up and sat me in her lap and told me that I must not feel so bad, that in a little while she was goin' to Rochester, and she would then take me along with her. She then took me by the hand and led me out into the orchard and around the flower garden and so over to her father's brother's House, but with all her fond care and good advice and sweet music, she could not make my mind any the easier. Home—Home still kept hanging on my mind.

I had now been with Mr. Lad three days when he one morning, being a little angry, ask me if I was ready now to go to work and learn to be a farmer. I told him no, that I was goin' to start for Home that very day, to which he said that I had been whining about Home long enough, and that if he seen any more of it that he would take me out to the barn and horse whip me. This made my passion rise a little, and I told him to raise a hand at me if he dared. At that he dragged me off to the barn, and taking a halter, he made both of my hands fast behind me and gave me a severe punishment with a black whip which he had hanging up in the barn, and ordered me into the House with my hands tied behind.

Oh, then was the hour that I thought of my beloved who was sleeping in the grave. Yes, then was the time that I needed a father's protection. The old villain, would he dared to raise a hand on me if my father had been alive, or would he dared to given me a word of insult? Would he dared to ordered me to the field to work under the hot burning rays of the sun, if my father had been alive? No, or he would shivered the head from his shoulders.

There he kept me tied till twelve o'clock, when I was unloosed by the hands of one of the girls. No sooner had I been unloosed than I made my way to West Avon, and stopping in front of a large mansion I ask one of the hired servants who lived there. He said that Esq. Osborne live there and was the possessor of a large tract of land. I open the gate and walk up to the door, and ask the servant girl if Esq. Osborne was in. She said he was not but would be in.

Presently Mrs. Osborne then came to the door, and she told me to come. She then sat down and talk with me awhile, and ask me where I lived and where I was goin', to which I unfolded the whole riddle to her. I had sat there talking to her nearly two hours, when Mr. Osborne came in. I arose from the chair which I was sitting in, and spoke to him in the following manner—

That I had just lost my father, and that my mother was left a widow, with five young children to bring up and to support, and that I had in the company of some other boys cut down some fruit trees that belong to a farmer who lived not far from my mother House, for which deed my mother has sent me out here to live with one Mr. Lad, and that Mr. Lad without the authority of my mother or without her knowledge had taken me out to the barn and tied me up and whip me.

After I had related the truth to Esq. Osborne, he told me to sit there in his House during that day, and on the morrow he would go Home with me and see my mother and get her to let me come and live with him. I was glad to hear such welcome news fall upon my ears, and I went out into the garden where a man was weeding and pulled off my coat and went to work and made myself as useful as I could until the shades of evening prevailed. I was then called into the House, where I ate a good hearty supper. I then wash my feet, and retired to bed where I slept away the gloomy hours of darkness.

Chapter V

I ROSE IN THE morning, and putting on my clothes I strolled out into the garden until breakfast time. It is now eight o'clock, and the stage was waiting at the door for me and Mr. Osborne. Everything being ready, the stage drove off, and at one o'clock in the afternoon I was seated in the cottage under the parental roof where my father gave me his dying blessing. My mother was not in. She had gone out on a visit and would not make her return until five o'clock. Mr. Osborne said that he had some business to tend to into the city and that he would return the next morning and see my mother, to which he left the House, leaving me and my sister alone by ourselves.

About three o'clock my sister and me went over to the spot where laid my father, wrapped in the cold icicle hand of death. There we stood, between the living and the dead, hand in hand, gazing on the green sods that covered all that was once dear and near to us, while the voice of my father seemed to echo afresh to me from the cold spot where he now laid. Leaving this sacred and hallowed spot, we made our way home. Reader, could you told the feelings of my mind as I march Homeward from my father grave, and the tears coming from my eyes? Or did my beloved father know the heavy heave of my bosom, or could he tell the wrongs and sufferings which I was goin' under through the means of my cruel hearted mother? Did he know that I would one day or another grasp the pistol which he used to carry with him nights, and with a high and an uplifted hand seek my revenge for the wrong that had been imposed upon me? No, Reader, or he would took the deadly weapon and sunk it low in the deep.

It was now nearly sun down, and my mother had not yet made her return Home, so my sister and me walk out to the woods which stood but a few rods from the House. As I was walking along, I opened to her the riddle of the punishment which Mr. Lad gave me, and the cause of my returning Home, and how cruel my mother had been in banishing me from Home to be brought up in the hands of a cold, hard hearted countryman.

"Curse that infernal woman," said my sister. "She will be the ruin and over throw of the whole family ere the age of manhood comes. Scoundrel," echoed my sister after I had told her my riddle. "Scoundrel—had I the power of a god or had I the strength of a man, I would make you bow in blood beneath my feet."

As she said these words, my blood began to run hot, and my temper began to hunger for revenge.

"Ere before the morrow sun shall set behind yon western cloud," said my sister, "you shall leave the country hound dead upon the ground stained with his gore."

The loud crack of a rifle brought us to a stand. Gazing in the direction to which the smoke came from, we press forward to the spot, where we heard the groans of a dying man who was just expiring.

"Oh, heavens and earth!" exclaimed my sister, as she stood upon a log and saw the fresh blood oozin' from the deep fresh wounds that was made by the cause of the burst of the rifle. "He is a dying!" shriek my sister, as the man laid there in the swamp, and a piece of the rifle sunken deep in his head, while across his breast hung a gold watch chain attached to a gold watch.

I ran with all my might for help and to give the alarm, but ere before help could be got, the cold night of death had approach, and his doom was sealed forever. The shades of evening had approach, and the coroner had sent several men from the city to watch over the body during the night.

Long before the dawn of day, a light tap was heard at my mother door, as though it had been the delicate rap of the hand of some female. My mother rose and open the door, and there stood the wife of the dying man, with her beautiful head bowed in deep mourning and grief.

"I told him, oh I told Mr. Wilkcocks to stay to Home with me and not go out a hunting," said the young woman, who had only been married but a few days, and seemed to be in great distress. I cannot tell the feelings of this young lady, but I leave it to the reader to imagine for himself. The morning light appeared, and at eight o'clock Mr. Wilkcocks was raised from his miry bed and carried home, where he was wash and laid out and conveyed to the grave. My pen nor pencil can't describe the feelings of this young lady as she followed the mortal remains of her husband to the grave.

It appeared, from the story that she told my mother, that Mr. Wilkcocks had went out in the morning with his rifle in company with some young men, expecting to return before noon, but his comrades returning another way Home, Mr. Wilkcocks struck off into the woods and come through, and striking off into the road that lead a pass my mother's House, he had loaded his rifle too much, and seeing game ahead of him he let flash, which caused his rifle to burst, and the pieces flew and sunk deep into his head, which caused his death. He was young and had just been married and started into business. Mrs. Wilkcocks was a young lady esteem by everyone that knew her. Borne down with grief and sorrow, she broke up House keeping and returned Home to her father and mother, where she soon died a few days after with a broken heart.

About ten o'clock the next day, Mr. Osborne made his appearance at the door, to which my mother sat a chair for him and ask him to come in. She then sent me and my sister out of doors to play while they held a long conversation about me.

I could plainly see that vengeance, eternal vengeance still burned in the bosom of my sister as she stood with her ear up to the door, a listening at the conversation. "I could plainly hear him say whip," said she to me, and at that she bowed with all of her force and bursted open the door and went in.

"Who and where is that damned infernal villain that whip my brother," said she in a rage of anger. "Show him to me, and ere the sun sets in the west the bowknife of my father shall be stained with his blood."

My mother stood speechless and dumb, not knowing what to say. She then called me up to her and ask me if I would like to go and live with Mr. Osborne—to which my sister replied that if she put me out to live with another white man that she would stain the floor with my mother blood. Mr. Osborne could clearly see what the consequence would be if he should undertake to take me away from Home, even by my own consent, so raising from his seat he made a low bow and left the House.

Chapter VI

IN DEEP SORROW my mother arose and put on her shawl and bonnet and left the house, saying with tears rolling from her eyes that she wish she was dead and in her grave, where her troubles would have an end, "for in sorrow will you children bring my gray hairs to the grave. I shall now leave you and never return to you again, and my prayer to God is that the hand of some kind stranger may pick you up as orphans and bring you up." Folding my little brother who was younger than me in her arms, she told us that perhaps we should never see her again. She then left the House, carrying my younger brother in her arms and leaving me and my sister to ourselves.

Three days had now rolled away, and our mother had not made her appearance, nor could she be seen or found or heard from, though my sister and me sought her with many tears. The fourth day had now arrived, but still no mother made her appearance yet. Where was she? Was she in the city? No, Reader, though we sought the city through and through, still my mother couldn't be found there.

With both hands in my pockets I went through the streets a crying. When a lady stepped up to me and ask me the cause of my weeping, I told her that I had lost my mother, to which she took me by the hand and led me to her House, where she gave me a piece of cake, and in the company with another lady she led me by the hand to the door of my mother cottage, where sat my sister, bathe in tears.

"Has mother come yet?" said I, and as she answered no, I bursted in a fresh flood of tears. I left the House and the two ladies a sitting there with my sister while I took a ramble in the woods, crossing an old swamp about a quarter of a mile from the House, and under an old elm tree there laid my mother, with her eyes half opened and my little brother, wrapped in her shawl, laying at her side.

Reader, can you describe the feelings of my heart as I stood there gazing at my mother, just on the brink of death? One day, yea one hour more, and the brittle thread of her life would have been snapped forever. Like a flash of lightning I ran off to the House and gave the alarm. The ladies came at her assistance and helped my mother Home. I then ran to the city after Doct. Backus,[4] and a begging him to save the life of my mother, the Doct. mounted his horse and in a few minutes was at the bedside of my mother, who had by this time by the help of the ladies been restored to a considerable degree. The Doct. left her some medicine, saying that he would call again the next day. After much rubbing and a little nourishment my mother began to speak, while me and my sister stood with tears rolling from our eyes. It was getting late, and the ladies after giving us a little advice returned to their Homes. The next morning I had the satisfaction of seeing my mother up and on her feet.

Worn with trouble and care and the disobedience of her children, she went off into the woods, and wrapping my youngest brother in her shawl, she there laid down to die.

Chapter VII

ALTHOUGH THIS WAS an awful shock to me, still it had no impression on mine and on my sister mind. The revenge which she still bore to Mr. Lad for whipping me still burned hotter and hotter in her bosom. One day, while my mother was gone out of the House, she came a running up to me with something in her hand under her apron. On my raising her apron, I found that she had been to my father old trunk and stolen his pistol and bowknife, and handed it to me, telling me to hide them and to be careful and not let mother know anything about them, and in the morning to rise before day and wake her up.

I retired to bed that night, a wandering in my mind what it was my sister wanted, and what under the heavens she was goin' to do with them deadly weapons of my father. Was it to destroy the life of my mother? No, for on the morrow when I arose from my bed and went to hers, and shaking her fickle form from a dull sleep, she rose and unraveled the whole sequel of the matter to me.

"Take them," said she, "and this little bundle, and before (pointing with her finger at the sun) before that sun sinks in the west, disguise yourself in that dress of mine which is in the bundle, and under the cover of darkness take the life of that infernal villain that had the boldness to horse whip you. Be careful as you enter the village that no human eye see you. Keep on the outskirts of the town until the dark curtains of the night appears, and let that pistol which I have loaded burst his brain, and let that knife with one stroke finish the work, and send that cursed infernal villain to his long Home, where trouble and cares will pierce his mind no more."

My hand shivered as she put the little bundle into my hand, but still I thought that I was doing no more than justice if I left him a cold corpse on the ground. Stuffing my pockets full of crackers and cheese, I began my march, with my little bundle in under my arm with a dress in it which belong to my sister. It was just coming day light, and it being cool I took the advantage of the day before the sun shone out hot. About ten o'clock I found that I had traveled thirteen miles, and had seven miles yet to trample. I sat down under the fence and began to eat some crackers which my sister had given me, and oh, my God, can you tell the feelings of my mind as I sat there eating my crackers? In loud peals of thunder I heard my father's prayer, playing in the flashes of lightning from beneath the ground where he laid. There I saw, dancing before my eyes, my mother beneath the tree with her infant at her side. . . .

But all of these sad reflections had no effect on my mind. I got up and began my journey again, and just as the hotel bell was ringing for dinner, I came in sight of the barn where I was tied up like a slave and thrash by the rough hand of a farmer who had no business nor no right nor authority to lay a hand on me, and as such reflection came rolling across my mind, my temper burned with rage and anger, and under an old tree I laid me down and slept till the moon throwed her silvery beams in my face.

I then arose from my lurking place, and untying the bundle I took my sister's dress and hood and slipped it on. I then wrapped the knife in my handkerchief and the pistol in my pocket and made my way to the House. Giving a rap on the door with my finger, the very girl that sympathized with me came to the door and ask me to step in. I told her that I was in a hurry and could not stay.

"Is Mr. L. in?" said I in a low voice.

"No," said the girl. "We expect him every minute."

As she said these, I rose from my seat and went out and stood listening at the door.

"Wonder who that little colored girl is," said the hired girl to one of the old man's daughters.

"Don't know. She must be some strange girl in the place that wants hire out."

By this time I heard the rumbling noise of a wagon a coming up the street. I knew that this must be none other than that marbled hearted man that lashed me in the barn. Throwing my sister dress from off me, I folded it up, and mounting the fence I cocked the pistol, and with an uplifted hand of revenge, I let fire and missed my shot. It was a dark night. I could hardly see my hands before my face. The old man hollered "Murder! Murder!" but before any aid could get to him, I drew the knife across his shoulders, which left a deep wound for months afterwards. By this time the country people had gather thick around, and the dogs a barking loud. I was taken and made fast by my hand and feet and taken to the constable house, where he made a bed on the floor for me and untied me for the night.

I was in a room by myself, with the door left open and the window made fast. I heard a loud snoring, and getting up from my bed, I walk out through the room where the constable and his family slept and open the door and walk out. I then went up to Mr. L— House, where the family was all sunk in sleep. I ascended the top of the kitchen roof, and taking a match from my pocket, I started a blaze. I then went to the barn, and putting a match to the hay, I soon brought it to the ground. The light of the flames played around through the windows of his brother's House, which brought the neighbors together. By this time his House was nearly level with the ground. The dawn of morning was just breaking forth, and I struck off into the road and walk some seven miles, when on looking behind me I saw a couple of horsemen come galloping up the road on full speed, with a rope in their hands. I mounted the fence and jump over into a large field. The horsemen dismounted, and letting down the fence came on a full gallop after me and made me their prisoner.

I was taken before Esq. Osborne, and from thence I was put into a wagon to be conveyed away to Geneseo to the county jail, where I was put under the care of Mr. Austin the sheriff till the appearance of court. I had now for the first time in my life become a felon of a cell for three long months. Being nothing but a boy, I was allowed to run about the hall all day, and my cell left unlock during nights. Many was the hour when Mrs. Austin would draw her chair up to the door and talk to me about my mother and my father, and I recollect that she told me once that for my disobedience to my mother that I had took ahold of the wrong kind of tools to play with, and in the course of a few weeks I was goin' to be taken from my mother and be sent off to the House of Refuge in the city of New York.

There was a fellow in jail with me, charged with stealing a horse, who was always full of jokes and fun and would often sit for hours with me and learn me how to play cards and show me several little tricks, which I soon began to get acquainted with. I now became harden in vice and crime. In the course of time I was tried and sentence to the New York House of Refuge until I was one and twenty.

The sun was throwing her golden rays on the fields, when the irons was put around my wrists to be sent off to New York. I had become so harden that my father advice and my mother prayer couldn't make me shed a tear, which the Reader shall plainly see, that when the stage drove up to the door for me to see my mother, perhaps for the last time in this world, I never shed a tear, while on the other hand my mother and sister was crying like a little infant. After hearing what my mother said to me and receiving a little testament from her, and they both imprinted a kiss on my cheek, and the stage drove off, and Thursday at eleven o'clock, five days after I started, I found myself within the walls of the House of Refuge.

Chapter VIII[5]

ON MY ENTERING the office my chains was taken off, and I was sent by the Superintendent Mr. Heart[6] with the steward to the wash room, where my hair was cut and my clothes was change.

Reader, go with me while I take you by the hand and conduct you through every department of the House of Refuge that stood in the Bowery in 1833, and give you a description of the rules and regulation of the House together with the diet—Viz. You are first led by Mr. Wood,[7] the Assistant Superintendent, to the hospital that stands above his office, where you see an old lady from the city, a nursing the sick. He then leads you through the sleeping Halls where you see every boy's bed made up in the nicest style with clean white sheets. From the Hall he directs you to the wash room, to which you turn into a little door at your left hand and enter the kitchen and the dining room. From the dining room you go to the school room where your eyes beholds copy boards hanging against the walls, and the floor nicely sanded with clean white sand.

You follow your guide a little further and he takes you to the female department, where you may see from a hundred to a hundred and fifty young females that has just began to enter upon the high roads of vice and crime and has been rescued by the hand of some watchman or constable from the broad road of destruction. From the female department he leads you into a beautiful flower garden that stands directly in front of the office, and if you be some great gentleman or lady from the city, he will allow your slender and tiny little fingers to pluck a few of the flowers. From the garden he directs you through the shops, to which you go up two flights of stairs and enter the chair shop. You then come down and go through the whip shop. From the whip shop he leads you to the brass foundry. From thence he takes you to the office, where he shows you the badge book with every boy's name on it and the character he bears, where he is from and where he was born, and so forth.

But woe to you, old chap, if you be a green horn that has come from the country to take a look and an insight of the place. You have no Superintendent nor officer to guide you and lead you through the several departments. There you stand in the center of the yard, on the play ground, with both hands stuff in your pocket, to be look on and gazed at and to become a by word by the inmates of the place. Tired and weary, a lingering on this enchanted ground, you make your way out of the gate with ten thousand curses and oaths at the end of your tongue, and blaspheming in the name of him that sits above your head, that you was much deceived and had to come away and leave the place without seeing and beholding some of those beautiful and handsome faces of the female sect.

Reader, I have now led you through every department of the place, and I will now introduce you to Mr. Samuel S. Wood, the Assistant Superintendent of the House, and Mr. Nathaniel Heart, the Head Superintendent, the only two officers of the whole establishment, and a school teacher that is hired by the committees of the House. There are three committees appointed, for the purpose of visiting the place on every Friday, and to hear the complaints of the inmates, if there is any to be made, and to inspect the House and the provisions and to look over the books, and so forth.

It was in the summer of eighteen hundred and thirty-three that I found myself crowded among seven or eight hundred boys, all clothed in white linen pantaloons and a little blue jacket which was changed twice every week through the summer for a clean suite. On the second day of my entering the place, I was called to the office before Mr. Wood and Mr. Heart, who asked me several questions and laid out the rules to me, and I was sent off to the chair shop, to toil and labor until I was one and twenty.

I had not been in the shop but two or three days before I began to learn the winks, the motion of the fingers, the shake of the head, and in fact all of the iniquities that prevailed in the House. On the

fourth day I was reported to Mr. Wood for talking in the shop during the working hours. Mr. Wood then came to my work bench and
told me that I must not talk in the shop during working hours until
I got so as I could do my task by eleven o'clock, and I could go down
in the yard on the play ground and play and do up my talking by
twelve o'clock.

Every boy in the House has a task given to him by the foreman
of the shop. If he gets that task done by eleven o'clock, he is allowed
to go down on the play ground and play marbles or a game at ball
until the bell rings at twelve o'clock. The Superintendent or the assistant then blows a little ivory whistle for him to go to the wash
room and wash his hands and face and to get ready for dinner. At the
rate of fifteen minutes, the whistle blows again and calls the boys on
parade, to which every boy falls in his place according to his size. Mr.
Wood then passes through the ranks with a rattan in his hand, to
inspect each boy's hands and face. If he finds the least bit of dirt on
the hand, he gives him a few smart quacks on the knuckles with his
rattan and send him back to the wash room to wash himself again.

After passing through this process, we march into the table with
our hands behind until the blessing is ask by Mr. Wood or Mr. Heart.
He then blows his whistle for us to eat, which he allows us twenty
minutes to swallow our dinner. He then blows his whistle again, and
with a loud shout he sings out "Time is up!," to which every boy
drops his knife and fork and turns his face towards Mr. Wood, while
he read a chapter from the bible and implores the blessing again, and
discharges us from the table and sends us down on the play ground
till one o'clock. He then blows his whistle again and marches us off
to the shop where we labor till three o'clock. Then another whistle
blows for us to go down into the yard for ten minutes. At the space
of ten minutes we return back to our shops again till four o'clock.
The bell then rings us to supper. After swallowing our dish of mush,
the Superintendent turns us out into the yard again where he joins
in our play till six o'clock. We then go to the wash room and wash
our hands and faces and get ready for school.

At half past six, every boy finds himself seated in the school room at his studies, some studying arithmetic, some grammar, some algebra, some Latin, and others learning pieces to speak and perform on the stage that stands at the north end of the school room. At eight o'clock, the Superintendent comes in and closes the school by singing a hymn and offering up a prayer. He then sends us off to our cells, where the steward stands by with the keys in his hands, ready to lock us up.

At half past five in the morning we are let out and called on parade. The roll is called by one of the inmates, to which every boy answers to his name, and we are sent to the school room to study till seven o'clock. From the school room we march to the dining room, where we have for our breakfast bread and molasses, and tea. After breakfast we are turned out on the play ground till eight o'clock, then return to our shops to perform our daily tasks.

The whole yard takes up about forty acres of ground, with a large vineyard attached to it at the south end of the wall.

I had been there nearly a year before I could learn all the little rules and regulations of the House—first, that I must not talk in the shop during working hours, and that I must not speak a lisp in the cell; that I must go to bed just as soon as my cell door was lock; that I must get up in the morning just as soon as I hear the bell ring, and make up my bed just as nice as though some king or queen was to sleep in it; that I must not spit on my cell floor, nor on the wall; that I must not look behind me in the dining room, nor in the chapel, nor in the school room; of which if any of these rules was broken, I would get twenty or twenty-five blows on the hand with the rattan, or stand in the middle of the dining room with my hands on my head and go back to the shop with an empty belly.

'TWAS A LOVELY day that Mr. Wood came strolling leisurely through the shop, and he casted his eyes towards me, and making some remarks to the foreman he made his way towards me.

"Well, Reed, how do you get along?"

"Very well, sir," I replied.

"Glad to hear it," said he. "Your foreman says that you have made great improvements since you have been here, and he tells me that you are the smartest boy he has in the shop. Can you read and write, Rob?"

"No, sir."

"Would you like to learn? I have just had a stage built a few days ago, and I want you to learn so as you can be one of the actors on it."

During the conversation the foreman stepped up, and with a grin and a wink said to Mr. Wood, "I think that I can make something out of that darkie. He is a smart nig. He gets his task done every day by nine o'clock, and throws me in an extra chair once and a while."

"Well, Mr. Semoure, I think I shall select some good boy to teach Reed and make a scholar of him."

"Do so, do so, Mr. Wood. I think he'll make a brave scholar."

"Here, Kimbell, I want you to take Reed and learn him how to read and write. I want to make an actor of him."

"Yes, sir," said Kimbell, with a low bow of his head.

Jack Kimbell,[8] as the boys use to call him, was a friend of mine. I thought that Mr. Wood couldn't pick out a better fellow among seven hundred boys than Jack Kimbell was. Jack was master of the stage, and every spare minute that Jack could get, he would run to me with his little pointer in his hand and show me which was A, and which was B, and by the space of nine months I was sitting at the head of the ninth class every night, reading and studying pieces from *The English Reader.*[9]

I had now made such an improvement in reading and writing by the help of Jack Kimbell and little Mike Flinn[10] that work aside of me, that it gave Mr. Wood a great encouragement. One year rolled away, and I found myself the master of a pen and the reader of a book, and a conqueror of arithmetic. Them was the days when I would challenge old England or America to throw down any history before me and let me read it through just once, and I was the boy that would stand before any historian that ever stood between England and America and argue with him on the subject of which I had been reading. I had such a greedy appetite for reading that I was called up before Mr. Williams[11] the school teacher one day and laid across the stool, where I got fifteen cuts with the rattan for having more than one book in my desk.

Many a time has the eye of the stranger as he has been passing through the departments of the house been casted towards me, while I have been stowed tight away in some corner of the wall with a history in my hand, reading and devouring on the life of some old hero whose bones lays bleaching beneath the sandy desert or that has found a watery grave. I say that I use to crunch on those old fellows until there wasn't a hair's breath of them left—Robinson Crusoe leaving the happy Home of his youth and childhood under the cover of darkness to become a marine of the sea, and leaving his father and mother to spend the remainder of their days in grief and sorrow on his account, and Pocahontas a throwing herself down at her father feet and bowing her beautiful head beneath the uplifted tomahawk to rescue the life of Capt. John Smith. Such was the books that the House of Refuge libraries use to contain.

After receiving a good common school education and being away from Home for two years without having the least encouragement either from Mr. Wood or Mr. Heart of ever returning Home, and being acquainted with the iniquities of the place, I cast my mind towards the land of my nativity, and the fond Home of my youth, and with such thoughts and reflections I was determined to try and make my escape, in company with Mike Flinn and Jack Kimbell, who had mention the subject to me once or twice before and was goin' to make a trial of it on the following Sunday. Mike was an Irish boy that had a father and mother that lived in the city on Chatham Street. Jack was a boy that was robbed of his mother in his infant days by the savage hand of death, and his father had took to a seafaring life.

'Twas on Saturday night on my goin' behind the barn that I found Jack Kimbell and Mike Flinn in a deep conversation. I step up to

Mike, and putting my hand on his shoulders, I told him that I had been in the Refuge now two years, and that I was determined to try and to make my escape that night at the west corner of the wall. By the time I had made known my plans to Mike, Jack Kimbell and Joe Long[12] stepped up, saying that we was studying some devilry, and that if it was a sure step that we had in view, they wanted a hand in it, too. Jack Kimbell and Mike Flinn had learnt me how to read and write, they had learnt me how to compute figures, and I thought that they could comprehend the plan of our escape better than I could, and I left the matter with them, to which they was to give me answer in the morning.

Sunday morning came, and with it a cloud and rain. The boys was all in the wash room, getting ready for breakfast. I was just coming out of the wash room door when Mike gave me the wink to be ready after breakfast. Mr. Wood had blown his whistle for the boys to come on parade, and as it rained he did not go through the inspecting of the hands and face but sent us in the dining room, where he offered up a prayer and gave the signal for us to eat. At the expiration of fifteen minutes, we found ourselves again out in the yard. I ran with all my might to find Mike and Jack, and on my goin' to the west corner of the wall, there stood Mike with the post in his hand that was driven into the ground to keep up some grape vines, and planking it against the wall he ran up it, and in a second time he was on the top, a helping Jack Kimbell by the hand. Then I made my trial, and by the help of the two boys, I made my escape.

We all three kept together, a crossing a large meadow and coming out on the Bloomingdale Road. We ran some fifteen miles and struck off in a piece of woods that laid hard by. Being tired and our feet well blistered by running, we went into an old farmer's barn and crept under some hay until night. We then made our way further up the country, where we entered an old cow shed to pass the night.

Fearing that our Refuge clothes would betray us in the open day light, I advised Mike to go out with me until we got something to eat. We both walk out together, and goin' a quarter of a mile up the road, we entered an old farmer's House and made known our wants to him. He loaded us down with provisions and ask us many question—where we was from and where we was goin'. We told him that we was boys that belong in Brooklyn and had come out to see the country, and that we was goin' to make our way back that night. It was getting to be late, and we had left Jack behind with a promise of returning in a half an hour, so bidding the old man good night, we tramp our way back towards the old shed where we passed a cold, chilly night. In the morning, taking our bread which had become hard and dry through the night and stuffing it into our pockets, we made our way back towards the city.

At three o'clock in the afternoon we found ourselves under the roof of an old Irish lady who appeared to be well stricken in years. How familiar she was with Mike's name, how quick she knew his voice, and with the affection of a mother how quick she grasped him to her arms and stamp a deep kiss on his cheeks, and a warm tear from her eyes came rolling down his brow.

"And who are these, Mike?" said the woman.

"Mother, my clothes and cap, quick, or the police will grasp me on the spot."

The woman had hurried and bundled up his clothes and, filling his hand full of silver and copper, give him another kiss, and we took our flight for the landing to get in a steamer that was goin' to sail for Albany—but just as we was stepping aboard, two constables wearing a star on their breasts, and Mr. Hayse[13] grasped us and lock us in the black Mariah and order the driver to drive directly up to the House of Refuge with us.

As he drove up in front of the office door, Mr. Wood step out of the office with a smile upon his face as gentle as the morning, saying to Mr. Hayse, "So, you have them boys here have you, Mr. Hayse?"

"Yes, sir, yes, sir," shouted Hayse with a loud laugh. "I have them."

"Where did you catch them, Mr. Hayse?"

"Catch them, sir? Why I catch them a loafing on the steam boat landing, half starved and covered with dirt and rags and in the same condition that you see them now."

After Mr. Wood had taken a fair examination of us, he ordered Mr. Samson the steward to take us up stairs and lock us up till Saturday night, and to give us nothing but bread and water once a day. Samson obeyed the orders of Mr. Wood, and we soon found ourselves lock up in our gloomy cells and left alone to meditate on the punishment we should get when Saturday night came.

Poor Mike and Jack was sobbing aloud and brooding over the punishment that was to follow on Saturday night, while I was making secret plans to make my escape. Kimbell was lock in a cell on my right hand, and Flinn was on my left. It was three o'clock in the afternoon that I called out to Mike and ask him how he felt.

"Happy, happy as a wood sawyer."

"Mike," said I, "Is there no way in getting out of these cells and make our escape?"

"Rob, I don't see no way, without we had some aid from—" There he made a deep pause and stop. I stood to my door and listen, and presently I heard the tramp of footsteps, tramping lightly on tip toe and stopping in front of Mike's door. Then I heard the voice of a boy.

"Mike," said I, "who is that?"

"It's Joe Long."

"Joe," said I.

"What?"

"Will you step here to my cell door?"

As I said those words, Joe slip lightly along to my door, saying that he could not stay but a minute, that he had heard that we was back and lock up, and that he had stolen out of the shop to come up and see us, and to see if we wanted anything to eat or any assistance in getting out of our cells and make our escape before Saturday night.

"Joe," said I, "can you get me a key hole saw?"

"Yes."

"And a brace and a bit?"

"Yes, but Rob I have stayed too long now. I must be for making my tracks back to the shop, or the foreman will miss me and report it to Mr. Wood. I will certainly be up here tomorrow at eleven o'clock, after my task is done, and bring you the necessary things which you want, and try to help you all out." Putting his slender little fingers through the door, he gave me a shake by the hand and bade me good bye.

Joe was an handsome English boy about the age of fourteen and the most interesting boy that ever I saw, with brilliant dark eyes, with long eyelashes, with magnificent teeth, beautiful mouth, and with refined manners, and I took him to be one of the effeminate looking, supercilious boy that ever I came across.[14] His father was a merchant, carrying on a large scale of business in the west. On a dark and a stormy night Joe left the parental roof where he had spent many a happy hour and strolled off to New York, where he fell a victim to crime and soon found himself an inmate of the House of Refuge.

In the meantime Joe came tipping along to my cell with the promised tools to cut our way out, that we might make our escape. A small hole through a thin panel door was to be made, large enough for the saw to go through, then a piece was to be cut out large enough for me to get through, all of which Joe done from the outside of the door. In fifteen minutes' time I was in front of Mike's door making a hole, while Joe Long was in front of Jack Kimbell's door assisting him. By twelve o'clock we was upon the wall, and ere the sun went down, we was on our march for the five points, where we was obliged to spend the night in an old barn that belonged to a colored man.

I awoke long before the dawn of day and gave the alarm to my companions that the morning light was fast approaching and that we had better rise and make our way out of the city of New York as fast as our feet could carry us, before the officers of the city was stirring about. We arose, and shaking the heavy sleep from our eyes, we began our march by striking across the five points and cross over on some road that led off into the country. On goin' up four or five miles into the country, we halted in front of a log cabin that was occupied by a Dutch family consisting of a mother and two daughters. I step up to the door, humbly imploring the good old lady for a morsel of bread to satisfy my hunger. She drew her table in the centre of the room and provided us a good dinner, which we devoured with a greedy appetite. We devoured our meal, and thanking the good old lady, we left the little cabin where plenty and contentment appeared to make its abode. The old lady was a tall, gaunt person, with her head and chin tied up with a handkerchief, and seemed to be suffering with the toothache. The other two females was very young and perfect personifications of German beauty, with blue eyes and blooming cheeks, red lips and a profusion of brown hair most classically braided and platted. That they were sister scarcely admitted no doubt to me, so remarkable was their resemblance to each other. A near inspection made it equally evident to me that one was much handsomer than the other. They were both tall and very slightly formed, and their dark cotton dresses were made and put on with an exactness that proved they were not indifferent to the advantages bestowed on them by nature.[15]

Bidding our Dutch hostess good day, we struck off into a large open field and consulted what was the best course to follow. Joe Long was for pushing back to the city and put off for sea. Jack Kimbell shouted that he would follow him, while me and Mike made up our minds to push directly for Albany. After consulting the matter over, we all four started back for the city. At six o'clock I found myself a standing on the corner of Chatham Street, where we held a long discourse.

"Come, Rob, for God sake," said Jack. "Join in with me and Joe and strike off to sea, for Mr. Wood will surely have the police on track for us before tomorrow morning."

"What do you say, Rob? Will you go or not?"

"No, Jack, I am goin' to return back Home to my mother."

"Fool to return back Home to your mother," echo Joe Long,

"without a cent in your pocket and with that Refuge suite on. Better by far join us and go off to sea, and become a sailor. Pshaw, won't go with us eh, Rob?"

"No, Joe, can't go to sea."

Grasping me and Mike by the hand, he gave us a hearty shake and bade us good night, promising to meet us on the corner of Chatham at early dawn.

The two heroes was now on their way to find some ship that wanted hands, while Mike and me was looking out some place to pass the dark and gloomy night. We stole along up the street until Mike got in front of an old building that look familiar to him. Stealing closely under the windows, he thought that he heard his sister's voice, in deep conversation with his mother. A tap on the window and a sharp whistle brought the two females to the door.

"And who are you," said Mrs. Flinn, "that dares come to my window at this time of night and disturb a peaceful family? Away with you, you imprudent rascal."

"Mother, dear mother," said Mike. "Speak low, don't speak so loud."

"My God," said the girl. "Mother, it's Mike." And she sprang out and grasped her brother in her arms, brought him in the House.

"And who is that with you?"

"He made his escape with me."

"God bless the boy, call him in."

Mike called me in, and the two females provided us with a bed on the floor, where we passed the night. In the morning we arose, and the good old Irish woman provided us each with a suite of clothes, and two clean shirts, and two dollars apiece, and exhorting us to make from the city as quick as possible.

It was late in the afternoon when we met Joe Long and Jack Kimbell, coming up Fulton Street in company with four young sailors, with their long white duck pants on and a blue broad cloth round about, with a row of pearl buttons shining and glittering in the sun.

"Well, Rob, we have hired out to one of the best captains that ever rode upon the sea. Won't go eh, Rob? D— fool. Rather be caught by that infernal rascal Mr. Hayse and be taken back to the Ref. than to put off for sea, eh? What do you say, go or not?"

"Goin' to sail in three days," said one of the sailors. "You had better go. My father the captain, and he'll use you well. Better go."

"Yes," said another sailor. "You will suit the skipper to a T, for I heard him say no longer than this morning that if he could get a smart colored chap, he would put him in the slush room to make duff, and take black Dick and put him before the mast."

"Suppose you come down and see the capt., Rob? I know that you will suit him. He is old chap that never speaks a cross word to none of his boys, and as for the old tarry cats, they haven't been taken down from the captain's room since the day they was hung up there. When the old mate wants punish any of the boys, he just calls them up on the deck in a rough and ugly way, and whispers a soft kind word in his ear and send him off with a loud coquettish laugh, and a heart full of good wish."

"So you won't go, eh? Well, Rob, come down and take a look at the ship while she is loaded, and get some dinner."

I followed them until I came in sight of the stern, where it said *Temperance*, for that was her name. There she laid, bowing her beautiful little temperance head to the proud waves that came rolling and dashing under her bow, and her deck as white and clean as the drifting snow. I thought she deserved the name she bore, for everything about her gave me evidence enough that temperance ruled and swayed among the crew.[16] While I stood gazing at her proud little head, the captain, a stout heavy man whose hair was tinged with a deep silvery gray and whose countenance seemed to tell me that he had faced many a storm, came up to me, and bringing his hard heavy hand upon me, which made me flinch, ask me how I like the looks of his little daughter.

I replied that I thought that she was a very handsome little creature.

"Yes, my boy, she has weather through many a storm and bluff many a heavy gale."

While I stood there talking to the captain, I happened by chance to cast my eyes over the cabin door and saw a tin label tack over the door with these words—"No Swearing."

"Well, my boy," said the sailors as they began to crowd around me. "Now what do you think of a sailor's life? Made up your mind yet to be a sailor? A good mate and a jolly hearted old skipper and a merry crew. Won't go, eh? There's that old mate yonder"—pointing to a stout old fellow that stood by—"and here is the captain. They both will protect you and take care of you, and as for myself, I will see that you are brought safely back to New York after three years' cruise."

By this time the cook, a heavy creole looking fellow, stuck his woolly head out of the door and shouted as loud as thunder that dinner was ready. The mate order the boys to take me along with in the forecastle and give me some dinner. It was a day which shall hang on my memory till my latest breath shall cease. After we had all tumbled down in the forecastle, the sailors all stood up, and taking off their hats they all joined in together and sung two verses, and the captain's boy ask the blessing over the meal which stood before them.

As I was eating a piece of the hard sea biscuit, I thought that a sailor's life must be one of the most hardest and perilous lives that a man could lead, although I saw nothing that mean in their humble fare, for they had pork and beef boiled together and potatoes and cold water and hard biscuits.

The dinner having ended, one of the sailors implored thanks, and then drew cuts to see who should tell a story.

The cut fell on the captain's boy, and he began his story, as near as I can remember it—

WHEN I WAS quite a boy, my mother died. (A heavy groan ensued as he got the word, died, out of his mouth among the sailors.) I say I lost my mother. I followed her to the sacred spot where her remains was to be laid cold and lifeless in the grave—until the angel shall come with one foot upon the land and the other upon the foaming sea, with his sword pointing upwards and swearing in the name of one that is mightier than himself that time is no more.[17] I stood at the side of my father as he held his hand into mine, and briny tears came rolling down his cheek and fell upon my brow, as the cold sods was covering all that was once dear and sacred to me.

May my mother's name be sacred to me yet, and sacred be the spot that covers her mortal frame. My father sold out his shop, and having no children but me, he betook himself to a seafaring life, and took me along with him as a cabin boy. After my father had been a dog before the mast for two years, he was promoted to a mate, and from a mate he became the captain of this little damsel where we now sit.

Well, three years ago we was out to sea, and a heavy storm blew up from the south-southwest. It was late in the middle of the afternoon. It was a horrible storm. The waves came beating and dashing over the deck, and expecting every moment to be lost—oh a terrible day indeed. The little creature was cracking and groaning beneath her weight. The sea was foaming and raging with madness, and the thunder was rolling, and the lightning was playing in the heavens.

"Who will go aft," the captain cried, "and clear away the rigging?"

The hardest and oldest old sailors refuse to go aloft, while I but a boy stood firm and bold at my father's side, while he stood pulling hard to at the helm.

"No one that dare go aloft?"

Yes, I jump into the rigging while my father pulled hard to at the helm, and the wind was swinging me between the heavens and the sea. In one hour's time we had her in her right position. Horrible day, boys, I tell you that was. Another such a day I never want to meet with again on life's bounteous ocean.

"I say, young chap, when you was aloft, a rocking in the rigging, and the waves was tossing your little cradle first up to heaven, then down in her watery elements again, was you not afraid that you would fall and crack your bones?"

Fear? No. What had I to fear when I was aloft, for my father was at the helm.[18]

———

THE SAILOR HAD now ended his story, and I thought it was time for me to make my tracks before night, to be ready for the evening boat that was goin' to start for Albany. I strolled up Fulton Street and entered a place where I saw a lot of sailors playing cards, throwing dice and such like. I step up to the table and look on until one of the party had finish the game. While I stood there, a darkie sailor dressed in a sailor's suite ask me if I wanted a hand, to which I answered him in the affirmative. I had sat there playing Old Sledge till the hall clock struck seven, and counting over my money, I found that I had won from the sailor seven dollars.

I walk over to Mike's House, and inquiring for him, his mother informed me that Mr. Hayse had just taken him from the upper chamber and made him fast to take him back to the House of Refuge, and Mrs. Flinn warned me to be on my lookout, for there was stars out on the look out for me and Jack Kimbell and Joe Long. She advised me to leave the city that night if there was any possible means of my getting away, and to give Jack and Joe the wink that the stars was on the alert for them. While Mrs. Flinn was laying out plans for my escape from the city, there happened to come in the House a tall Irishman by the name of McCollough, who had a son in the Refuge himself. He asked me many question about his son William,[19] to which I answered them all. He then took me over to his House, where he provided me a good supper and a good bed and told me to fear nothing during the night, but to repose myself comfortably as I could. I turned in my new bed and slept till near eight o'clock the next morning.

Mrs. McCollough came to my bed and told me to get up and eat some breakfast, and that she was goin' to rig me out with a suite of her son clothes, and that I must keep in the house all day and not go outside, and at night her husband was to see me safely aboard the boat and send me Home to my friends. Mr. McCollough had gone off to his work and left me in the charge of his wife until he returned at night. I sat a looking out of the window between the hours of ten and eleven, and Mr. Hayse came in the house behind me on his tip toes, and tying my hands behind me, he order me to follow him. Mrs. McCollough ran and shut the door and turned the lock and put the key in her pocket, swearing that I should not stir a step until her husband should be sent for.

"Mrs. McCollough," said Hayse, "if you don't want to bring any trouble upon yourself and husband, I think that you had better unlock that door and let me go about my business, or I shall call you before the court of justice where you will have to answer for your conduct towards me."

"Conduct, you good for nothing infernal rascal?" said the woman. "You are dragging every body's children off you meet with in our street, and transporting them to the House of Refuge. That poor innocent young girl that you drag a pass my door the other day because she wouldn't let you—. Ah, you cold hearted brute, you are robbing hundreds of families of their children."

"I say, Mrs. McCollough, will you unlock the door and let me pass out peaceably about my business?"

By this time a large crowd had gathered around the door, and a loud voice was heard to exclaim, "Make room!" No sooner had the words fallen from the lips of the enraged man, he bowed himself with all of his strength and press his way to the door, and ordered Mrs. McCollough to open the door. The hand of the female unlock the door, and McCollough entered the House with oaths and blasphemies. Takin' Hayse by the collar of his coat, he demanded of him, who had authorized him to come and disturb his wife and bring such a crowd of citizens around his door in the open day light?

"Sir," said Mr. Hayse, "I entered the threshold of your door peaceably and quietly to take and arrest this boy Reed, who has made his escape from the House of Refuge twice, and I am authorized by the magistrates of the city to take him wherever I can find him and take him back to the House of Refuge. And furthermore, Mr. McCollough, I am authorized by the same to arrest and bring before the higher powers any person or persons that dare molest me in taking this boy back to the Refuge, and it will be the best thing that you can do to let go of my collar and let me pass quietly out of the House with this boy. As far as I am concerned, Mr. McCollough, there shan't a hair in his head be hurt."

McCollough now let go of the policeman collar, and accosted him in the following manner, with sharp and angry words, viz.— "Mr. Hayse, do you not remember some two years ago, when I was gone from Home, that you came under the roof of my House and snatch the only son of my bosom from my side? And that cherry cheek young girl that you drag by the hair of her head a pass this very door? Oh, you infernal, hard hearted brute, you now want to take that poor black boy off to the Refuge, where he must stay for years and drag out a poor and a miserable life. Oh, you infernal black hearted villain, I will never let you have any rest. I will haunt you till the day of Judgment, and when cold and lifeless I lay beneath the sods I will haunt and torment you day and night. I'll give you no rest, till you enter the cold mansions of the dead."

Thrusting my hand into my pocket, I drew out seven dollars and plank it on the table, and told Mr. McCollough to let the policeman pass, that he couldn't no more than take me back to the House of Refuge, where I would have to go under the treatment of the cats, and that if nothing happened, I would meet him again in the course of a few months. With tears streaming from my eyes and my hands tied behind me, Hayse pressed his way through a thick crowd that had gathered around the door and led me back to the House of Refuge.

As I entered the office, there sat Mr. Wood and Mr. Heart, who examined me very close and ask me several questions, then ordered me off to the kitchen to get my hair cut and my clothes changed for a suite of Refuge clothes. At twelve o'clock, while the boys was eatin' their dinner, Mr. Heart, the Head Superintendent, a fine venerable old gentleman, entered the dining room with a pair of cats in his hand, and calling me by name, he ordered me out in the center of the room where stood a large post, and in sympathy and with good feelings he order me to take off my shirt.

I took it off and tied my suspenders around my waist and walk up to the post. He then tied my hands around the post, saying to the inmates that he wanted them all to take warning by the punishment which I was to receive for making my escape, and hoped that it might be a lesson to them hereafter.

I stood firm, without uttering a word or making a groan, until he given me twenty-five. I then told him that I thought I had enough for this time. He then gave a smile and told me that he would try me once more and untied my hands and told me that I was not to speak a word to no boy for the space of four weeks, and that no boy was to speak to me. If they did, they should pass through the same treatment. For four long weeks was I kept in profound silence and lock up all day on Sundays, with one piece of bread a day, till the expiration of the four weeks. At the end of that time, I was permitted to talk and to associate with the rest of the boys.

The day that my time was up to talk, the boys surrounded me, and praising me up for standing the cats so well without shedding a tear, and among them was Mike, who began his playful jokes by saying, "You never flinch, eh, Rob? Brave boy. You never made a groan under the old cat's paw when she was scratching your back. Never flinch, eh? Bravo, good boy, Rob. We are enough for them yet. Wait till some rainy day comes, Rob, and by the heavens, we'll play the slip jack on them yet."

"By Jove," said McGollin, "didn't Rob stand them cats good. Twenty-five lashes right on the bare back, and never made a bulge."

"When the old cat," said Mike, "was scratching in his back pretty deep, he had to sing out enough."

"And you, Mike," said I, "and how did you stand the darling little puss, when Mr. Hayse brought you back?" To which he gave me the following narrative, viz:

"The moment I left you on the corner of Chatham Street I went Home, and I had not been in the House not more than one hour before in came Hayse and a watchman with him, and laying their pruny hands upon me led back to the Refuge, where I was lock up till the next day. Mr. Wood then brought me down into the dining room and asked me where you was, and where Joe was, and Kimbell."

"And did you tell him, Mike?"

"Tell? I told him nothing."

"Then what, Mike?"

"Why, he told me to strip off my shirt and hug the very post that Mr. Heart tied you to. He then tied me, and the first blow that he struck upon my poor back made me wish with streaming eyes that I didn't go to sea with Joe Long and Jack Kimbell."

"Did you holler, Mike?"

"Yes, Rob, and I drop a fainting on the floor, and great drops of blood came running down my back, and Mr. Wood having some sympathy for me untied me and let me go."

"So the little kittens did make you bow at the feet of your tormentor, did it?"

"Yes, Rob, and it would make an angel bow too, if he had received the like."

"Well, Mike, what then?"

"Mr. Wood put me in profound silence, forbiddin' me to speak to any boy for four weeks."

"Did he lock you up on Sunday, Mike?"

"No, he wasn't quite so cruel as that."

Reader, these cats are made out of cat gut with a small knot made at the ends of them and wound around with a small wire, then rubbed well with shoe maker's wax and attach to a piece of rattan that has a pretty good spring to it, so as when the officer strikes, it leaves a deep cut in the back, causing the tender skin to burst while the blood flows freely down the back from the cuts it leaves, leaving the back entirely striped with red.

For my part I felt sorry for poor Mike. He was a boy that was fair and beautiful, and when I look upon that fair white skin of his all cut in pieces and lacerated with the cats, it made me bow my head in sorrow. Mike was a boy that was growing up for vice and crime or to stand one day or another upon the platform of virtue and truth. His parents was poor, yet they had warm blood running through their veins and hearts that could feel for those that were press down beneath the galling hand of oppression.

Oh, you dare devil Yankees, who run down the poor Irishmen as they land upon your docks, and point the finger of scorn at them, and look upon them with a sneer of disgrace, while he or she stands shivering in poverty and clothed in rags of disgrace and shame, while love and freedom is planted deep in his breast, and he is passed by the rich and the poor, who refuses to give him one word of consolation. So 'twas with Mr. McCollough and Mrs. Flinn as they stood upon the dock in the city of New York—left their native soil on account of low wages and emigrated over in this country—and stood poor and helpless on these shores, with no one to extend them their hand, here in a strange land and strangers to all the laws and governments of the land. Poor Pat, me heart beats in deep sympathy for thee as you step your foot upon the soil of freedom. Take courage, me brave Irish lads, and with your strong arms of industry, you will soon press your way through the smiling ranks of poverty, and in after years, if you leave the intoxicated drinks alone, you may be seated in the chair of honor, swaying over a nation that once laugh at your deep poverty and shame. Pat, methinks I see thousands of your race, like yourself once clothed in rags and shivering in shame, now holding high stations in life, and your little ones smiling under the roof of peace and contentment. Yes, me brave Irish boys, me loves you till the day that I am laid cold under the sod, and I would let the last drop of this dark blood run and drain from these black veins of mine to rescue you from the hands of a full blooded Yankee.

Reader, have you never been in some deep distress and trouble, and in your anguish of sorrow has not the warm hand of an Irishman grasped you and help you out of all your affliction? Or have you not been weary and hungry, and not a cent in your pocket, and you have stop under the humble roof of some Irish families, and the hand of the female has spread before you a frugal meal? Or have you not been pulled by his rough hand in kindness to go and take a friendly drink with him? Has he not in some cold midnight hour drew you from some miry ditch and led you away to some quiet place where you might repose yourself in safety and security? Methinks I hear ten thousand voices goin' up with shouts and saying, that Pat once rescued me.

I remember once, on a cold winter's day when I ran away from home, that the wind was howling and whistling without, and the snow was drifting high against the fences, and as the day sunk away and the darkness of the night was fast approaching, that I entered a rich man's House and begged him in the name of heaven to let me just step into the kitchen and warm my feet, for I was five miles away from Home. He refused me, and I turned with tears in my eyes towards the parental roof of my mother's House, making my way Home as fast as I could. I was bare footed and not a thing on my feet. My mother had taken my shoes away from me and had lock them up to keep me from sliding on the ice. On my running up the road some two miles, I saw on the left side of the road a little shanty. I ran up to the door and gave a hard rap, to which an Irish woman came and open unto me and ask me in the name of God what had caused me to leave my Home on such a cold day as that. I told the good woman and the man of the hut that I had run away from Home.

Pinch with cold and hunger, the good woman of the House went out to the well and drew a pail of cold water and told me to put both feet in the pail. I followed her descriptions, and after keeping my feet in the water for a half hour, I took them out, and she fell to a rubbing them with both of her hands until my feet began to burn and smart with pain. She then wrapped my feet up in a blanket which she took off from her bed, and left me a sitting by the fire until she got me some supper. It was getting late in the evening, and the night was growing cold, and she and her husband took part of their bedding off of their own bed and made me a bed on the floor, with my feet towards the fire. In the morning the good Irish woman and her husband provided me with a pair of socks and a pair of old boots, and packing up some bread and butter for me in a piece of paper, she begged me in the name of God to return back home to my mother, and imploring me to be a good boy—"for," said she, "I have never known nor heard of children yet that has run away from Home but what they would or have come to some bad end."

Reader, if you are on the right side of an Irishman, you have the best friend in the world. Meet him on the highways, and he is your friend there. Meet him toiling and laboring beneath the hot sun of a summer's day, and he is still your friend. On the right side of him, and he will spill the last drop of blood for you that runs in his veins. I would rather suffer wrong from the hands of an Irishman ten thousand times, than to suffer once from the hands of a full blooded Yankee—but I must now return to my story.

———

THE COLD WEATHER was now fast approaching, and the nights was getting longer, and more time was allowed us for study. The stage had been put up in the north end of the school room, and Mr. Wood and the teacher told the boys that they who made the best improvement in learning pieces for the stage should be rewarded with a handsome present. I had now determined not to try to make any more escape until the opening of the spring, and then if possible to make my escape and return immediately Home to my mother. Poor little Mike was determined to try it once more, and if he succeeded, to go right off to New Bedford or to Boston and put off for sea. I took Mike one day behind the barn and held a long conversation with him.

"Mike," said I, "you are determined to try it again, are you?"

"Yes, Reed, I shall try it next week, the very first rainy day that comes, and if I have good luck in scaling them walls again, I shall put right off to sea."

"Mike, why will you throw yourself away so foolishly to follow the life of a dog? You are but a boy, and to throw yourself to the waves of the sea is all madness. Listen to me, Mike. It is now getting to be cold, and you had better stay here with me till spring and go with me and Thom McGollin and McCollough and put off for the west. What do you say, Mike, will you do it or not?"

"Yes, if you promise to take me along in the spring."

I gave him my hand in token of the promise, and we parted, with our minds made up to tend to the studies of the school during the winter and prepare to perform on the stage, to which one hour was granted us for that purpose once every night through the week, excepting Saturday nights and Sunday. Mike and Wm. Tealling[20] and me was studying an Indian piece to perform on the stage in the presence of some ladies and gentlemen that was coming from Philadelphia in the course of a few weeks on a visit, and for that purpose a suite of Indian clothes was made for all three of us over to the female House to perform in. I was to be the Indian, Mike was to be a young female laying in her bed with an infant in his arms, and Tealling was to be the little infant, wrapped sweetly in the arms of his mother, in deep sleep.

The day that was appointed for us to be ready had arrived, and the school room was lit up that night with extra lights, and there was to be no studying that night. Mr. Wood called us three out and gave us the warning that the company had come, and to step out and dress ourselves as soon as possible, while he stepped to the office after the spectators. Being all ready, the three little bells rung, and the curtains drop. There laid little Mike on a bed, dressed in the attire of a female, with his cheeks painted red, and the little infant Tealling wrapped in his arms in deep slumber and sleep, while I was dress in a little red gown coming down to my knees and a pair of buck skin leggings on with little bell buttons attach to them, and my face painted red and black. A large scalping knife stuck in my belt. The little bell rung again, and then the piece began, which end by my cutting a bladder that was full of red water representing blood and tied close up under the chin. The bell rung again, and the curtains drop, and we went out of the back door into the wash room where we change our clothes, and came upon the stage, where we spoke a piece call Old Snacks and the Steward, and as I had a clear silver voice for singing, Mr. Wood permitted me to close our piece by singing at the close of each piece.[21]

In this way did we pass the long winter night away until the return of spring. I was then determined to trust to luck and chance again.

ONE SPRING MORNING — AND oh how fair are our spring mornings, bursting on the sober face of nature like the coquettish laugh of a beautiful woman, short but delicious[22]—I say on one fine spring morning, Mr. Heart the Head Superintendent came into the school room, and with tears rolling down his cheeks he gave us his farewell prayer. I shall never forget that solemn hour as long as I live, when nearly seven hundred of us boys was all gathered together in one large room, and the old gentleman standing before us, telling us that he must now leave us, that he was goin' to resign his office and that Mr. Wood was to take his place.

"I have been here with you now for fifteen years. I am now goin' to move to New Haven, and my prayer is that God may bless you and be with you. I must now leave you, and some of you I shall never meet again until I meet you at the judgment bar of God. I now leave you in the hands of God."

Tears was seen to flow from every boy's eyes in the room. As for myself, ah, me thought, while the good old patriarch was speaking, that he must have been standing by the bed side of my father and borrowed those sacred words from his lips just before he expired, for they seemed to me to be very parting words of my beloved father.

Mr. Heart had now left us, and for weeks afterwards every boy in the House felt as though he had lost an earthly father. Yes, Mr. Heart, though years has pass away between us and your body lays deep in the dust, yet my good old father I still remember you, with your silvery hair tinged with the touch of time. I have not buried in oblivion forever those kind feelings and sympathy you had toward those little ones that was placed under your care. Though I am wrapped in sins of disgrace, and clothed with shame and dishonor, and harden in vice and crime, and have become the felon of a gloomy cell—yet my prayer is that your soul is in those highlands above, where not a wave of trouble care shall ever cross your peaceful breast.

Deep sadness had taken place in every boy's heart when Mr. Heart left—but we still had a friend left to us yet who stuck closer to us than a brother, who sympathized with us in our sorrows, and who felt every heavy wave that came rolling in our bosom, and that was Mr. Wood. He stayed with us about two years, and falling in love with some lady, he too gave us his farewell speech and left us, and a man by the name of Terry took his place. Then, oh then was the worst days that ever I seen. Things went up side down when Mr. Wood and Mr. Heart went away. Terry began to rule the boys with a tyrannical hand, and punishing the boys on the bare back every day with the cats for little things that Mr. Wood wouldn't blow his whistle at. Day after day did cries and bitter lamentations go up from the inmates, with hopes that Mr. Wood would return back.

By the heavens, Mr. Terry called Wm. Smith from the table one day and ordered him to take off his shirt because he had heard Smith say in the yard that he hope the day wasn't far distance when Mr. Wood would come back again. Smith took off his shirt, and Terry catted him on the back till his poor back look like a piece of raw beef, and Terry gave out orders that if any boy heard another boy wish that Mr. Wood or Mr. Heart was back, to report it to him, and he would lacerate his back so with the cats that he wouldn't make another wish in a hurry.

This the boys couldn't put up with no longer, and there was continually a fight with Terry and the boys every day. There was more boys catted in one week, while Terry was there, than Mr. Wood had catted in three years. One day a little English boy by the name of Esq. Miller[23] had spilt a little salt on the table, and Terry happened to pass along and see it. He called Miller from the table and slap him some twenty time aside of his ears with the palm of his hands. After dinner was over, the boys was let out in the yard to play. Miller staggered along as far as the female department and sat himself down on the steps, where he sat in silence alone, mourning over the treatment which he had just passed through. Presently I saw a crowd of boys gathering around him. I ran with all my might to see what the trouble was, and there laid young Miller, stretch out on the ground with his little hands shut tight together and the froth a foaming from his mouth. The boys pick him up and took him to the hospital and laid him on a bed while the nurse, an old lady, wiped the cold sweat from his brows.

The next day I seen Miller in the yard, but he did not look to me as he did the day before, for there had a great change taken place in his face. Them cheeks of his, which was red as a rose only the day before, was now pale and white as a sheet. I asked Miller if he had ever had any fits before in his life, to which he replied he had not. After I had ask him that question, I casted my mind back and remembered of reading some of Doctor Brown's lectures,[24] where he says that the causes of fits arises from parents inflicting hard treatment upon their children in early life, such as slapping them in the face and on the head and boxing their ears with the flat of their hand—and as I look upon Miller's case, I was led to believe that the learned Doctor was right, for Miller became a subject to fits for years after.

This Mr. Terry was an old Presbyterian minister who had taken hold of the horns of the altar, but in after years had been banish from the pulpit. Oh, how many ministers now days are kneeling down on their knees behind the pulpit and praying for the sick and the afflicted, for the orphan and the widow, for the prisoner and the captive, the soldier and the sailor who is tossed upon the waves, while no feelings nor no sympathies ascends upon to the throne of grace for those whom they are praying for? Oh, ye leaders of the blind, be careful while you are on your knees and uttering those sacred words and imploring blessing from above on the behalf of those afflicted people whom you are praying for, that the brittle thread of life don't snap and send you away to take up your portion with hypocrites and unbelievers. Then, with solemn and mournful prayers, you'll cry for the solid rocks and the firm mountains to fall and crumble down upon your defenseless pates.

To RETURN TO my story—it was about one month after this that a boy by the name of Peter Mackerboy[25] hid himself behind a swill barrel that stood at the lower end of the yard, just as Mr. Terry blew his whistle for the boys to come on parade. The roll was called, and Mackerboy was missing, and no answer was given to his name when it was called. After the boys had all got seated in the school room, search was made for Mackerboy, and he was found and brought in the school room. Mackerboy had only been in the House but a few days before he undertook to make his escape.

Mr. Terry ordered him to take off his shirt. Mack told Terry that he didn't come to the House of Refuge to take off his shirt. As he said them words, Terry struck him across the face with the cats. Mack grasped a slate from the desk and threw it at Terry with all of his might. No sooner had the slate got out of his hand than he drew a long knife from the sleeve of his coat, and with the fierceness of a lion he made a plunge after Terry, and they two closed in together. Terry got the upper hand of Mack and was just about to bring him to the floor, when a noble hearted boy by the name of Wm. Tell[26] sprung from his seat and grasp Terry by the hair of his head and brought him a sprawling and crawling on the floor, a begging and pleading for mercy. Mack twisted the knife from the unfortunate man's hand who laid at his feet and was ready to make a deep plunge, when a hand of another boy by the name of Murphy grasped the uplifted hand that the knife was in, and reason with the enrage boy for a moment, and he let him up after getting his full satisfaction, and stripped off his shirt and walked up to the post to receive a punishment with the cats, from the hands of Terry.

Terry made his hands fast around the post with a handkerchief and gave him about one hundred blows. He then called Wm. Tell out and told him to take off his shirt. Tell strip himself like a man and hugged the post while the tyrannical old scamp catted him till there was not a white spot to be seen on his mangled back. When I have often look back to that day and on that awful scene of misery, I have often wondered with amazement how Wm. Tell could stood up to that post so and take such a punishment as he did without saying one word or uttering one mournful groan, till he had received one hundred and some odd blows. Mack and Tell was then taken off to their cells and lock up. On the following day they both broke out of their cells and made their escape.

Mackerboy went to England, and Wm. Tell ship as a sailor and went off to sea. In the year of 1853,[27] I met him in the city of New York, now a heavy stout man, dress in his broad cloth with a gold chain a swinging from his watch pocket, and the captain of a vessel that laid in the harbor, loaded with a cargo for the East Indies. He grasp me by the hand when I stepped up to him and called him by name, and by the heavens I thought the fellow would squeeze my paw off of me. He conducted me aboard of the vessel and took me into his cabin, where sat a young lady whom he introduced to me as his sister. He then drew out the table and asked me to amuse myself by takin' a game of cards with him until his wife returned, and talk over some of our by gone days. Just as we had finish the game, in came a dashing young girl who looked to me as though she was just entering her teens, dress in rich silks and velvets, and a gold chain hung around her neck, attach to a gold watch, while her bosom was shining and dazzling with some of the richest pearls of the ocean.

I took dinner with Mr. Tell and the two young ladies, and was about to leave and make a visit up to the House of Refuge, when

Captain Tell sung out and told me to wait a few moments, and he would accompany me up to the place and see how things look. On our way to the Refuge, Tell and me in a deep conversation about the fight he had with Terry and about the catting that him and me had received from Terry, the hardships which we had gone through, and ended by hearty laughs and jolly jokes. We reach the place, and giving the bell a loud ring, the gate keeper came and open the gate. We inquired if there was a gentleman there who acted as an officer by the name of Mr. Samuel S. Wood. The keeper of the gate stared us most suspiciously in our faces and said that there was no such officer there. We then ask for admittance, which he refused to give us until we had told him that we was once Refuge boys in the old Refuge that stood up in the Bowery, and that we was under the care of Mr. Wood, and that if he was in, we would be glad to see our old friend and Superintendent once more, telling him that we would give him two dollars if he would let us in, or if he would just step up to the office and tell Mr. Wood to come to the gate. I knew that if Mr. Wood was there, he would grant us free admittance, and been glad to see us, and given us the privilege of looking around to see if any of our old comrades still remained behind, but the gate keeper confirmed to us with a solemn oath that Mr. Wood was not there, nor there had not been such a gentleman there by that name since he had been there. We then desired him to go to the office and give in our names to the Superintendent and inform him who we was, and to look on the old record books and see if he could find our names and numbers still a remaining among any of the old records. The gate keeper said that he would oblige, and he went off and was gone about ten minutes, and then made his return, and open unto us and bade us to enter in.

We stepped in and walk up to the office and told the Superintendent that we was once boys in the House of Refuge, under the care of Mr. Wood and Mr. Heart, and would like to have the privilege of goin' through and look each boy in the face to see if any of our old companions yet remained among the large number. The Superintendent was a stranger to us both, a man that we had never seen before but appeared to be a very fine gentleman. He conducted us through the whole establishment, and not a face could me and Captain Tell discern that was there when we was.

"My God," said I in a loud voice to Captain Tell, "is possible that not but a few years ago we was crowded and numbered among seven hundred boys, and not one of them is now left, among this vast crowd, to join us in our jokes of by gone days and to tell us of the sorrows and troubles to which he has pass through since we left the solitary old place?" No, Reader, out of nearly four hundred, now there wasn't one left to give us any account of the Mysteries and Miseries that was prevailing within the walls of the old mansion. All had gone—from the inmate of the place up to the officer was nothing but strangers to us.

The Superintendent then conducted us to the office and opened several record books to see if he could find our names or numbers, but not a sign of them could there be found. Where was our names then to be found, if not on them books? It's true, we was once boys in the old Refuge that use to stand up in the Bowery, and it is true that me and Wm. Tell was both boys under the care and superintendence of Mr. Wood and Mr. Heart, but where was our names and numbers to show this to the Superintendent, who was pawing over his record books and looking earnestly for our names and numbers? Reader, our names ere long ago has been given to the flames, and the devouring fire that swept the old Refuge and brought her a quaking and crumbling to the ground melted everything to ashes. Years has passed away, and the old record books has become ashes under the feet of travelers. Had Mr. Wood been there, he would had no need of looking over those old records to search for our names, but he would known us on our first entering the door.[28]

The Superintendent, after spending some time in vain a looking over the books to find our names, I told him the old books of records was all burnt up at the time the old Refuge burnt down. He then closed the books and came to the conclusion that I must be right. He then fell in a conversation with us and ask us how we liked Mr.

Wood. I told him that I thought he was a very nice gentleman, a man of good feelings and full of sympathy, also a man of good sound judgment, and that he knew how to use it, and that he never ruled without law or reason, and never inflicting a punishment on a boy, only when he deserved it, and not inflicting any more on a boy than he is able to bear, and that he was a gentleman that sought the welfare of those that was under his care, and trying to implant in the bosoms of them little ones a moral reformation, and sowing the seeds of religion and truth in their hearts.

"But," said the Superintendent, "how did you like the Rev. Mr. Terry?"

"He was a hard hearted man," replied Captain Tell—"a hard, brutalizing old fellow. He had no feelings to show, nor no sympathies to give. Hard hearted old scamp, he took more delight in catting the boys than he did of eatin' his meals. The old chap would sway seventy or eighty on a boy's back, and then fall down upon his knees and ask heaven to pardon him for all the blood he had drew from those little innocent boys' backs. During one of his long prayers one night, when they use to hold the school in the halls, Terry was praying with all his might, and a young fellow by the name of Petterson[29] came up behind him and drew a knife across his throat, which nearly proved his death. Never as long as live will I forget that dark and doneful night when I seen the blood a running from his throat, a making deep stains in the floor."

Captain and I arose and took another look at the old mansion and made our way back to the ship, where I stopped with him for three days. On the fourth day I march towards Home. I have often thought how it was that Wm. Tell, once a boy with me in the House of Refuge, was now grown up and become a heavy stout man, and become the captain of a large vessel, with a large capital of gold piled away in his trunk, and yet could be a card player at the same time and the possessor of a handsome young girl who was wearing and flourishing in the robes of extravagance. How many females are there now a living who, once flourish in the ball room with their silks and satins on, are now weeping under the cold, pinching hand of poverty? The cold icicle hand of time soon turns their plenty into poverty, and those gay dresses soon turns and fades away and becomes signs for other people to gaze and stare at.

I MUST NOW return back to the significant Mr. Terry, where the reader will see that I was still a boy in the House of Refuge on the day that Peter Mackerboy and Wm. Tell received such a hard punishment, and with raw mangled backs they was driven off to a dark and a gloomy cell, where they made their escape on the following day.

It was about two weeks after Mack and Tell had got punish that Mr. Wood made a visit up to the Refuge. It was the hour of eleven. I had just got my work done and was coming down stairs when I met Mr. Wood. I was glad to see him, for he had been gone about one year, and I gathered around him with the other boys to take a look at our long and absent friend. Mr. Wood, seeing me among the crowd that stood around him, ask me if I was here yet. I told him that I was and that there was no chance of my getting out.

"Well, Reed," said he, "if I had stayed here till this time I should have bound you out or sent you off to sea."

I then told Mr. Wood that I wish he would come back and take his office again, not meaning any harm or hurt in what I had said, but upon my soul. Just as soon as Mr. Wood got through with his visit and had got outside of the gate, Terry called me in his office and gave me twenty-two blows on my bare back with the cats and sent me back to the shop to my work till dinner time, and when the boys all got seated at the table, he called me out from the table and made me go without my dinner for just a asking Mr. Wood if he was coming back again.

After dinner, I called Thom McGollin[30] and Bill McCollough one side and told them that if I lived to morning that just as soon as we was unlock, I was determined to make my escape and pass right over into Jersey City and get my living by gambling. Thom ask me if I was in earnest.

"Yes, Thom," said I. "I am in earnest."

"Then I'll be with you," said the two boys.

"But don't forget," said I, "to take Mike with us."

The day passed away, and night rush on. Heavy drops of rain fell during the night and continued during the day. Early in the morning in that beautiful and sober month of May, four of us in number rounded the west corner of the House while the boys was down on the play ground, and goin' to the west corner of the wall, we swung the rope and made our escape.

I was determined this time to keep out of the way of Mr. Hayse, for I knew if I could only keep out of his way long enough to cross the river on the Jersey side that I was all right. It rained hard during the day and there wasn't many people to be seen in the streets. Crossing a large track of land, we fell out into the road that led to the city. It was now nearly noon, and we traveled on till we reach Mrs. McCollough's House. We all four went in, and in the flash of lightning did Mrs. McCollough provide us with food and money to make our escape in to Jersey. Mrs. McCollough had a sister a living in Jersey, and she charged her son William to go right to her, and she would take care of him until she herself came over.

After getting our necessary things from this kind hearted Irish lady, we cross over into Jersey. As I was walking and wandering up the street, I met a black fellow who had made his escape from the Refuge about a year previous to the time to which I am now speaking of, and had been lucky enough during that time to keep out of the clumsy hands of Hayse. This young fellow proved a friend to me. He took me to his mother's house and had me provided with a suite of clothes and advised his mother to let me stay and remain there until I got a goin'. He also lent me five dollars in money.

The next day I met McGollin and Mike. I ask them where they snoozed during the past night. Thom replied that they had snoozed away the dead hours of the night under an old coal cart. We all three stood together, awaiting for McCollough to come, but he did not make his appearance until late in the day. We then walk in a saloon that was kept by an old lady and called for something to eat. The old woman took such a fancy in Mike that she picked out some of the nicest nicknacks that she had in her saloon and spread them out before him and sat down aside of him, a telling that he was to stop and remain with her. Well might the old hag fell in love with him, for Mike was as beautiful as a flower and had the features of the feminine sect. After Mike had got through a eatin', the old woman ask him if he would stay with her and be her son. Mike told he would, and the old woman went out to buy some nice broad cloth to make him a new suite of clothes.

While we was sitting there, there came in a dozen or more sailors and went into the back room a playing cards.

"Now," said I to Thom, "is our chance." We stepped into the room and ask the boys if they would give us a hand in. They said they would. We sat down and played all that day and all of that night, not even stopping the game to close our eyes in sleep. In the morning I counted over my cash and found that I had come out ahead the amount of thirty-nine dollars, and Thom was fifty-two dollars ahead, and McCollough was seven dollars and a half. I had just six dollars when I commenced, and divided it equal between the three of us.

In the morning the party broke up, and the sailors returned to their several vessels, promising to meet us on the following night. We step up and paid the old lady for our meal which we had got from her the day before and left her and Mike a flourishing behind the counter in deep love with each other. Promising to make our return in the course of the day, we walk up the street aways and turned into a tailor shop and got measured for a new suite of clothes, paying the tailor for them before they were done, and walk out, telling him that we would call for the clothes on Saturday afternoon. We then went up to the colored woman's House where I had passed my first night, and Thom being flush struck a bargain with the old woman for two months' board and threw her down eight silver dollars in cash. We then went back to the saloon, where we found Mike and the old woman wrapped deep in each other's arms and solacing themselves with love.

For three months we had kept together and shunned the hands of the police men. At the end of these three months, I had won money enough to buy me four new suites of clothes and a trunk and enough to convey me back to my native Home, to which McCollough and McGollin was to go with me as far as Albany. It was on a Monday morning that we arose at early dawn and pack up our trunks, and to get ready for the steam boat that morning to commence my Homeward march. Having all things ready, we went down to the saloon where Mike was to take, as I thought, the last farewell shake of the hand, but to our great surprise as we entered this place of hell, there stood Hayse and six more policemen, with Mike bound hand and foot, and that clumsy old hand of Hayse seized me again, while four other policemen seized McGollin and McCollough and took us back to the Refuge.

Mr. Terry stood in the office door as we entered the gate. We walk up to the office, and Terry ordered the steward to have us wash and dress in our Refuge clothes by twelve o'clock. At the hour of twelve the bell rung for dinner, and the whole four of us was called out in the center of the dining room, and Terry orders us to take off our shirts. McGollin told him that he didn't come back to take off his shirt.

"Do you hear me?" said Terry in a rough and an ugly manner. "I say take off your shirts."

We stood still and firm, without moving a hand, until Mr. Terry stepped up to McGollin and struck him across the face with the cats. That McGollin could not stand, but seized Terry by the throat and brought him to the floor. No sooner had Terry been brought to the floor than McCollough rush in and struck him several blows in the face. Terry hollered for help, but there was not a boy in the house that would rise to lend him a hand. The foremen of the shops heard his cries, and they run to his assistance and pulled the two boys off. We then stripped off our shirts while the tyrannical old scamp gave us forty-five blows apiece. I had always thought that Mr. Roe,[31] who use to have the management of that institution, was a very severe man in punishing the boys, but he was a man of humanity aside of Terry.

The next day after we had received our punishments, I witnessed a scene which I never want to see again on this side of the grave. It was at the hour of eleven o'clock. The boys had got their tasks done and had gone down on the play ground, a playing a game of ball that is called knuckle all over. Mr. Terry had come down there to join them in their sports. As the ball came in the grasp of Terry, he grabbed it up and threw it with all his might and hit Wm. Burris[32] in the back. Burris snatch the ball from the ground, and thinking that turn about was fair play, he let fire at Terry and hit him on his leg. The play continued in a friendly way between the two for some time, until at last Burris threw the ball in a playing manner and took Terry aside the head. Terry couldn't stand the heats and burns from Burris any longer, but thrust his hand into his pocket and blew his whistle for the boys to come on parade and march into the dining room. He then called William Burris out and ordered him to take off his shirt. Burris took off his shirt, and Terry made his hands fast to the post and punished him on the back with a little black rattan until there wasn't room enough to make another red mark on his back.

I remember once when Mr. Wood was about to punish me in the same manner with a little rattan on my bare back, that I begged him to put my punishment over until he got a new pair of cats made. He granted my request and unloosed my hands from the post and postponed my punishment until the next, by which time he had got a new pair of cats made, and he rewarded me with twelve lashes on my back according to my just deserts. Mr. Wood and Mr. Heart were men of feeling, men that did not sway their authority with the cats like Mr. Terry in a tyrannical way but in a way of good feelings and sympathy, always looking the poor little sufferer in the face with a smile and a laugh at every blow that he gave him and speaking a soft and a kind word to him. Thus was it with Mr. Heart in the same way, striking the little scamps a few soft blows on the back with the cats for some high crime that they had done, until the little devils hollered and squeak out enough. He would then untie their little paws and let them go.

Gloomy days hovered over our heads when Mr. Wood and Mr. Heart left their office and resigned it into the hands of Mr. Terry. As soon as those two officers had left, the contractors broke up their shops, and the boys went to work a burning down the whole institution in four short hours. No less than sixty thousand dollars' worth of property all crumbled away to ashes, and we was obliged to take up our night lodging in the shops and in the barn.

A few days after Mr. Hayse had brought me back, Terry called me into his office and ordered me to take my shirt off. I took my shirt off and tied my pants with my suspenders around me and folded my arms, ready to take a punishment, for what I knew not. Terry then took down a new pair of cats that hung up behind the office door and demanded a gold watch from me which he said that I had brought in with me. I denied openly to Mr. Terry that I had never brought any gold watch in with me nor that I had never had a gold watch of my own in my hands since the day that my father died.

"Do you deny such an open falsehood as that to me, sir?" said Terry in a rough voice.

"Yes, sir, Mr. Terry," said I. "I certainly do, sir."

"Turn around there, sir." As he said these words, I turned my poor back around to him, which was already sore as a boil, and he gave me about three dozen lashes, and still demanding the watch from me.

"Mr. Terry," said I, "will you let me speak one word, sir?"

"Yes, speak," said he.

"As true as there is a God in heaven, Mr. Terry," said I, "I have had no watch. Neither do I know anything about the watch which you are demanding from me."

The tyrannical old fellow ordered me to turn my back to him again, and the old whelp gave me a dozen more and ask me if I was ready to deliver up the watch. I declared to Mr. Terry by all that was sacred in heaven, and in the sacred name of my beloved father that laid beneath the ground, that I knew nothing at all about the watch. The tyrannical old demon ordered me to turn my face to the wall and put both hands upon my head. I did so, and he went out and was gone about twenty minutes and returned with a nigger as black as midnight a following him at his heels. Terry and the nigger whose name I shall call Thom King[33] entered the office where I stood, and Terry ordered me to turn my face towards him and King. As I turned around, Terry accosted King in the following manner—

"King, I want the whole truth about this matter, and I want you to tell me now just what you seen."

The infernal nigger turned his face towards Mr. Terry, and looking me directly in the eye began his story. "Mr. Terry," said the black hearted scamp as he rolled the white of his eye at me, "I was down on de play ground behind de barn and I seen Rob pull a gold watch out of his pocket. Den he shoved it into his pocket again."

"Are you sure, King?" said Terry.

"Yes, sirs, just as sure as I am standing here, sirs."

"Well, King, do you think that you can find that watch and produce it to me, to make your story true?" said Terry.

"Well, sirs, I am not sure dat I can, but I think," said King, "dat Hank Strongman has de watch in his possession now, for I seen him and Rob holding a very long conversation behind de barn over de watch."

"Sure, are you, King?" said Terry.

"Oh yes, sirs, very sure."

Terry then ordered me to turn around, and he gave me two dozen more right in the presence of that black hearted and infernal lying nigger—and then demanded the said watch from me.

"Mr. Terry," said I, "may the all vengeful hand of God fall on me and crush me at your feet if ever I brought a watch inside of these walls with me."

"Turn around, then," said Terry, and he gave me about sixty or seventy blows more, which brought me faint and senseless to the floor, and the blood came streaming from my back. How long I had laid there in that condition I am unable to tell. As I opened my eyes, I saw King and Terry a raising me from the floor and seating me in a chair. I was so weak and faint that I was not able to put my shirt on alone. There I sat until Terry had called poor Henry Strongman[34] in, who was to go under the same innocent punishment that I had already gone through and bow himself beneath the bloody strokes of the cats, innocently and wrongfully, while that infernal black whelp stood by, a looking on our pains and miseries. Terry ordered Strongman to help me on with my shirt. Poor Strongman, though a strong hearted boy, stretch forth his hands and help me on with my shirt, while the back of it stuck fast to my back, stained with innocent gore.

After I had got my shirt on, Terry ordered poor Strongman to take off his shirt. Strongman stripped himself like a man and stood in the center of the floor, with his arms folded, demanding of Terry what he was to be punish for.

"Strongman," said Terry, "I wish to put a question to you, of which if you tell me the truth it will save you from a severe punishment, but if you tell me a lie, I shall punish you till there ain't a drop of blood left in you."

Poor boy held up his head like a man and told Terry that it was never a shame to face the truth.

"Well, sir," said Terry, "I want you to tell me about that watch that you and Robert had behind the barn day before yesterday."

"Watch?" said Strongman. "I do not understand your meaning, Mr. Terry. Explain yourself, if you please."

"Strongman," said Terry, "this is a serious matter, and unless you present that gold watch to me which you and Robert had behind the barn, I shall punish you till you can't stand up. There stand King, an eye witness, who seen you and Rob have the watch in your hands."

"Is that so, King?" said Strongman to the lying devil.

"Yes," said the thick lip nigger, "it is so, Strongman, and you know it."

"I have no more to say, Mr. Terry," said Strong. "If I am punished, it will be inflicted on me wrongfully, and remember that if you spill my blood and stain your hands in my innocent gore, remember that it will follow you to the judgment. I have never seen Robert with a watch, nor do I know anything about it."

Terry ordered him to stand around and incline his back a little over. Poor Strongman obeyed the mandate, and look me innocently in the face with streaming eyes, and bowed himself beneath the suffering weight of the cats.

Reader, could you told the feeling of my heart and mind as I sat there, wrapped in fountains of tears? Could you told my sympathies as I look upon that beautiful milk white skin of Strongman's, who was to be lash and striped like a slave, and that innocently, too, for that which he knew nothing at all about. My tears, my sympathies, nor my panting heart could avail him nothing. While poor Strongman was getting tortured and mangled, I, oh I bowed my head and closed my eyes, that I might not look on the awful scene of misery, nor stand a witness against Terry at the day of doom. Terry gave Strongman about one hundred and twenty blow, and told him to prepare for more on the following day if he did not present the watch, and sent us both out of the office a staggering beneath the weight of weakness. We then crawled down at the lower end of the yard and laid down in the sun, with our backs cut all to pieces.

I did not care so much about myself as I did about poor Strongman, whose skin only an hour before was clean from stripes and as white as milk. Then was the day that I wish for to see Mr. Heart or Mr. Wood, that I might make my appeal to him, that I might bring mine case in plain open day light to him, who would have went before Doctor Mott and the committee and brought our cases before him and investigated the matter over and seen if Mr. Terry had had any right in punishing us, in the brutely way that he did, for what a lying nigger had said. Although Mr. Wood had resign his office, yet his heart flowed in sympathy towards us, and he was still living in the city, a seeking our interest and everlasting welfare.

As I rose upon my feet, I look up the walk, and lo, I seen King come poking slowly along with his head bowed towards the ground, and afraid to mix and mingle in with the rest of the boys, but stood with both hands in his pocket, a leaning his back against the females house, sneered and scorned by every boy in the House for telling such an up and down blasphemous lie on two poor unfortunate beings that was shut up in a prison like himself. But the Reader shall now see what an awful end King came to, two days after Strongman and me had received our punishments. The old Refuge had been set on fire by some rude hands of some of the inmates.[35] The boys was put to work a picking up the bricks and piling them up by themselves. Among the number was Thom King. It was just supper time, and Terry had blown his whistle for the boys to wash and get ready for supper—but Mr. King took no heed to the whistle, but thought that he would step inside the old building and fetch out one more load of bricks before he wash himself. Just as the King of liars was stooping down to pick up a brick, a large stick of timber fell from over head, and made a large hole in his skull. King was taken up and carried to the hospital. The Doctor was sent for, and he pronounced his case desperate, that he wouldn't live to see the morning.

As I and Strongman heard the Doctor utter them words, we both stepped up to Mr. Terry, and taking our caps off of our heads, we ask the Rev. gentleman Mr. Terry if he would allow us to go up and see King a few minutes before the night of death over took him. As we said these words to Terry, he turned as white as a sheet in the face and said, in a most affecting manner, that we might, after the boys was all shut up in the barn. The hour arrived, and in company with the Rev. Mr. Terry, we entered the hospital, and there sat the nurse,

an old lady, a wiping the blood from the wound which King had received. All was still and silent as death.[36] The cold night of death was
fast approaching him. There he laid, stretch out in full length, with
his mouth wide open, a gasping for breath. As the dying nigger open
his eyes, he saw me and Strongman a standing around his dying
couch. The impudent and black infernal black hearted nigger had
the impudence to stretch out his black paw to us and exclaim that he
was goin'. Refusing to take his black paw, I told him that I had come
up to see him before he died.

"King," said I, "have you got your reason yet?"

"Yes," said the poor infernal nigger.

"Do you understand what I have said to you, King?"

"Yes," he answered, with tears streaming from his eyes and rolling down his black cheek.

"King, I see that the cold icicle hand of death is ready to snatch
you away. Soon your lamp of life will go out, your brittle thread will
soon burst, and your spirit will go up to that God who gave it, to
receive its just rewards. I want to ask you one solemn question, King,
before you die, right here in the presence of Mr. Terry. King, will
you answer me that question?"

King said he would.

"Tell me, King, did you ever see me and Strongman with a
watch?"

"No, Rob," said King, "I never did."

"Then why did you tell Mr. Terry so? How could you been so
wicked, King, as to stand by and see our poor backs hacked up in the
way you did? Have you anything to say or any excuse to make,
King?"

"No," said King, "I have none."

"Tell me, then, what possessed you to tell such an infernal lie?"

"I done it," said King, "thinking to gain the favors of Mr. Terry.
But Rob, I am a dying. Oh Strongman, for God sake," said the dying
imp, "save my life."

"No, King, I cannot save your life. It is not in my power. Your doom is sealed up forever. This night, yes this very night, King, you must die. There is no help for you. This night you will see that innocent blood of ours that was spilt in the office day before yesterday. Yes, King, our blood will haunt you till the day of judgment, and many will be the long and lonesome nights that you will gaze upon our sore and striped backs."

"Too much for me to hear," said King. "I am a dying. My soul will go to hell. Hand me a drink," said King.

As he said these words, the infernal wretch stretch himself out and yielded up his ghost, and his black spirit took its everlasting flight in the presence of him who had sent his judgments down on the pate of King for telling an up and down falsehood on Strongman and me. Gone—yes, forever gone, to receive his just due and deserts from the hand of that God whom he had so justly receive his rewards.

The next morning Terry told the boys that Thom King was dead and that his body would be brought out into a coffin and placed in the center of the dining room, that he wanted the boys to pass out in a single file and take a look at one of our number who but a few hours ago was alive and joining in our sports and play, and that we should always remember that we, like King, might be apt to be called suddenly away at any moment of the day; that we, though young and flourishing with good health, we was not a bit too young to die; that when the angel of death came with his glittering sword, he showed no partiality to no one, old or young, rich or poor, black or white, bound or free. After he had got through with his discourse, he ordered the boys to rise and march quietly and peaceably out into the yard.

The next day King's body was brought down in a pine coffin and placed on two stools, and the boys passed out, taking the last look at that infernal nigger who but three days before stood and smiled on my sufferings. As I passed his coffin, there he laid, in the same condition that he did when he died, with his mouth wide open and his eyes half closed.

Reader, I have now unfolded to you the mysteries and miseries of the New York House of Refuge. Now I would candidly ask you, what is it that brings so many young boys to this place, where they have to go under the cruel hand of torture and punishments, where their backs are cut and mangled up with the cat of nine tails? I answer, it is because they break over the fond restraints of a mother or a father or sister, and leap over the wall of instruction, and in early boyhood they leave the parental roof of their happy Homes, and go a rove about the streets without a place to lay their heads, or enter into some large city where they learn to drink and gamble, and enter the House of infame until they fall a prey to vice and crime, until the heavy hand of the policeman takes them away to the House of correction, and even when there his little hands grasps at some novel, and he read over some infernal lie of some burglary, or the exploits of some highwayman, such as Jack Sheppard and Dick Tarpin.[37] Who ever knows it to be a truth that there ever was such a highwayman as Sixteen String Jack, or Dare Devil Dick? Who ever knows that one half of the robberies that are written in novels have been committed? The little youngster gets a hold of these novels, and he swallows them with a greedy appetite as though he was reading the life and the adventures of some great man of his country. He goes on a studying such foolish tales until he gets the whole robbery perfectly by heart, and he steers out into the world with his mind stored full of novels and desperations, until he commits the novel crime which he has been a reading and finds himself a shameful and a disgraceful young man, shut up in a dark and a gloomy prison, cause of many old gray heads to bow beneath the shameful disgrace of shame and woe, as the reader shall shortly see.

I despise the looks of a novel. The cursed infernal things, I can't bear the sight of one. They are a curse to every one that reads them. I never could bear the looks of them. They are pack full of lies. They are a store House of lies. I never could take any comfort in reading them. Give me the history of some great and good man who is laboring for the welfare of his country, like Wm. H. Seward, who is fighting against the world of enemies every day for the promotion and benefit of his country, and laboring with a strong arm for to crush vice and crime and morality under the feet of the world. That is such a book which I love to read. Novels are books that will bring many a young man to a gloomy cell, and many a weeping mothers to their graves.[38]

———

I MUST NOW bring the reader back where he left me, a taking the last look at my old friend Thom King, and with my back sore and raw with the prints of the cats, and Strongman shivering under the gnawing pains of a mangled back. Two days after the death of Thom King, I called Strongman and a French boy behind the barn, where we had held so many counsels together, and told them that there was nothing in the way to hinder us from making our escape and return immediately back Home to our friends, and not to stay in the city of New York one hour if we could possibly help it. After I had schemed out my plan in getting away, Nicholas Miller[39] the French boy and Strongman promised to be ready at nine o'clock. At the hour of nine I saw Strongman and Miller together. I step up to them and told them that I was now ready to make another start, let the consequence be what it would. As I said these words to them, we all three push up behind the garden fence and walk up to the building that had been burnt down, and taking up a long stick of timber, we plank it firm against the wall, and I made my escape with Strongman and Miller.

The first place we made for was the Hudson River. We was bound to leave for the happy Homes of our native lands. It was near twelve o'clock when we got to the steam boat landing. There we all three stood, without a shoe to our feet or a cap on our heads, no coats on our backs but a coat of red stripes which the cats had made, and not a single cent of money in our possession. The reader may sympathize with us and imagine what a sad condition we was in, two of us with our backs sore and raw with the cats, and the back of our shirts stained and gored with blood.

How to get Home or what to do, I knew not. I seen the steam boat getting ready to start. Passenger after passenger step aboard, one after another. One short hour, and she would be a puffing her way up the river, with her bow pointing right towards the land of my nativity. While I was standing in this pensive and lone condition, a young gentleman dressed in the fashion of the day, with a heavy gold seal attach to the chain of his watch, came up to us and told us that if we was goin' to take passage aboard the boat, that we had better be a looking to it, for the boat would start in five minutes. This gentleman proved to be the captain of the boat.[40] We all three step aboard and went and sat alone by ourselves, free from all the passengers at the bow of the boat. As we sat there, the captain, a fine sympathizing young man, stepped up to us and accosted us in the following manner—

"Well, boys, where are you bound for?"

I rose upon my feet and told him that we was three boys who had just made our escape from the House of Refuge, and that we wanted to be carried back to the land of our nativities. I then pulled off my shirt and showed the captain my back and told him that Strongman was in the same condition, that it was caused by the means of a good for nothing, lying nigger, who but a few days ago ended his life in the walls of the Refuge.

"Poor boys," said the captain. "I feel sorry for you all. And as I am not a goin' to sail no further than Harvest Straw, I will let you go as far as there with me, and then I will try to put you on some boat that will convey you back to your natives Homes."

He then left us and went away and called the cook and told him to see that we had something to eat brought to us after the passengers got through their dinner. The cook made a bow with his head and returned back to his room, and brought us provisions enough for a horse to eat, and sat it down before us and went back to his room. Strongman and Miller ate with a ravenous appetite, but for myself I could not eat, for this reason—that my little heart beat wildly with joys to think that I was bending my way back to the happy Home of my childhood and friends.

Oh, how my eyes beam and sparkled with joy on the distant shores, as the little steamer plough her way through the water! Reader, could you only seen the feelings that came mingling and playing around my heart as I went along on the river, your very heart would sympathize with me. Homeward bound—yes, Reader, Homeward bound, as I thought, after being gone for three long years. Homeward bound to see my mother, and to grasp the hand of my sister once more and mingle in our childhood sports again, and to visit the sacred spot that held my beloved father. But oh, alas, alas my future enjoyments and prospects of reaching my native Home was cut off in one short day—

For just as the blazing sun was sinking behind the distant hills and mountains that stood on the bank of the Hudson River, the steamer came playing up at the dock in the little village of Harvest Straw. It was a cold night in spring, without a shoe or a cap or a coat on my back. Strongman and me went a strolling along up the hill, while Miller went off in another direction to see if he could find a place for us to lodge during the night, for it was too cold for Strongman and me to take up our lodging on the wet ground and in the night air, in the condition we was in. As we stroll along up into the town, we saw but one tavern in the whole place, and that was a large hotel where none but ladies and big bugs put up, and me a poor boy just nine years old. To go and beg a night's lodging there, I thought, it would be a piece of insult to the landlord of the House, but there I stood, with both my hands in my pockets, and bare footed and bare headed, with no coat, and standing on one foot while I had the other pressing against my leg, a shivering with cold, not knowing where to lay my head during the night.

Yes, Reader, there we both stood, a leaning against the corner of the House, with raw backs and shivering with pain and cold. Night was fast approaching. Night was throwing her dark mantle over the land. There I stood, while tears of grief and sorrow came mingling down my cheek. As I stood there in this doneful condition, a lady and a gentleman glided swiftly a pass us. My tears and grief called their attention. The lady and gentleman was on their way to the hotel. It was the captain and his sister who had brought us to Harvest Straw. The American Hotel was always their stopping place when in port.[41]

As the captain and his sister pass us, the cry of deep woe and wailing brought him back to us, and he spoke to us in the following manner—

"Well, boys, you are here I see."

"Yes, sir, captain," said I, "we are here."

"And where is the other boy, Miller?"

"He has gone to find a place for us to stay tonight."

"Have you no money, boys?"

"No, sir, captain, not a cent."

"Stay here, boys, and I will return back to you in five minutes."

"Captain," said I, while the tears came pouring down my cheeks, "captain, is there no boats that is goin' to sail for Albany tonight that you can put us aboard of, that we may reach our native Homes?"

"No, boys, there is no boats as I know of that will sail tonight, but stop here a minute."

The captain and his sister glided along till they entered the hotel. The bright lights of the lamps shone through the windows, and we could see, from the distance we stood, young gentlemen and ladies a playing cards and turning roulettes. The captain was gone about fifteen minutes, and then made his return.

"Come, boys," said he. "Follow me."

Strongman and me followed the captain to the hotel, and he led us in the kitchen, where there was seven girls making a great noise among the dishes and knives and forks, as though the little creatures was in a hurry to get their plates washed and their work out of the way.

"Poor little fellows," said the girls, as they sat a chair in front of the fire for us to warm our shivering limbs.

As we sat there, the girls one after another brought us a few nick-nack to eat and then began to question us about our Homes and the place of our nativity and the friends we loved so well. After sitting there a full half hour, I crammed my pockets full of cakes and rose up and ask Strong if he was ready to go (for I felt as though I wanted to wing my way out of the House and find some lone spot where I might give a full vent to my tears).

"Go where, boys?" said one of the girls.

"Out doors, madam," said I.

"It's too cold for you to go out tonight, in the situation that you are now placed in." As she said these words, I heard the tramps of many feet tramping through the hall and making their way towards us in the kitchen.

"Well, my boys," said the captain, "how do you feel now? Had any supper? Feel sleepy and tired? Here, Esq. Johnson,"[42] said the captain to the landlord, who was a heavy stout looking man with a cigar in his mouth. "Here, as you never have had a colored person in this town before, and as you have no sons, I will make you a present of this little colored boy."

Esq. Johnson step up to me and patted me on the head and ask me how I would like to stay and live with him. I was so over powered with tears that I could not speak.

"Poor boy," said he, turning to the captain. "I dare say that he is a smart boy."

"He looks to me like a smart, intelligent boy," said the captain. "Get up, boys," said the captain, "and let Esq. Johnson see your backs."

We both rose from ours seats and stripped off our shirts, while a crowd of ladies and gentlemen gathered around us to see our man-gled backs.

"Poor suffering boys," said the ladies. "How them little fellows have suffered."

"Yes," said Mrs. Johnson as she huddled her shoulders up to her neck.

"Father," said the little damsel, "them boys must have a very soft feather bed to lay on tonight on account of their backs."

"How happen your back cut so raw, boys?" said Esq. Johnson, who had taken a seat aside of me.

"Sir," said I, "two weeks ago I was in the city of New York. I had made my escape three months before this from the House of Refuge, and two weeks ago, in company with two other boys, I started with a trunk of clothes and some money to go back Home to my mother. But just as I was ready to step aboard the steamer that was goin' to Albany, the hard, pruney, clumsy old hand of Hayse grabbed me and took me back to the House of Refuge, and for making my escape I was brought up to the post with my shirt off and received thirty-nine blows on my bare back with the cat of nine tails, and two days after, a big liver lip looking nigger by the name of Thom King had told Mr. Terry the Superintendent that I had brought a gold watch in with me and that this boy Strongman was knowing to it and had a share in it. Mr. Terry then called us into the office and question us both very close about the watch, to which we could not give him any information concerning the piece he demanded from us. He then ordered us to take off our shirts right in the presence of Thom King, and gave us about one hundred and fifty lashes a piece on our bare backs."

"And where is that Thom King now?" said Esq. Johnson.

"The all vengeful hand of the Almighty (said I) grasp a stick of timber two days after and threw it on his black pate, and that very day the cold night of death over took, and he now lays with the pale nations of the ground, taking up a bitter and a horrible lamentation among his inmates in hell."

"But how came you to get out again?" said Esq. Johnson.

"Sir," said I,

"God he proved a friend to me
as shortly as you shall see
I climb the plank and scaled the walls
and gain'd my liberty.[43]

"The very timber that fell on the head of King and that was yet stained with his blood, I plank it firm against the wall, and in company with this boy Strongman and Miller we made our escape, and tonight we find ourselves under the peaceful roof of your building."

"And where is the other boy, Miller?" said the Esq.

"I don't know, sir. He went off to seek a place for us to sleep during the night."

"Well, Esq.," said a gentleman that stood by a whiffing smartly on a Havana. "I guess you have got a smart black boy there. You had better keep him and bring him up."

"Just what I am goin' to do," said the Esq. "And as I have no children but one daughter, I will take the boy into my family and make an adopted son of him, and if he is smart I will give him a chance to get a college education in the course of a few years."

During this conversation, the captain's sister and Mrs. Johnson and her daughter had slip out to the druggist store and bought a box of ointment and prepared it for our backs. Oh, how I thought of my mother as these ladies came pressing towards us, with a tea cup in their hands. Yes, Reader, my mind went back to my infant days, when I laid helpless and needed the care of my mother. The gentlemen thrust their hands in their pockets and made up a donation of nine dollars for us and left the kitchen for the women to go through their process of anointing our backs. Mrs. Johnson spoke to us in a motherly way and told us to take off our shirts and turn our backs to the fire. We obeyed her motherly orders, and one of the hired girls took a piece of silk and wash our backs in warm water. The deep cuts in our backs was filled up with clog blood. Oh, how my back did smart, as Martha bathe it in the water. It felt as though a hot iron was laid upon me.

After she had pass through the process of washing, Mrs. Johnson took her finger and dip it into the salve and rub it gently across my back. After serving us both so, the little girl went and brought two night gowns and put them on us and conducted us up stairs, in a room where there was a feather bed made up for us. We both got into bed and laid a rolling in pain during the night. Though I was tired and weary, yet I could not sleep. I thought of the poor French boy Nicholas Miller. Where could he be? Or what could the poor boy be a doing, or where had he strayed to? How sorry I felt that he had separated from us and gone off in another direction. How my heart heaved with sorrow that he did not keep close to us, though he was a stout healthy boy and not a print or a scratch of the cats was there to be seen on his back.

Thus did I lay all the night long, a listening to the voices of the sportsmen that was gambling in the next room to us, and the cheerful notes of the females a singing their night airs in the parlor below.

The morning broke upon me with no sleep, nor no rest during the night. At nine o'clock, Mrs. Johnson and several other ladies and gentlemen entered our room and look at our backs. They all agreed that we should keep our beds through the day and that a milk poultice should be made for our backs. The ladies left the room and went down to prepare the poultice. I sent word down by the captain sister to have him come up before he sailed. The captain came up in a hurry, saying that he was goin' to start for New York at ten o'clock. I now learned that he only made his trips between Harvest Straw and New York.

"Captain," said I, "for God sake don't let Hayse know anything about my being here."

"No, boys," said he, "you needn't never be afraid of my making your burdens any heavier or your punishments any sorer than they are now." He then took us by the hand and told us to be good boys till he returned from New York.

"Captain," said I, "will you be so kind as to go to Mrs. Flinn on Chatham Street and get a trunk and some clothes that belongs to me, which that lady has in her possession?"

"Is she a true woman?" said he.

"Yes, sir, she is the best friend that I have. I made my escape with her son twice, and she fight for me like a heroine for two hours with Hayse."

"Sure that I can trust her?"

"Yes, sir."

"She won't betray you?"

"No, sir."

"Then tomorrow night you may look for your trunk and clothes." As he said these words, he left the room, and Mrs. Johnson came up with two milk poultices and laid them on our back. Thus did she do, day after day, and like a good old mother extended her hand, night after night, until there wasn't a mark of the cats to be seen on our backs.

Captain Smith returned the next day with my trunk and clothes and twenty-five dollars in money and a letter from Mrs. Flinn, warning us to keep clear from New York and not to make our appearance in the city, for Hayse had been at her House twice a looking for us.

———

I MUST NOW introduce the Reader to Nicholas Miller, who had parted from us on the first night of our landing. The boy had strolled far out of the town, until he came in sight of an old barn where he entered and covered his feet up in the hay to get warm, intending to return to us the same night, but his feet paining him so with cold, he bursted in a flood of tears and came down from the hay mow and entered the man's house that own the barn and beg for a night's lodging. The people of the house prepared him a bed on the floor for the night, where he says he had a pleasant night's rest. Miller spent one month with that family, a working on the farm and fearing that he might be caught again and taken back to the House of Refuge. He shook hands with me and Strongman one morning and crossed the river on the Sing Sing shore and took a boat and went off to Avon Springs, tending bar for one Mr. Comstock.

On my opening my trunk, I found three new packs of cards that I had bought in Jersey and four new suites of clothes and twenty-five dollars in money. I gave Strongman two suites and divided my money with him. He then went out and hired to a rich man in the village by the name of Levingston.

One morning, as I stood in the kitchen a talking to Martha, John the bar tender came in with a pitcher in his hand and told me that he was goin' to leave in three days and was goin' to return Home to Michigan where he lived and was never coming back. He advised me to stay and live with Esq. Johnson, "for," said he, "the Esq. is a fine man and will take good care of you. He told me to take you behind the bar tomorrow and learn you how to tend bar. The people in the town thinks a great deal of you because you are the only black person that ever lived in this town before. You must be smart and active and keep yourself nice and clean. Esq. is goin' down to New York next week and buy you some new clothes."

These words of John pleased me very much, and I long to see the day dawn when I should become the adopted son of a gentleman. After the bar tender left the kitchen, Esq., Johnson daughter Sarah, who was goin' in her fourteenth year, came running in the kitchen and told me that her father wanted to see me. I went into the room, and there sat the Esq. and Mr. Levingston in the presence of three young ladies.

"Well, Robert, I am goin' to put you a tending my bar in the morning. I want you to be up bright and early, and John will show you. I am goin' to New York in a few days and buy you up some new clothes. I feel very proud of you, and if you be a good boy I will try to give you a college education in the course of a few years and try to make a man of you, that you may stand high in the ranks of society in after years."

As the old gentleman spoke these words, my heart leap for joy, and I long and wish to see the morning dawn. Early in the morning I arose and dress myself and went down in the bar room, and John gave me my orders what to do, and showed me the different decanters of liquor which I was to deal out. After showing me and telling me what my duty would be and what Esq. Johnson would require of me, he pack up his clothes and got ready to start for Home.

While he was getting ready, a thought struck me, that John was to pass right through my native town, and now would be my time to write a letter and send it Home to my mother by the hands of John, that she might know where I was and what I was doing. This I immediately done, and handed the letter to John, who promised to deliver it right in the hands of my mother himself, and send me back answer in three days after date. After eating his breakfast, he shipped his trunk on board of the steam boat and started for Home to greet those long absent friends.

I was now placed in a situation which I did not like, and I was determined to tell the Esq. the moment an opportunity offered. In the afternoon I went in the kitchen to get some ice, and Mrs. Johnson ask me how I like my new berth. I told her that I should like it very well if it wasn't for dealing out liquor to men.

"Pshaw," said she. "You must not mind that. You will get use to it by and by, and then you won't mind it no more than John did."

"Don't you remember, mother," said Martha, "that John had the same feelings and the very same way about him when he first came here to live with us, and we use to plague him so much that such feelings soon wore off of his mind?"

"Yes, my dear," said Mrs. Johnson. "Robert will soon get use to it and he will like his place very well."

No, Reader, the situation and the place which I was placed in I did not like, and as I now had my trunk and clothes and money enough to carry me Home, I was determined to start the next morning, if I had to foot it all the way.

While I was a musing over these thoughts, Mr. Levingston step in and walk up to the bar and called for a cigar. I hand the gentleman down a box of cigars and a box of matches. After lightin' his cigar, he commenced a talking to me—

"Well, Rob, how do you like your new station?"

"Not very well, Mr. Levingston," said I.

"Why not, Robert? I am sure you have very easy times here."

"Yes, sir," said I, "but that is not the thing of it, Mr. Levingston. This dealing out liquor to men I don't like at all."

"Why, my dear little fellow," said he, "it will be nothing but play to you after you get use to it."

"I don't want to get use to it, Mr. Levingston," said I. "I had rather do anything else around the House than to do this business, and unless Esq. Johnson takes me away from the bar room, I shall leave the place and return Home, or go back to the city of New York."

"Foolish boy," said Levingston, drawing a newspaper from his pocket. "Foolish boy you are, to return back to New York. Never would you think about New York if you only knew how Hayse is haunting you night and day, like a hound that is in chase of game in front of him. Listen boy," said he, as he spread open the New York paper and began to read the following advertisement to me—

"Three boys by the name of Henry S., Nicholas M., and Robert R. made their escape from the House of Refuge on Thursday last. If any persons or person will return the said boys back to the House of Refuge or give the subscriber any information of where they can be found he shall be liberally rewarded."

I took the paper from Mr. Levingston's hands and read the above advertisement and seen Terry's signature to it, and handed the paper back to him.

"Poor foolish boy, you want to run right back into the fire again, do you?" said Levingston. "There ain't a better man and a kinder gentleman in the whole world to live with than Esq. Johnson, and my advice is to you to stop and stay here with him, and he will take good care of you and protect you as he would one of his own children."

"Mr. Levingston," said I, "I will stay with Esq. Johnson if he will only change my place and take me from behind this counter—or other wise I will leave day after tomorrow with Captain Warner, who is goin' to sail for Albany and has promised to take me along with him."

"Well," said Levingston, "I will see the Esq. and have a talk with him and see if I can get him to change your place and give you something else to do."

As he said these words, in came Captain Smith and Esq. Johnson with a cigar in their mouths. It was near tea time, and the captains of schooners and brigs and other boats was crowding fast into the bar room, calling for liquor and cigars, ordering wines to be sent to such and such a room where they would be passing the night away in gambling. This operation kept me a flying around till the bell rung for tea. Then I had a few spare moments left me to myself, in which I could just run across the road and speak a few words to Strongman, who promised to meet me that night after the hour of eleven—for the Reader must understand that I had been order not to close the House nor go to bed till half past eleven. After telling Strongman not to fail in coming over, I hasten back to my station, and there stood three young gentlemen in the bar room, waiting for me to attend to their calls. These was the sons of a rich planter that lived in St. Louis, who had come out to spend the summer with Esq. Johnson.

"Come, Rob. Come, my boy, this won't do," said they, with a laugh on their faces long enough to reach to heaven. "You must on your guard, boy. We been waiting some time here for you. Hand us over a decanter of wine."

The young men drank and threw me a half dollar and told me to put it in my pocket and keep it myself, that it was a present for me.

"See, Rob, that you bring a bottle of wine and seven glasses of brandy and sugar up to our room in a hour from now, and tell the Esq. to charge it me. Take that quarter and shove her in your pocket."

The three youngsters left the bar room and went up stairs and began their night reveling by playing the game of faro. After they had gone I had a thousand other calls, which I was unable to attend to alone. The Esq. had gone up stairs with four other gentlemen from New York who had come in on the steam boat that day and was busy a paying at the roulette wheel, and had left me alone to do up the evening business. If I had had ten thousand hands that night, I could used them all. I was nothing but a boy at nine years old, and I found the work was too hard for me to perform alone. I cursed the day that John left the accursed place for me to fill. Bells ringing and calling for glasses of lemonades for the young Miss So and So. A bottle of wine to be sent to such and such a room for the Honorable Mr. So and So and his wife. A couple of decanters of brandies for captain A and captain B. A dozen cigars and a box of matches for them gentlemen from New York. And then the little steamer that had brought me from New York to Harvest Straw came puffing and blowing along, as though she was laden with a heavy load of hungry passengers who would be making their way up to the Hotel and calling for an extra meal. The captain and his sister must have a superior supper from any the rest, and it had to be cook just so, or in just such a style, or they would not touch it, and the poor girls would have to hear from it the next morning, and to give a correct answer why Capt. Smith and his sister's supper wasn't done up in a French style.

I must inform the Reader that I was sick of my place, and at half past eleven, when Strongman came over to see what I want of him, I called him up into my room and told him that if I lived to see morning that I would leave my place, and brought before his mind the advertisement which Mr. Levingston had read to me.

"It nothing but an old advertisement," said Strongman, "that was put into the papers about a month ago. I do not fear it, and by the eternal G—," said Strongman, drawing a horse pistol from his coat pocket which he had bought that day—"by the eternal G—, if ever that Hayse or any other living man lays a hand on me to take me back to New York, I will blow his brains out and leave him cold and senseless upon the ground, if I swing between the heavens and the earth for it the next minute."

I seen that Strongman had acted the part of the wise man, that he had got his House in order, less at any time the enemy should come upon him, and was ready to face the storm the moment it began to blow up. This made me to look around me a little, and to get ready, too, so if Hayse did happen to hear of our whereabouts, and should under take to retake us back to New York (which he would certainly do if he had heard where we was), to shoot him dead on the spot and pay him for the injuries and sufferings which I had gone through.

"In the morning, Strongman," said I, "I leave the place."

"D—d accursed fool you are, Rob, to be scared by a man. Stand your ground and don't stir a single step. Lose your life before you run for that infernal black hearted devil."

"That, Henry," said I, "is not what I am afraid of. That is not what troubles my mind. It's being up so late nights and dealing out liquor to men that God has made in his very own image is not what is quack up to be. Dam— the infernal stuff, Henry. I hate, I hate the smell of it. I can't bear the looks of it, Henry, and you know I can't. Don't you recollect, Henry, when we was coming up on the steam boat how drunk and bloated that old devil look that stowed himself away in one corner of the boat?"

"Yes," said Strongman. "I remember him."

"Well, Henry," said I, "that very old scamp was once an angel made in the image of his master above. He had a golden crown sat upon his head. He ate at the same table with his master, and his face shone so once that you and I couldn't look him in the face without dazzling our eyes. Nay, Henry he would took it as a piece of impudence if we had said to him, 'Old fellow though you look so bright and dazzling now, though you are eating the fat of the land and though you have a crown of gold tip upon your head, remember, old chap, the days will come when a fiery looking king (alcohol) will come out against you and with his sweeping sword will clip that crown off of your head.' Yes, Henry, that very old devil we seen on board of that boat was once beautifuler than them little stars you see out of my bedroom window, but look at the old brute now. Like another Nebuchadnezzar he is got his glory and his crown taken away from him, and he is sent out into the meadows to eat grass like an ox.[44] Mr. King Alcohol had a fight with that old fellow one day and gave him a heavy blow on the head and smashed his crown all to pieces and left him a wallowing like a sow in the mire and dirt.

"Why the old villain, 'pon my soul, Henry, the old chap puts me in mind of one of them little devils that the savior pulled out of Mary Magdalene. But after all, Henry, I believe the chap can get his crown back again, if he will only get up and wash himself and not meddle with Mr. King Alcohol any more. For he is a mean old devil. I have seen the old bugger play with little boys and girls, with men and women, and the dam'd old scamp turned around the next minute and burnt them so severe that the best physician that was ever on earth couldn't heal the burn. No, the tallest angel in heaven couldn't heal the smart nor scratch out the print that this fiery devil had made.

"Nor is that all, Henry. This old King is more than a thousand years old, and he is a thief, a robber, a base dishonest robber. I remember a rich man once, Henry, that smiled and laugh at poverty. He was so rich that if you pointed your finger for him to look and take a peep at poverty's door, he would turn his head in another direction. Well, one day his sons and his daughters made a great dinner and give this Mr. King an invitation to step in and sup with them. The old King accepted the invitation and stepped in. The old man and his sons and his daughters, who was swinging and swaying themselves in their broad cloths and silk dresses, made a great fuss around the table in preparing and getting things ready. The girls began to whisper in each other's ears, whether it was best to put some of the red fire on the table and entertain their guest with some of their father's best wine.

"While the whisper went around, the old man's sons descended the cellar and brought up two or three bottles and sat it on the table. Dinner being ready, the visitors drew up their chairs, and the gentleman of the House began to pour out his wines and to give his visitors a long introduction of its qualities. All the rich ladies and gentlemen that sat around his table (the Reader must remember that the guests that sat around the table was all rich ladies and gents) began to praise the lord of the House up concerning his wine.

"'How pleasant it taste,' said one of the ladies.

"'Yes,' said the young gentleman that sat at her side. 'It looks nice and sparkling.'

"'Yes, ladies and gentlemen,' said Mr. King, that looked so red and that showed so many handsome colors and tricks in the glass. 'Beware of me, for lo,' said he, 'I come a creeping slowly along. I am a lover of every body. I amuse myself with ladies and gentlemen, with the rich and the poor, at the card table and in the palace. I play and mingle around the heart and make it merry. Beware of me, for lo, I come in a moment when you think not, with my glittering sword which you see in my hand stained with red. Yes, beware of me, for I only make one dash, and you are gone.'

"The party ate and drunk. Visits from each other continued for a month.

"A few days after, I happen to pick up a newspaper accidentally, and I casted my eyes on one of the columns, where the rich man's House and property was to be sold, under sheriff's sale. I look again a few days after, and I saw the same haughty rich man covered with rags and sunk deep in the ditch of degradation and woe, laugh and scorned at by the rich and the poor, by the friends that had ate and drunk at his table. The creeping hand of poverty found its way at the door of his House. The rich and the poor refused to lend him any aid or to draw him from the sloth of despond. Time, that bright and sparkling moment which says, in notes of thunder, I wait for no one, came dancing along, and I seen the rich man and his whole family carried off to an untimely grave.

"I bethought myself and ask myself, What has done all of this? What has caused all of this poverty and accursed shame? What has caused this low degradation to fall upon the youths and the beautiful female flowers of this country? What has caused so many fair and rosy cheeks to fade away to an untimely grave? What is it that has caused so many orphans and widows to go a mourning through our streets? What is it that has caused many a weeping mother and sister to visit their unfortunate son shut up in a gloomy prison?

" 'I said me, King Alcohol,' looking me boldly in the face. 'I have done it. I show no partiality to no body. I am no respecter of persons. I enter the King's palace and peasant hovel. I stain my sword with the young and old.'

"No, Strongman," said I, "the damned black hearted old thief shan't steal me. He shan't rule and have dominion over me. Neither will I have any more dealings with him after tonight. And if I live to see the morning sun arise, I will leave Esq. Johnson House forever if he don't get another bar tender."

"Hold, Rob," said Strongman. "Listen to me and take my advice. Stay where you are now for one month, and by that time I shall have money enough to start the world with. I shall leave Mr. Levingston store and get my living by gambling."

"No, Henry," said I. "It is immaterial to me whether you go with me or not. I shall buy me a pistol in the morning and keep it charged and ready to lay the first man cold that lays his hand on me. I have suffered enough. I might as well die in the hands of the law than to suffer under the tyrannical hand of Terry. Capt. Warner has promised to take me to Albany. I then can get aboard of a canal boat and go Home—"

As I said those words, a heavy tap was heard at my bedroom, and as I had not gone to bed yet, I open the door, and the young man demanded me to go down and bring up four cigars and three bottles of wine.

"Stay, Strongman, until I return. I shall only be gone a minute."

I went down below and fetch up the cigars and wines, and the young man plank me out a one dollar bill and told me that it was a present for me, for obliging them so late an hour in the night. As I look up at the clock, I found that it was four o'clock, and I had not closed my eyes once in sleep during that night. Every room in the House was lighted up, and the sportsmen was drinking and smoking, playing roulette, throwing dice, playing the beautiful hand, faro, and cut throat. As I entered their rooms, I saw no less than seven and eight hundred dollars piled on the roulette table. The three young gentlemen from St. Louis occupied this room. It was so near morning that I thought I wouldn't go to bed, and Strongman and me went down in the nine pin alley which belonged to Esq. Johnson, where a dozen or more of gents was rolling on a marble bed. For the first time in my life I went a betting on spares, till the hour of six, and during that time I had won seven dollars.

I then went in and open the House for the day. The bell rung for the ladies and gents to get ready. I hand Strongman a cigar and told him to meet me at nine o'clock, for I was determined to leave. Another bell rung, and the boarders came rushing down stairs into the bar room, calling for their morning drinks before breakfast. After dealing out, as I thought, the last draughts that ever I would deal out again to a man, I made my morning's bill for the liquor and drinks and cigars that I had passed around during the last night and handed it to Esq. Johnson's daughter and told her to hand it to her father, telling her that I was goin' to leave. She look me in the face and laugh and ask me if I was in earnest or only joking.

"No, Martha," said I, "I am not a joking. I am in earnest."

"Why, Robert, what do you want to leave for? Has any one been abusing you?" said she. "If there has, I want to know it."

"No, Miss Martha," said I, "there isn't no one been abusing me or saying anything to me to hurt my feelings."

"Well, why is it, then, that you want to leave us?"

"Well, Martha, if the truth must be told, I might as well be plain with you in this matter at once. The place," said I, "which I now occupy, I do not like it. I like the family very well and would be glad to live here as long as I live. I don't like to be a dealing out liquor. The devilish stuff, I cannot bear the smell of it, and I despise the looks of it, and if the Esq. don't take me away from behind the counter, I shall leave this very day."

"Well, Robert, I will see Father and have a talk with him," said the girl. "You shan't stay there unless you want to. My father wouldn't put you there in the first place, only the boarders wanted him to do it, and to gratify their wishes my father put you there. Don't go way until I see my father."

I promised the girl that I would stay until she consulted the matter over with him, and I returned out into the bar room, and there sat some of the big bugs and their sons, a smoking their cigars and looking over the morning news. "Well, Rob," said one of the St. Louis boys, whose name I shall call George M—. "So you are goin' to leave this morning, are you?"

"Well, I don't know for certain yet, George," said I.

"Oh, foolish boy you are. You never said he had a better man to live with in the world than Esq. Johnson. I have known him for twenty summers and have put here with him for seven years. Stay where you are, and many is the bright dollars and quarters that you will pick up here. Let me tell you, Rob, the boarders all likes you and thinks a good deal of you. It wasn't no more than a half an hour ago that I heard them a quacking and praising you up, and telling Esq. Johnson what a smart little colored boy he had. You better stay where you are, Rob. The old man is rich and will take good care of you. He owns most every store and House in the town."

"Yes, boy, you had better stay," said Thornton. "Esq. Johnson may make a rich man of you yet. Stay where you are, and I will give you my word and honor that Esq. Johnson will prove to be a father to you, and Mrs. will be a mother to you, and as for Martha, she will prove to be a sister to you as long as you stay."

"Mr. Thornton, I will stay, if the Esq. will take me out of the bar room—but if not, I shall put my trunk and clothes aboard of Capt. Warner's boat and leave."

By this time Miss Martha had made her appearance and told me to step into her room. I followed the young girl into the sitting room, where sat seven or eight ladies, two gentlemen, and Esq. Johnson.

"Well, Robert," said Martha, "I have consulted with my father about your case. I have talk the matter over with him, and he says that Monday he is goin' to start for New York, and he would like to have you to tend the bar room until he comes back, and when he returns he will bring a man with him to tend to the bar room. Be a good boy, Robert, and stay here with me until my father makes his return Home, and I will be sister and a protector to you during the time you stay here with us, and in the course of a few months I will take you Home to see your mother, and when you return back, I will see that my father bestows a good education upon you."

"What do you say to that, Robert?" said Mrs. Smith, who sat by and over heard the conversation.

"Say to that?" said Judge Smith⁴⁵—"why I am sure," said he, "that Robert wouldn't lose the chance of a good education for all the world, would you Robert?" said Judge Smith.

I held my head down like a boy that had been doing something wrong and replied, "No, sir."

"I have no doubt but what Robert will stay here with his mother and sister," said Mrs. Johnson, "until the Esq. returns from New York."

I now began to think what Mrs. Johnson had done for me and Strongman on that dark and cold night when we first entered that town, poor and helpless, without a cent in our pockets or a place to lay our weary heads or a mother to heal our lacerated backs that had been tortured by the stroke of the cats—and with tears sprinkling down my checks, I promised Mrs. Johnson that I would stay.

"Poor, unfortunate boy," said Wellington, as I bounded slowly out of the room, that I might go and find some lone place to give away to my grief and sorrow.

Just as I got out of the door, I heard the voice of Wellington, calling after me. I turned and open the door, and wiping the big tears from my eyes, I stepped up to the gentleman, who began to ask me the following question, viz.:

"Where is your native place, Robert, when you are at Home?"

Stretching my arm out and pointing towards the Home of my

nativity I told him that in yonder's western land in the city of Rochester was the place of my birth and the happy Home of my childhood and youth.

"Is your father yet alive?" said Judge Smith.

"No, sir, my father lays moldering away to dust."

"And your mother, Robert?"

Ere before he could get that sweet and affectionate name, mother,
out of his mouth, I told him that my mother was alive when I left the
land of my nativity.

"And what is it, Robert, that has brought you so far from your
Home?"

Here I again bursted out in a full flood of tears and was ready to
make my escape out of the door, that I might go and seek a place of
reflection in some lone and solitary spot, but Martha taking her
apron, she wiped those sorrowful tears from my eyes and tried to
soothe and assuage grief by telling me that in the course of time I
should return back Home, loaded down with riches and with a good
education.

Reader, can you imagine the sorrows of my heart as Judge Smith
and Mr. Wellington, who was both rich and wealthy men, sat there
a talking to me? Ah, when these two wealthy lords mention the name
of my beloved father and the tender name of my mother, how my
soul melted away within me. All the soft feelings, the kind instructions, yea the last farewell counsels of my dying father all rose up at
once in my mind, which caused the silver cords to be loosed and the
pitcher broken at the fountain. Yes, Reader, these was my deep and
dearing thoughts when I stood, a poor helpless and shivering boy, in
the presence of these ladies and gentlemen.

"I understood you to say, Robert, that your mother was alive
when you left your Home," said Mr. Wellington to me.

"Yes, sir," I replied. "She was alive."

"How long is been since you heard from her?"

"It is now nearly four years since I have seen or heard from my
mother."

"What was it, you said, that brought you down this way?"

"Sirs, four years ago I lost my father."

"Poor boy," said Wellington as I said them words.

And the big drops of tears began to gush from my eyes again, as I continued my narrative: "But breaking through the restraints of my mother, and leaping over the fence of her kind instruction, and breaking her counsels, and leaving the Home of my boyhood, and plunging my hands deep in the sink of vice and crime, I became the vagabond and the inmate of the House of Refuge, where I was tortured and ill-treated through the means of Thom King, who for telling a lie on me and Strongman is now taking up his abode with Ananias and Sophira[46] his wife."

"What lie did he tell on you Robert?" said Mrs. Wellington.

I went on and related the story as the reader has seen in the fore goin' chapters—and in the presence of these ladies and gentlemen, I pulled off my shirt and showed them my back, where the marks of the cats was yet plainly to be seen.

"Curse the scoundrel," said Wellington, "that would torture and torment a boy in that manner. I would follow the scoundrel that would serve a son of mine in that manner," said Wellington. "Yes, I would follow him till the day of judgment. Yes, I would haunt him till his infernal spirit took its everlasting flight."

After putting on my shirt, Judge Smith began to ask me about the rules and the regulations of the House of Refuge, and the diet and schooling and so forth, to which I unfolded to him the whole mystery and miseries of that cursed and infernal hold since Mr. Wood and Mr. Hart had left, how it was swayed and ruled by the hand of a tyrannical old demon who was treading the wine press of blood under his feet, i.e., and rearing up children that had either been neglected or that had broken through the restraints of their parents for a dark and gloomy cell in a state prison, or preparing them to make their speech upon the scaffold that has been prepared for some highwayman, there to swing between the heavens and the earth.

"So you did like Mr. Wood, did you, Robert?" said the ladies.

"Never," said I, "will that institution get another officer that used the boys well as did Mr. Wood. Yes, Mr. Smith, I like Mr. Wood," said I, "for this reason: he was kind and obliging, never inflicting hard and cruel treatment upon a boy's back for what another boy said."

"I think," said Judge Smith, "that Mr. Wood and Mr. Hart are both very fine men. I have known them for a number of years."

"Yes, it is Mr. Wood that first gave me the little education that I now possess. It was the same gentleman that made so many improvements in our school house. He put a stage for us to speak poetry and pieces on, and a thousand other improvements did Mr. Wood make while he was there."

"Can you read, Robert?"

"Yes, sir, I can read, write, and cipher."

"And they say you are a good singer in sacred music."

"Yes, sir, I can sing a little and speak poetry."

"Ah indeed, Robert," said Mrs. Wells. "I am a great woman for poetry. I love to hear good poetry."

"Well, Robert," said Wellington. "Suppose you step in the center of the room and gives us a piece of your poetry which you learnt in the House of Refuge."

I step out in the center of the room, where sat some half a dozen ladies, and making a low bow to the ladies and gentleman I began the following piece of poetry—

'Twas in the glade season of spring
Asleep at the dawn of the day
I dream what I cannot but sing
So pleasant it seem'd as I lay.

I dream'd that on ocean afloat
Far hence to the westward I sail'd
Where the billows high lifted the boat
And the fresh blowing breeze never fail'd.

In the steerage a woman I saw
(Such, at least, was the form that she wore)
Whose beauty impress me with awe
Never taught me by woman before.

She sat, and a shield at her side
Shed light, like the sun on the waves,
Then smiling divinely she cried,
I go to make freemen of slaves.

Then swiftly dividing the flood
To a slave culture island she came,
Where a demon her enemy stood,
Oppressing his terrible name.

But soon as approaching the land
That goddess like woman he view'd,
The scourge he let fall from his hand
And the blood of his subjects imbrued.

Then raising her voice to an air
The sweetest that ear ever heard
She sung of the slave's broken chain
Wherever her glory appear'd.

Awaken, how could I but muse
on what such a dream could betide?
But soon mine ear caught the glade news
which serv'd my weak thought for a guide.[47]

After I had got through with the piece, Mr. Wellington put his hand in his pocket and drew out a hand full of gold, and fumbling his cash over and over, he at last pitch me a five gold piece, and Mr. Wellington told me not to fail and come in the sitting room at half past two.

"I say, Esq.," said Wellington, "you had ought to give that boy a good education. I am sure that he will appreciate and take the advantage of his time. Poor boy, see how hungry and thirsty he looks for to get knowledge. He seems to be a panting for knowledge and groaning for an education. What say you, Esq.? I will pay half of his school expenses if you will pay the other."

"What say you to that, Esq.?" said Mr. Smith.

"Well, I think the boy is yet too young."

"Too young, Esq.? Not at all, sir. Not at all a bit too young," said Smith. "That boy may grow up and become a smart man yet, if he only haves a good education bestowed upon him."

The bell rung for dinner, and the parties broke up and entered the dining room.

I went out and casted my eyes up and down the street to see if I could see anything of Strongman. While I stood there, Judge Smith, who had swallowed his dinner, came out on the stoop and ask me what kind of a profession I would like to choose, and I told him that, if I had the means, I should go off somewhere and study for a Methodist minister.[48]

"Well, Robert," said he, "I think that you have chosed and made choice of a very good profession."

Yes, Reader, then in my young and early days was the time that I was panting beneath the burning heats for an education. Then was the time that I would almost laid my life down, if I could only been sent to some high school for two or three years, and there spent my time in learning some good and useful knowledge, which might do me a deal of good in after life—but no, there I was, a boy in the school house of hell and misery, learning all sorts of devilment, and treasuring up for myself wrath against the day, wrath. I had been with Esq. Johnson now nearly six months, and I had given up all hopes of ever getting any education from him, except it was from the card table or dealing out liquor, and I sat myself down, and made myself contented as I could, indulging myself in sin and deep cruelties, caring not what become of me or what I done.

Amusing myself in this manner, I left the bar room and steered directly for the post office, where I expected a letter either from my mother or the former bar tender that had promise to call at my mother's House and send me back answer. On calling for a letter, the post master handed me out two. I went directly and found Strongman and open the letters and found that one was from my mother and the other from Mrs. Flinn, warning us to stay where we was and not to come down to New York at all, for Hayse was haunting us night and day. After reading these two letters, I went across the way and bought me a heavy horse pistol, which I carried loaded with me night and day, with a determination to blow out the first man's brains that undertook to lay a hand on me to take me back to the House of Refuge.

After purchasing my pistol, I went back to the House and went into the sitting room where Mrs. Wellington and the ladies sat a discussing over a piece of music. As I entered the sitting room, Martha handed me two dollars which the ladies had given her to give to me for speaking the piece of poetry. Ah, young ladies, said I to myself, if you could only see me act out the part of the female highwayman, or sing the song of William Riley,[49] I rather think that your eyes would open a little and your soft hearts would beat as the air tingling upon your ears—but thinking that the piece which I had spoken was enough for that day, I turned and left those delicate little creatures to themselves, and stepped out into the bar room, and stepped behind the counter and handed Esq. Johnson a cigar.

"Well, Robert, be a good boy till I come back," said the Esq. "I am goin' to start for New York in the morning. I shall be gone three days." He then step into his pleasure carriage with four other gentlemen and drove off to take an afternoon ride.

The morning came at last, and Esq. Johnson started for New York, leaving me in care of the bar room alone until he returned.

Three days passed away, and I look for the Esq. and saw him trudging up the hill with some fifteen or twenty ladies and gentlemen. As he entered the House, he introduced Wellington and Judge Smith to those heavy looking old bugs, who had come up the river for none other purpose than to gamble and sport. (These are some of those dandy looking chaps that passes through this county and puts up to your large Hotels under the pious and fictitious names of gentleman sportsman, who pretend to play the honest hand of faro, and at the same time they are playing the dead drop game on you and cheating you out of your money.) Them was such gentleman, Reader, which I had to wait on night and day, goin' from one room to another in the dead hour of the night with a bottle of wine or brandy.

Among the large company of ladies and gentleman that came up with Esq. Johnson, I could not see nor discern the new bar tender which he had promise to bring with him. No, Reader, I look and I stared, first at this gentleman, then at that gentleman, as they came flocking up to the counter a calling for liquor and cigars, demanding this room and that room to be dazzling brightly tonight with light.

The Esq. walk in the bar room, and ordered me to take the horse and buggy and go down to the steam boat and get them two hundred bottles of wines and a trunk full of new clothes which he had bought for me and bring them up to the House.

"I say, Esq. Johnson," said I in a rage of madness. "You took damn good care to bring up your cigars and wines from New York, but not your new promised bar tender. Hell and damnation," said I, uttering an oath and dashing a tumbler to the floor which I had in my hand, full of cordial—"hell and damnation if I stay in the House another minute. My father didn't tell me, when he gave me his cold hand, to stand behind a counter and deal out liquor."

As I said these words, I went up in my bedroom, and shouldering my trunk I walk out into the street and took up my lodging that night with Strongman.

Early the next morning Martha, the daughter of Esq. Johnson, came over to Levingston's House and inquired of the servant girl if I was up. The girl came up stairs and gave a rap at my door, telling me that Miss Johnson wanted to see me. I got up and put on my clothes and came down stairs and stood before the presence of Miss Johnson, who began to tell me that her father had hired a man in New York, and that he would be up on the next steamer that came in.

"Martha," said I, "I came here a poor helpless boy among strangers and in a strange land, not having a place to go to or to lay my head, until your father saw me, a wanderer in the land, and took me in, of which I am under a thousand obligations to him for doing so, and I am willing to stay with your father until I am one and twenty if he will only change my work and promise to give me a good education, if it ain't no more than a common school instruction."

"Very well," said the girl. "You stay here until I go over and consult with my father." She then left me and made her way back to her father's House.

While she was gone, Mr. and Mrs. Levingston told me that I was a foolish boy in acting thus with Esq. Johnson, for they are the best people in the world to live with. "If you only knew how much the Esq. thinks of you, Robert, you would never leave him. He thinks a good deal of you because you are the only colored person in the town, and I heard him say that he was goin' to make a gentleman's son out of you. Be a good boy now, and go over with me, and I will see that your work is change."

As Mr. Levingston said them words, I told him that I would rather be a barn boy, to be working around the barn, than to be around in the bar room. He then took me by the hand and led me over to Esq. Johnson House, where I saw Martha and her father in a deep conversation concerning me. I went in the back kitchen and sat there until they had got through with their conversation, and I was called in the room before Esq. Johnson and Mr. Levingston, who made me a present of two new suites of clothes, a pair of fine shoes, a new cap, and a silver watch. I must confess that the present which these gentlemen presented to me gave me some encouragement, and

I concluded that I would stay with Esq. Johnson and to tend to what ever duty called me to, until a better offer presented itself before me.

I must now occupy the place of a dog and become the villain of cruelty and the scoundrel of vice and crime, while the advice of my dying father comes in blazing flames, a playing and dazzling before my eyes. Yes, I've got to leave those good and religious principles which my father tried to inculcate into my mind, and throw them all away, and become the dare devil of misery and degradation, as the reader shall here see.

———

AFTER I HAD made an agreement with Esq. Johnson, I went across the road and consulted with Strongman, whether it was best for us to return to New York and seek our revenge on Terry, and give our selves up to the chief magistrate.

"I don't understand you, Rob, in what way you wish to take to seek this revenge," said Strongman. "Please to explain yourself."

"I mean, Strongman," said I, "to let us both cross over in a yawl boat on the Sing Sing shore, so as to be ready to take the swallow when she passes and go right down to New York and secret ourselves away until the hour of nine, and about that hour of the night Terry will be coming from the school House to his own family residence. See that you have your pistol well primed, and as he steps at the door of his residence, I will step up to him and fall into conversation with him. Then, during this conversation, I will pull the pistol from my pocket and let it flash at his heart. As soon as you hear my pistol crack, you present yours at his brain, and I will finish the last stroke."

"And what if someone hears the report of our pistols, Rob?" said Strongman.

"I have a heavy charge in mine, Strongman, and if I present it and discharge it so as it will touch the heart, it will lay him cold as ice at our feet, and we can make our escape before any one gets the scent of his blood. What say you, Strongman? Be quick and give me answer, for I am ready to have my revenge out of him for all the pain and misery that ever he has brought upon me. What say you? For god sake, Strongman, don't make a coward of yourself. Talk fast and give me answer. What say you?" said I, while my blood was burning and boiling within me, longing to seek revenge on that cruel hearted man who had shed our innocent blood for what a lying nigger had said. "Tell me, Strongman, ere the hour of one, and if you will agree with me we will commence the march of death this very night. Tell me, what say you?"

"Well, Rob," said Strongman, "that will be shedding blood."

"Oh, you poor miserable fool, have you not never read the law of Moses, where he says blood for blood?"

"Yes, you poor cruel hearted dog you, Rob. Do you not know that he was speaking to a nation of people at that time that was continually making war, and shedding blood of the neighboring nations, and Moses was speaking under the old dispensation at that time?"

"No more of your scripture language to me, Strongman. Let me know the secret of this matter, for I am in a hurry and can't stop here a dallying away my time. Quick, ere the steam boat comes and we are left behind. What say you, Strongman? I am in earnest about this matter."

"It looks to me like a too hard and horrible crime, Rob, for the old rule, you know, says that thou shalt not kill."

"Great God, more of your scripture lessons. Did that old tyrant think that it was a hard crime when he was pelting us with the cats? Or did he think that he was doing justice before God, when he was shedding our blood for the sake of gratifying a black hearted nigger? Damn you, Strongman, you haven't blood and rage enough to seek revenge and return the injuries back that has been inflicted upon you. A thousand times better for you, Strongman, if you will take that pistol which you carry loaded in your pocket, and sink it to the bottom of the Hudson, than to go through the streets with it loaded and not use it."

Poor Strongman held his head down as I said them words, not knowing what to say or what to do. In rage and madness I made my way back to the Hotel, a leaving Strongman a standing there to come to some proper conclusion of the matter.

As I entered the hall, I heard the voice of "Murder! Murder! Murder!" come pealing in my ears in a most a pitiful manner. Then like a heavy roll of thunder I would hear the same words repeated again. Then all at once the voice would die away in a silent and a doneful manner. I made my way towards the room from whence these words and groans proceeded from, and to my great astonishment and amazement there laid young Mr. Wellington on the bed, and a dozen of men binding him hand and foot and making him fast to the bed.

My God, said I in a low whisper as I entered the room. Who is that they are binding and making fast in cords? What young man is that that has been playing with wine until it has mocked him and made a fool of him? Who is it that has given himself to wine and strong drink, until the serpent has foamed from the bottom and stung him with his deadly quiver? Who is it, who can it be that has such sorrow? What young man can it be that is wrapped in such woe? Let me see—let me take a peep at him and see if ever I have seen that once fair and beautiful youth. I look, and lo, I saw a young man that was void of understanding, who had passed the bowl around and round until it came to him again, and he drank to the very dregs until the iron hands of the tremors had clinch their tight hold on him and made him holler out "Murder! Murder! Murder!" How he look, his very eyes look like a blazing flame of fire, his cheeks as pale as death.

It is impossible for me to give a correct description of Mr. Wellington as he laid on the bed, bound hand and foot. To give the Reader a right description of this young man and his look, I've got to go down for a few moments into the mighty deeps, and pull up an old hidden treasure, and draw from thence a couple of old manuscripts which the reader perhaps has read over and over in the days of his childhood when he sat at the side of a praying mother. Here is my old manuscript, Reader. Let us look and see what it says.[50]

And when he was come out of the ship there met him a man a coming from the tombs, and the old fellow took up his dwelling among the tombs, and he was so enraged with madness, and so strong in degradation, that he had lost all of his good principles and reasons that he once possessed, and become so brutalized, that no man—no, not the strongest man in the land, and the heaviest fetters that Paul and Silas wore—couldn't hold this old fellow. And he was such an ugly looking old fiend, that the very beasts of the field was afraid of him and went and plunged themselves in the sea where they all perish; but an old acquaintance of his happened to pass that way, and looking upon his form, and the situation in which he was place, and the low degradation to which he had sunk himself in, commanded a legion of little devils to come out of him; and the little imps obeyed the voice of him that spake as never a man spake, and that poor, hard, rough looking old fellow who only a minute before was transformed in an image of hell, was now fix and clothed in his right mind, and his face shone like an angel. Yes, you thirsty old rum sucker you, who has throwed off the image of a man that the almighty had given you, and made yourself equal with the beasts, there is yet hope for you. And though you may be sitting among the tombs and biting and tearing your flesh, there is a hand that can snatch those little glass devils from your bosom, and make you to sing to every one that passes you and say, "My name is Legion."

I must now fold up my little manuscript and sink it deep in my bosom, hoping that it may serve me and do me some good in after life when I shall have any occasion to plunge for it again. I must now return the reader back to Mr. Wellington, and the dark and horrible scene that lays before him. I have been trying to compare him to one of those little imps which the savior tore from old Legion bosom, but the situation in which he was in could not be compared to him, so I must bid my old friend Legion adieu, and introduce my Reader with the sequels of Wellington.

NIGHT CAME ON—YES, Reader, the most darkest and blackest night that ever I saw—and I for one had to set up with him and deal out a regular portion of wine for him at certain hours of the night. He would some times be a calling his father by name, and then cursing us because we wouldn't bring a tender sister of his at his bedside who had laid low in her grave for more than four years.

"How can I go, Mr. Wellington," said I, "and bring your sister from the grave? How do I know where she lays? Gladly, Mr. Wellington, would I obey your orders, if it laid in my power, but low her beautiful head lays beneath the reach of my arm, and I cannot fold her in your arms."

Thus did he go on for a week continually, night and day, calling on names of some old companions that had found their way to a drunkard's grave years ago. There I sat, night and day, a dealing out whiskey and brandy to him to quench his thirst, plunging myself deeper and deeper into crime and making myself harder and harder by every glass I gave him, while the words of my dying father began to grow colder and fainter into my bosom.

On the fourth day Mr. Wellington began to get better, and Mr. Livingston and Esq. Johnson came up into his room, and calling him by name they ask him if he knew them. Wellington replied that he did. "Will you untie me, Esq.," said Wellington, "and let me loose, that I may get a little exercise? For I think my reason has returned to me a little since morning."

"Yes," said Esq. Johnson, and Livingston and Esq. Johnson untied him and let him loose and told me to stay by him and not to let him come down below. Poor Mr. Wellington, how my heart flowed in pity for him as I look at his eyes all swelled up and black as ink, while the eye balls rolled and shone like a blaze of fire. Yes, Reader, I pitied him, as he pitied me and Strongman when he saw our back torn to pieces by the cats, and I was under an unbounded obligations and gratitude for the blessing which he had bestowed upon me, and

I thought it no more than my bounded duty to administer to his wants and wait on him during the time of his illness.

"How do you feel, Mr. Wellington?" said I as he paced the room backwards and forth, almost on a run. "How do you feel?"

"Miserable, Robert, miserable. Awful pain in my head. How do I look in the face, Robert?"

"Horrible, Mr. Wellington, most horrible, sir," said I.

"Will you bring me up a little hot water, Robert, that I may wash, and comb my hair, for me, that I may try to look a little better?"

"Yes, Mr. Wellington, I will do it." And I sprung like a streak of lightning and got the water and wash his hands and face, and comb his hair.

The poor fellow then took a peep at himself in the glass and said, "I don't look like the same dashing young man that I did a week ago, do I, Robert?"

"No, sir, Mr. Wellington, but I hope that you will before Saturday night."

"Damn the liquor," muttered Wellington to himself as he took another peep in the glass at his face. "Damn the Liquor. I wish there wasn't another drop in the world." As he said these words, he bursted out in a flood, and I open the door to go out, that I might find some little lonesome corner to drop the tears that began to come in my eyes.

"Hold, Robert," said he, "don't go out and leave me here alone. Oh, damn the cursed and the infernal slings. What would my father and my mother say if they saw me in this condition? What would my sisters say? Does my wife know it, Robert?"

"Yes, Mr. Wellington, and you have almost broken her little heart."

"Has she been up here today, Robert?"

"No, sir, she hasn't been up here since day before yesterday. She has been sick in her bed ever since you have been ill."

"Great God," said Wellington, "what shall I do? Oh cursed and infernal destroyer of man, you shall never get the upper hand of me again. Neither will I sip at your fountain again. Oh, that I had took the advice of the companion of youth, and all would been well today. Cruel destroyer and hard hearted man slayer, I challenge you to deceive me again, and in the name of heaven I swear I won't drink no more."

Oh, how my heart beat with gladness when I heard that word. "No more"—yes, Reader, it was a sacred word which he had vowed in the presence of angels and had sworn in the name of heaven. "No more, no more" kept striking on my ears. "No more. You won't drink no more, will you Mr. Wellington?" said I in my boyish way. "You won't drink no more, will you?"

"No, Robert. Go down and tell my wife that I won't drink no more."

Oh, how I open the door and flew, as though I had wings, to carry that sacred word, "No more," to Mrs. Wellington, and as I entered her room and repeated the words of Wellington to her, she flew from her bedroom, with her hair hanging over her face, and fell in the arms of her lover. As I entered the room, I seen Mrs. Wellington's head laying on the bosom of her husband, and her black and glossy hair a hanging over her face, which prevented me of seeing the scoalding tears that came rolling down her cheeks. Wellington held a tumbler in his hand that was filled with brandy, which I had brought up in the morning, and taking another sacred and solemn oath in the presence of his wife, he held up the tumbler and said, "Oh, cruel master, thou manslayer of thousands, never shall you beguile me again." And he dash the glass to the floor, breaking it in ten thousand pieces. What joy must have played and mingled in the bosom of that young lady during that sacred moment, and what joy and music must have been floating in the meeting House above. What a happy temperance meeting they must have had there, and the heavens must have rung with the airs of the temperance host as they sung those temperance songs which no drunken devil on earth would ever dare to sing.

Though the weary hours of time hangs heavily upon me, and my mind may be casted back to the Home of my nativity, yet never will I forget that doneful scene that came flashing and playing before my eyes, and remembering that drunkenness will fetch a man to poverty sooner or later. During the three last months that Mr. Wellington stop at the American, I do not remember of his drinking a drop of liquor, nor would he even drink water out of the tumbler that had the smell of liquor in it, after he had felt the awful effects it had upon him.

During the latter part of August, Esq. Johnson closed the House, and I hired myself out to a couple of travelling sportsmen as a waiter and a stool pigeon, and went off with them to Oswego, where they put up at the Welling House. Strongman had gone off during that summer to St. Louis to capp for four gentlemen that was travelling through the Southern states and playing what was called the beautiful hand faro. Thus spending three years with Esq. Johnson, and studying the rule of vice and crime, I became a well educated scholar, always ready to plunge my hands deep in the sink of crime. Being well dressed and clean about my apparel, and with one hundred and sixty dollars in my trunk which I had made and saved by gambling with the common sailors that use to come up into the town for the sole purpose of gambling—I say, being thus equipped and passing as these two gentlemen's private waiter, I was allowed to put up there with them and to take my regular meals at the second table.

'Twas a cold evening in the month of September, between the hours of ten and eleven as I was crossing the toll bridge that run across the river, that I heard the voice of a female exclaiming in a low and a feeble voice and saying, "Let me alone, sir. Let me alone and let me pass peaceably along about my business, or you will be sorry for it. Let me alone, or I will call for the captain of the watch. Let me be, and let me pass quietly to my Home."

I had just made my way from a grocery that laid on the tow path, where I had been playing cards till that late hour of the night, and was just pressing my way across the bridge to the Welling House, when I heard the weak voice of this unprotected girl, a begging with tears in her eyes to let her go, that she might pass peaceably to her Home. On my hearing these words from the mouth of the girl, I trod lightly on my tip toes until I approached within ten feet of the infernal fiend that had the rascality and impudence of molesting a harmless and an unprotected girl who was on her way Home.

After advancing so near to them so as I could get a good sight and observe what was goin' on between the two, I stood my ground and drew my pistol from my side coat pocket, with a determination to shoot the scoundrel dead at my feet if he undertook to force and intrude upon the girl in an unmanly way, against her own free will. There I stood, with my pistol cock, ready to let flash the moment the villain undertook to lay the girl beneath his power. Yes, Reader, there I stood for the first time in my life with a cock pistol in my hand, ready to protect a harmless and a virtuous female.

"Come," said the heavy voice of a negro, as he grasped his heavy arm around her waist. "Come, yield yourself to what I want you to do, or I will force you with the strength of my arm."

"I will not, sir," said the girl. "Let me go."

"Bow and submit yourself to me," said the negro, "or I'll commit the crime by force and throw you into the river."

"I will not," said the girl, "if you kill me dead on the spot and sink my body low beneath the rolling waves."

As the girl said these words, the negro laid his heavy clumsy hands on her shoulder, telling her that she must bow herself to him. Who, oh who could describe the heat of my temper at that awful moment, as I sprung over the railing of the bridge like a deer before the hound, and my pistol in my hand already loaded and cock, ready to lay the offender speechless at my feet?

"Scoundrel," said I, as I pulled my cap over my eyes, and pointing my pistol at his breast, "Scoundrel, how dare you intrude on my sister in this manner at this hour of the night? How dare you lay your cold, quivering hand on her?"

The drunken wretch drawed off with all his might to strike me, but being a boy quick and active, I dodged his blow, and the blow fell heavily on the girl's arm. I could not stand to see that, but giving the girl a push with one hand out of the way, I drew my pistol and shot the negro in the shoulder blade, which caused him to lay down on the bridge and holler for the watchman to come and rescue him from a total death.

I stood my ground and was loading my pistol again to give him the second charge if he arose and undertook to commence a fight with me. The loud yell of the negro (Jones, for that was his name, which I learnt afterwards) brought several watchmen and woke the neighbors from their peaceful sleeps. There I stood, nothing but a boy, with my pistol in my hand, ready to give Jones another charge, but some of the by standers wrest the pistol from my hand, and I was taken off to the jail that stood under the market to pass a long and a miserable night, without a blanket or a bed to lay my head on.

The next morning at eight o'clock I was called out to get my examination, and to give an account of my being out so late an hour of the night, and the reason that I had shot Jones. The examination went on as follows:

"Your name, sir," said the justice of peace.

"My name, sir? Robert R—."

"Where do you reside when you are at Home, or, in other words, where is your native place?"

"In the city of R—, sir," said I.

"What is your business that you follow?"

"A waiter, sir."

"On whom do you wait, sir?"

"I wait on Mr. Eldad and Mr. West, a couple of distinguished gentlemen from the city of New York."

"Then you are a private waiter to those two gentlemens, are you?"

"Yes, sir."

"Where are they, or where do they stop?"

"At the Welling House, sir."

"Well, what was it that brought you out so late an hour of the night?"

"Business, sir."

"Business, eh?"

"Yes, sir."

"What kind of business?"

There I stood, a boy only at the age of twelve, without a lawyer or an intercessor to speak or plead in my behalf, and ashame to own or to tell what my business was that brought me out so late on that dark and doneful night. Bowing my head down with shame and contempt, I gave way to a flood of tears, not knowing hardly what was best to say or how to answer the Esquire's question, which he had put to me so sharp. Again did he ask me what it was that had brought me out so late an hour of the night. A trembling and shivering over the Esquire's questions, and keeping my eye on the loaded pistol that laid on the table in front of me, I thought whether it was best to tell him the business that had kept me out so late an hour of the night.

"Will you answer me that question, Robert?" said the Esq.

"No, sir, we will not answer that question," said a lawyer, jumping up from his seat.

"Are you goin' to take his case in hand?" said the Esq.

"Yes, sir, I am, and I am goin' to defend the boy. I reject the question to which you just put to him."

"Then you will allow me to ask the offender why he made a hole in Jones' shoulder blade with that pistol that lays on the table, will you, sir?"

"Yes, sir, oh yes, sir," said the learned counsel. "Certainly I will."

"Well then, Robert, what induced you, or what cause had you, to sink that ball in Jones' shoulder?"

"Sirs," said I, as I stretch out my arms at full length, and filled with joy and gladness that I had the privilege of speaking for myself, and holding my head up and looking more than two hundred spectators in the face that had already crowded into the room to hear the examination—"Sirs," said I, "as I was crossing yon bridge, between the hours of ten and eleven o'clock last night, I heard the feeble voice of a girl, saying in pitiful notes of distress, 'Let me alone, and let me pass to my Home.' And as I approach near and nearer towards the spot from whence them direful cries descended from, I heard the fickle voice of the girl again in low and solemn tones, saying, 'Let me alone.' I could not bear to hear such groans proceed from the mouth of an unprotected female, and bounding over the railing of the bridge, I drew yon pistol and let flash at Jones, and rescued the girl from the prowling hand of a negro, and perchance from a watery grave."

"Show me that damn and infernal nigger," said Mr. Smith, "that had the impudence to lay his black knuckles in the face of my daughter. Where is he? Show him to me, and I'll take his life if I spill every bit of this English blood which I have got in my body. Make room till I get my hands on the infernal hound."

As Smith said these words, he came pushing his way through the crowd to see if he could see Jones, but no, Jones was not to be seen among that multitude of people. It was a good thing that Jones wasn't there, for I believe that Smith would taken his life on the spot. But where was Jones all of this time? I will go on with the examination and refer him to the reader in the after page.

After telling my story to the court, Mr. Smith stepped up to the lawyer, and putting several bank notes into his hand, told him to do his best for me and, if there was any possible means, to get me discharged right on the spot, and I should be handsomely rewarded for rescuing his daughter from the foul hand of a negro. The girl was then called on the stand, and was ask what brought her out so late an hour of the night, and to give an account of herself.

"I had been out," said the girl, "on a visit to my friends and to spend the afternoon with them, but it got quite dark before I started for Home, and having some distance to go, night overtook me, and I was left to gropple my way home unprotected, through the dark and under the curtains of the night. As I was crossing the bridge, the heavy hand of Jones was coiled tightly around my waist, and demanding me to yield and bow myself down to low and shameful sin and degradation, and to throw my virtue and humanity away to him."

"What reply did you make to him, Cinthia, when he put that question to you?"

"I told him that I wouldn't bow myself down and yield to him if he killed me dead on the spot and gave my body to the waters that came rolling beneath my feet."

"How long had he kept you there in that situation?"

"I cannot tell exactly, sir, but I should think it was about an half hour till that young boy came mounting over the railing, and pretending that I was his sister and that he was my brother who had come to save me from the cruel hands of a man that would committed a crime on me and would took my life, as he afterwards told me."

"After Robert had mounted over the railing, Cinthia, what did he say to Jones?"

"He drew the pistol at him and ask him how he dared to molest his sister in that manner."

"Then what took place?"

"Robert demanded him to let me pass quietly along about my business, and raising his hand with all of his force, he drew off to strike him, to which Robert drew his pistol and shot him, and the monster came falling like a stone at my feet."

The watchman that took me was called to give in his evidence and to relate the circumstances as far as he seen it.

"Well, Mr. Curtiss, what did you see?, and please to go on and relate the circumstances."

"I stood on the corner of the American Hotel, and I heard the dead cry of 'Watchman! Watchman! Watchman!' sinking deep into my ears and dying away at the distance. I made my way towards the place from whence to the voice proceeded from and found Jones a laying drunk on the bridge and wallowing in his blood, and the boy a charging his pistol, ready to give him the second pull."

"What did you do then, Mr. Curtiss?"

"I took the pistol from the youngster's hand and led him away to the black hole under the market."

"What did you do with Jones?"

"I returned immediately to rescue Jones and place him in a cell for safe keeping until the morning, but on my returning to the spot, I found that the crew he sailed with had got wind of the case, and they took him on board the vessel that he sailed on, and this morning I learnt that the vessel was loaded and sailed away this morning at three o'clock."

"Did you learn the name of that vessel?"

"Yes, sir."

"What was her name?"

"*Thomas Hart*, of Buffalo, sir."

Mr. Curtiss then took his seat, and Mr. Eldad and Mr. West, whom I was hired out to and who intended to pass the fall and winter there, was called on the stand, and the following questions was put to them—

"Do you know that boy, Mr. West?"

"I do, sir."

"Where does he live?"

"He lives with me, sir."

"Your private waiter, I suppose, sir?"

"Yes, sir."

"What business do you follow, Mr. West?"

"Rejected the question," said the lawyer.

"Do you know what it was that brought him out so late last night?"

"Hold on, reject that."

"You say that he is your waiter."

"Yes, sir."

"Are you travelling gentlemen?"

"Yes, sir."

"Where do you stop?"

"At the Welling House, sir."

"What business do you follow for a living?"

"Reject that question altogether."

Mr. West then took his seat, and Eldad was called up and ask the same questions, to which he answered the same as Mr. West did. Thus did the examination end, and the learned counsel got up and told the Esq. that he didn't nor couldn't see no grounds where on he could hold me and send me back to jail, for I had done a good deed which I ought to be rewarded for, in rescuing a poor defenseless girl that was making her way Home alone, unprotected by the arm of a man, and perchance she might have lost her life. Also that I was nothing but a mere boy, among strangers and in a strange land.

"Take the case," said he to the Esq., "take the case Home to yourself. Suppose that one of your own children had been abused in thus manner by the rude hand of some midnight villain, and the offender came along and seeing no one to rescue the child, he'd stepped in between the breach and opened a way of escape for your child. Would you not stretch out your hand and reward him for saving your daughter from the low depths of degradation?"

After the lawyer had went on in thus manner, a pleading and interceding for me, that wicked old Esq. had to fence up ground enough for to send me back to the jail until the court sat, and give my case over into the hands of a judge and jury, saying that he would have to give a strict account if he discharged me, and for using a pistol and shooting a man or a brute with it. I was demanded back to the black hole where I had to wait for my trial till the month of December.

It was late in the afternoon when I was taken back to jail, and at the hour of six Mr. Smith brought me down a straw bed tick and a feather bed and a bedstead which was put up that night, and Mrs. Smith sent me three warm meals regular every day for three months and done my washing and ironing. About nine o'clock Mr. Bronson and Mr. Crocker and several ladies came in the jail to see me, and telling me that I shouldn't want anything good as long as I stayed in jail, and not to give way to fear nor let nothing trouble me, for there shouldn't a hair in my head be hurt, nor there was no one that would go before the grand jury to get me indicted, nor no one to swear against me.

"Jones," said Mr. Bronson, "lives in Canada, and he dare not come over on this side of the Ontario, or he will take up his abode in a state prison. Furthermore they have got to have him here before they can convict you. All the people," said he, "takes an interest in your case and are trying to raise means to get you out before court time."

I told Mr. Bronson that I was very much oblige to him for seeking an interest in this case, and hope that he would call and see me every time an opportunity offered itself, and to have my trunk and clothes sent down to me in the morning. Being late, they presented me with a light and charged Mr. Rolmer the jailer to grant me the privilege of having a light every night, and what ever I wanted from the grocery, to send and get it and have it charge to them. After giving out their orders to the jailer, they left me for the night to think and condole over the sad condition which I was placed in. Mr. Bronson and Crocker was very rich men, and although they tried to make my condition as comfortable as they could, yet my mind and my bosom was heaving with sorrow and grief. Early the next morning, Mr. Bronson had sent me my trunk and clothes and a chair and more bed clothes, and for three months every day I had friends who was strangers to me to come and visit me, and fairly loading the old jail down with nicknacks.

A young Scotch girl about seventeen years of age and myself was the only prisoners that was in jail, and we had the hall to ourselves, with no one to trouble us or to say a filthy word or sing an undecent song to us. We was lords and queens of all we surveyed, living together in harmony and peace, and sharing everything that was good with each other, passing away the lonesome hours that came hanging heavily on us by playing the game of old sledge. Poor Fanny Miller, I shall never forget her as long as I live. I fancy that I see her now, with her handsome rosy cheeks, and I think the handsomest little creature that ever I seen. Yes, I say the *pulcherrima mulier in mundo*, with her jet black hair falling over her neck in glossy ringlets, and eyes as black as indigo.

On the fourth Sunday that I was confined in jail, Fanny and me had been playing cards during the forenoon, and in the afternoon we sat down to read. I had a book called *The Swiss Family Robinson*[51] a reading, and Fanny had her bible. I had been reading about two hours, and casting my eyes toward Fanny, I saw large drops of grief come pouring down the girl's cheeks. Thinking that she might be sick or unwell, I ask her what the trouble was.

"Robert," said she, "I am thinking of my Home."

Of your Home, poor girl, said I to myself. "Of your Home, Fanny?"

"Yes, Robert, if you could only see the tears that I have shed before you come here, you would pity me."

"Poor girl, Fanny," said I. "I do pity you now, and God bless you, girl, I wish you was Home today."

"Yes, Robert, if I was only Home with my poor mother, how happy I would be."

"Where do you live, Fanny?"

"I live in Kingston in Canada, and if ever I get out of this place, I shall return right Home to my mother, if I can raise money enough to carry me there."

"I have money in my trunk that sits there, Fanny, and when your time is out, I will give you enough to pay your expenses Home. How came you to come from Canada and come over here, Fanny, so late in the season and without any money?"

As she wiped the warm tears from her eyes, she gave me the following and true narrative of the whole circumstance which had not only brought her from her friends and Home, but the cause of her spending three long months in a county jail. Thus did she commence, and said—

"I fell in love with a young man whose parents was rich, and he himself in good circumstances, and promised to marry him, but another young man that came over from the states stepped in between the marriage breach, and pointed out to me the riches his father had bestowed upon him, and the pleasures I should enjoy if I would only seek his hand and marry him."

"Well, did you do it, Fanny?"

"Hold, Robert, till I tell you."

"Go on, Fanny. Go on with your story."

"Well, without advising with my mother or my friends about the matter, to see which of the two lovers I had better marry, on I rush, right in the vigor of youth and beauty, until I proved my over throw."

"Got married to your second lover at last, did you, Fanny?"

"Yes, Robert, I got married to him at last, and cross the lake with him and came over to Syracuse, where my husband put up to the largest hotel that was in the town and called for a private room, and a private waiter to attend to our calls. On the fourth morning after we had put up to the hotel, my husband arose very early in the morning and dress himself in a very great hurry, telling me that he had some very important business to tend to that day, and that he wouldn't make his return till late in the evening. I urged him hard to stop and get some breakfast, but he told me that his business was so urgent that he couldn't stop a minute, and he flew out the door like a flash of lightning, or like a thief that was hurried by his pursuers. What can this mean, said I to myself, that my husband is taking such an early flight, without his giving me the least notice of it? Has he been a robbing, or has he been a murdering some one, was my anxious inquiry. No, neither of these crimes had he been guilty of, but a far worse crime than either murder or robbery was he guilty of."

"And what crime was that, Fanny?" said I.

"The villain married me for better or worse, richer or poorer, seduced me from my first lover, took me from my happy Home and brought me here in a strange land and among strangers, and left a written note on my stand saying that he was goin' to leave me and never return to me again. Look, Robert, oh look at the shame and the disgrace that he has brought me to, and the misery that has followed."

"Did he not leave you any means, Fanny, where by you could get a living, or to pay your board?"

"No, Robert, not one red cent did the poor unfortunate wretch leave me, nor was he worth the clothes he had on his back, as I afterwards heard. He was a young man of poor parents, and after the death of his parents, he followed the canal for a living, and came over to Canada in a rich suite of clothes and a few dollars in his pocket, a seeking my love and affection and quacking himself up to be some rich and wealthy man's Son."

"So the young chap got the upper hand of you and deluded you after all, eh, Fanny?"

"Yes, Robert, and I was oblige to leave the Hotel where I was boarding under the cover of darkness, without paying or having a cent to pay my board with, and I made my escape here to Oswego, not having a place or not knowing where to lay my head."

"Why didn't you return back Home, Fanny, to your mother?"

"I hadn't the means to get Home with, and if I had returned Home, I should been a shame and a by word to every one that passed me. So I didn't care what become of me or what I did, as long as I could get a living, and being advise by another young girl who was dressed in dazzling silks every day, I took her advice and followed her secret habits."

"So, Fanny, you bowed and yielded yourself down to shame and disgrace at last, did you?"

"Yes, Robert, for this girl opened a wide and a beautiful field of riches and pleasures before me, and I gave myself away for the first time in my life to entreaties until I found myself lock up here in a county jail for the term of ninety days."

After the girl had got through with her narrative, I arose from my seat and began to pace the hall to and fro, and having a good voice for singing, I struck up the following song, which me and my sister use to sing in our happy days, when cares nor toils could find no hiding place in our breast, nor trouble to molest our joyful days.

The Author's Song, to Fanny Miller

Come all ye females of a fickle nature
don't never turn your first love away,
for many is the brights and shiny mornings
that turns to a dark and a dismal day.

I thought that now was my time to throw into her bosom a few fragments which I had had lock up in my heart from my boyhood. Yes, Reader, now was my time, while her heart was yet warm and soft, and while nature was giving away to grief and tears, and I commenced, and said, "Where does that young girl live, Fanny?"

"Robert, I heard she was out late a few nights ago and was found dead in the canal the next morning."

"So you see, Fanny," said I as I gave her some of these old fragments, "so you see that her way was crooked, and the very pit that she dug for you she fell into herself. And that flowery field of riches and pleasures she showed you, Fanny, did you not know that within that field laid the bleaching bones of many strong men that she has already slain? And that dazzling silk dress that glisten your eyes so when she was pointing you to the path of ruin, did you not know that that was her dress of her everlasting shame and contempt, which an old writer spoke of some years ago, or have you never read that they that go in unto her never returns again, and that her steps leads to the gates of Hell, and that her ways leads down to the cold chambers of death?[52] Or have you never read, Fanny, how she has brought many a young man to a morsel of bread? Have you never look over the old record book and found those old documents? If not, I will throw one at you, which was given to me by one of the noblest men that ever lived. He says that her House is the way to Hell, leading down to the chambers of death. So you see, Fanny, just by taking one false step, you lost your character and fame forever."

Now as I saw the girl had some feelings of reforming I was determined never to play another card with her or to bring them out in her sight again, as long as I stayed in jail. I gave up my bed to her, which had been provided for me, and chose to lay my head on the cold oak floor, rather than to see her lay her beautiful head so low. It was no more than what I had done and could do again, with the sad remembrance that one who was mightier than I had taken up his cold lodgings on the mountains, with nothing for his cover at night but the damp air and the cold drops of the night, and in the mornings he was heard to cry that the foxes have holes and the songsters of the air have nest, but I, even I have not where to lay my head.[53]

Days rolled on, and we amused ourselves together by singing and takin' turns of reading to each other, until the expiration of her time. It was a cold December's morning when the turnkey came down and unlock the door to let Fanny free. Poor girl, said I to myself as she was throwing a thin shawl over her shoulders and getting ready to go, poor girl, I am afraid you will forget yourself and give way to temptation. You have no place to go to and no money to help you with. Let me see, Fanny, let me look, let me remember my promise to you, you fair little creature you, for your little limbs are too tender to stand the cold winter blast. I unlock my trunk and lo, in one corner of it there laid heaps upon heaps which I had given to me before I left Esq. Johnson's. "Come, Fanny, and I will share with you. Poor girl, I pity you from the bottom of my heart. I have been place in the very circumstance as you are, far from Home and without means to get Home with, and I know how to pity you, especially at this present season of the year, with the cold blast a grumbling and growling in your face."

Thrusting my hand into my trunk, I drew out fifteen dollars and handed it to her, telling her to go and find a place to board and not fail to come and see me at least once a week till my time was out. While I was telling her, Mrs. Bronson happen to step in to see how

I got along and if I needed anything. She look at Fanny and then stepped up to her and told her that she might come and work for her during that winter, and if she was a faithful girl, she would pay her one dollar a week. The girl accepted the offer and went Home with Mrs. Bronson, and for three times a week did Fanny visit me as long as I stayed in jail, bringing me all kinds of nicknacks. I don't remember of ever giving her a word of insult or saying a filthy word to her or trying to take any advantage of her during our confinement together in jail.

Poor girl, she had gone out just in good time, for two days after she had gone, a rough looking set of criminals had come from Pulaski to Oswego to get their trials, and they was continually a gambling and disputing about the money on the board, and it would end in fight—and my heart mounted with joy that Fanny had gone and wasn't there to take jeers and filthy abuses.

Time rolled on, and there being no indictment found against me, and through the influence and kind intercession of Mr. Bronson and Mr. Smith, I was discharged, but not allowed to have my pistol again, and a donation of thirty-five dollars from the ladies' society. Shouldering my trunk, I cross over to the stage office to start for Home that night. On inquiring at the stage office which way Eldad and West had gone, I was informed that they had gone on to Rochester and had left word for me to come right on as soon as I got out of jail. Unlocking my trunk to get some money out to pay my fare Home, I found that some of the prisoners had unlock my trunk with a false key and taken out some twenty dollars. I returned to the jail and informed the sheriff of it, and a search was made and the money found stuck in one of the cracks in one of the cells, no one knowing who put it there. And that evening at eight o'clock, after giving Fanny a call, I was on my way home, and the next night I was at the outside of my mother's cottage door, after being absent from Home and not seeing either brother or sister or mother for six years and seven months.

There I stood. Yes, Reader, there I stood, a lingering between two doubts, whether it was best to give a light rap at the door, or to stand right up like a man and walk right in and make myself known as a lost prodigal who had just made his return Home. No, Reader, I must stand here at the door a minute and see if this is the same old latch which I once use to raise. I must stand and listen and see if I hear the same voice that I heard six years ago. I must walk lightly around the House on my tip toes and examine the old roof and see if it actually is the same old parental roof that covered my head six years and seven months ago. Let me take a secret peep into the window and see if my mother does live in the very old cottage yet. Perhaps I may be mistaken. Some other family may be living here, and the tread of strangers' feet might have trodden on my mother grounds since I have been gone. Let me look, let me see, let me take another glimpse through the window, while the pale light of the moon plays her silvery form about me. Heavens, heavens, I see the wrinkle face of my mother by the light of the pale empress of the night. Let me, under the silvery light of yon moon, go and find a lone and a silent place to weep. Let darkness cover me, and thick darkness shelter me, and let all nature be rapt in silence till I approach the cottage door again, with these scalding tears that's running from my eyes again, and I am standing at the old cottage door of my boyhood.

Hark, for I am sure that I hear the cheerful voice of my mother. I guess I will raise the latch and see who will be the first one that opens the door. The door opens, and I am folding my sister in my arms, and trying to hush the loud shrieks of my mother. Give back, give back, ye dark and black clouds, and let yon pale moon break forth, that I may look at that old oak tree that stands in front of the door, where me and my little sis has sat under its green boughs many a summer evening, watching the fragrant leaves, and the lofty old fellow submitting himself and making his obeisance to every breeze of wind that comes sweeping over its boughs. Many was the evenings, just as the sun was sinking away in the west, has me and my sister sat beneath its shady boughs and sung—

Good night, good night my own true love
how swift those moments fly
we soon must part this heretic
the hateful watchman cries.[54]

Casting my eyes to the west part of the house, I see the bed on
which my father died on. I am now listening to my mother as she is
trying to set me in the right way again, and putting me in mind of my
father dying advice, and she leads me away by the hand and pours
out a prayer to the almighty in my behalf. Hark, what doneful sound
is that I hear, as I pass the bed on which my father died? Great God,
it's the prayer and the voice of my father, calling afresh to me from
the lonesome tomb. Where shall I flee to? Where shall I go that I
may shun that voice? It comes a pealing upon my ear like a heavy
clap of thunder, and the voice of my father is haunting me tonight,
and his advice and prayer seems to prick my very heart.

I'll retire to bed, and ere before the morning light comes peering
into my room, the advice of my father may all die away, and I will lay
a brooding on vice and prepare myself as a student for crime. I am
now under the roof of my mother's cottage, ready to close my eyes
in sleep, and must bid the reader a good night, while I lay a dreaming
of the sufferings and cruelties which I have gone through, and preparing myself one day or another to be a harden convict and the inmate of a gloomy prison, where I must be loaded down with shackles
and bending beneath the heavy weights of balls and chains.

Introduction to the Reader

You MAY NOW see the shame and the disgrace that is brought upon
a boy that is sent to the House of Refuge. The world and society is
looking up to the day with open eyes, when a reformation will take

place within them walls and among them boys, and religion and truth spread itself among the inmates of the place, but never, no never will that day come, as long as a novel can get on the inside of them walls. Curse the infernal things. They are grasp by the hands of young children just as soon as they learn their A.B.C., and they learn him to lie, cheat, steal, drink liquor, rob, murder, and plunder, and in the very brightest and best of his days he finds an empty cell in a state prison, all through the influence of reading Novels, and following the practice and vice of some one that he has been reading about that has committed such and a crime or made such and a crack in the city of New York or London. No such a thing, my good Reader, no such a crack was never made. They are seluding you and driving you into vice until your hands commits a crime and you find yourself a cold inmate of a prison, and there dragging out a poor miserable life of a dog.[55]

After getting fairly settled at Home, and seeing my friends all well and comfortable, I made my way to the city and hired out as a bar tender in a saloon to one Mr. Hallet. Not having much to do one day, I thought I would take a stroll towards Home. On one of the back street that led up to my mother's House, as I walk slowly and leisurely along up the walk, I found that there had been a great improvement in building on that street since I had been gone from Home, and found that many of these buildings was let out to those who kept a House of infame. As I was walking slowly along, I saw a beautiful young girl sitting in the door, and a young man who went by the fictitious name of Iverson a walking up and down the walk, a passing the door several times and continually glancing his eyes on the girl who seemed to be his victim. I passed on until I had reach the door of my Home.

My sister had dressed herself to go out and take a walk, and ask me if I would like to walk out with her. I replied that I would. We walk down the same street again, and there stood poor Iverson, charmed with the looks of this girl, a leaning on the fence with his hand under his chin. My sister being acquainted with this girl, she stop and talk with her at the gate, while I walk towards Iverson, who was very richly dress, with a gold chain a swinging from his pocket. As I passed him, he made a low bow to me with his head and ask me who that young damsel was that sat in the door. I replied to Mr. Iverson that I did not know, and that she was a stranger to me, and that was my sister that was talking to her.

"Don't you know," said Iverson, "what she does or what she follows for a living?"

I replied that I did not.

"Well then," said Iverson, "as your sister stands there and is acquainted with her, suppose you walk up there with me and pretend that I am an old acquaintance of yours, and give me an introduction to the two girls, and I suppose that they won't take it as an insult."

"Your name, sir?" said I.

"My name is Mr. Iverson, from Baltimore."

Mr. Iverson and me walk side by side until we had come in front of the two girls, and calling their attention, I told them that I would make them acquainted with one Mr. Iverson from Baltimore, to which the two girls returned their compliments, and Miss Mutermer,[56] whose name I shall now introduce to the reader, ask Mr. Iverson if he wouldn't step in and take a chair. This pleased Iverson to the very heart, so as his eyes seemed to dance with joy and gladness. No sooner had the invitation been given him to come in, that he swung open the gate and walk in and sat him self down on the lounge, and began to talk about the weather and about times, and telling the girls what a fine and flourishing city Baltimore was, and closed up the conversation by asking the girls to step up to the table, where sat a decanter of brandy, and take a drink with him in honor of each other's health.

Iverson poured out a full glass for himself, and giving a low nod with his head to Mrs. Mutermer, he drank the liquor down as though it had been water, and put his hand into his pocket and threw Mrs. Mutermer a dollar bill, telling her that he did not wish no change back. My sister got up and walk out the door and pressed her way back Home, leaving me there with Iverson and Miss Mutermer. Mrs. Mutermer took a glass of water and came and sat herself down on Iverson knee, and throwing her arms around his neck and her head on his breast, exclaimed that she was tired. Five minutes passed away, and Iverson had her curled in his arms and promenading her off in a back room, where they was gone for fifteen or twenty minutes, and they then made their appearance with their faces covered with guilt and blushes, which seemed to tell me that something wrong had gone on between the two. Pulling his cap over his eyes as though he was ashamed to let people see that he had just come from the House of infame and profanity, he made his way out of the back door and leap over the back fence, and so made his escape through lanes and alleys until he gained Washington Street, which led him into the city.

Three hours rolled away, and Iverson made his return back to Miss Mutermer's house with a face as red as fire, and his eyes flashing and turning as red as blood. I was playing cards with Miss Mutermer on a center table that stood in the center of the room when Iverson entered the door.

"I say, friend," said Iverson to me, "that damn infernal little French ___ has got my pocket book with one hundred dollars in it. Have you seen her with it since I left the House?"

"No, Iverson, I have not seen it, nor do I believe that Ann would be so mean as to take your pocket book."

"I know better," said Iverson in a rash tone. "I know better. She has got it, for I had it in my pocket when I got in ___ with her, and remembering of giving her a two dollar bill from it, just what she ask me for."

"Mr. Iverson," said I, "perhaps you may be mistaken about your pocket book, for I don't think the girl has got it."

"Mistaken? My dear boy, I can't be mistaken," said Iverson, letting his temper cool down a little. "I can't be mistaken, for when she got in the ___ I pulled out a two dollar bill and put it in her hand and put the pocket book back in my pantaloons pocket and got in ___ with her. Let me see," said Iverson, "perhaps might drop it in the bed. Perhaps it might have slip out of my pocket in the bed. I'll go and see." As he said these words, he flung open the bedroom door and search the bed high and low, but could not find no pocket book.

"I say, Ann," said Iverson in an anger of rage, "I want that pocket book and money, or by G— I will stain the floor with your blood. I treated you like a lady and paid you just what you ask, and you took that pocket book from my pocket when we was in ___ together, and now I ask you like a gentleman to present it to me in less than five minutes. There is no one else got it but you, and I want it."

The girl raised the very hand which had committed the crime on Iverson, and with a solemn oath and an uplifted hand to heaven, she swore in the name of him that sits upon the throne forever and ever, that she did not know anything about the lost property. Iverson went off a grumbling to himself until he reach the police office, where he made his complaint and secured two officers with search warrants.

While Iverson was gone, Mrs. Mutermer slip the money into my hand, and a red silk handkerchief that belong to Iverson, and gave the pocket book to the devouring fire, to crumble up to ashes. I made my way out into a large meadow that stood directly in front of the door, and raising a heavy stone, I planted the money under it until the news of it all died away. Returning back to the house, I sat down and began to play cards again with Miss Mutermer until the policemen entered the house and began to search. They search every spot and corner in the house, except the bed. Iverson had not told the officers that he had been in ___ with Miss Mutermer, but had hid that as a secret from them.

Miss Mutermer was taken before the justice of peace, and Iverson called on me as a witness against Miss Mutermer. The examination went on, and Iverson was called on the stand first. "Well, Mr. Iverson, you say you lost one hundred dols and a handkerchief in Mrs. Mutermer house, do you?"

"Yes, sir," said Iverson.

"Well, go on and describe what kind of money it was, whether it was gold, silver, or bills," said Esq. Maure.

"All bills, sir," said Iverson.

Esq. Maure: "Well, what bank was these bills on?"

Iverson answers: "Can't tell, sir."

Esq. Maure: "What was you doing in Miss Mutermer's House, or what call had you in there at all, Mr. Iverson?"

Iverson answer to Esq. Maure: "I am the son of a wealthy merchant in the city of Baltimore and have a known brother that resides somewhere in this city, but can't tell exactly where. I heard that he lived on the street that Miss Mutermer lived on, and I made my way up that way. Being tired and weary of tramping all day, I stepped into Miss Mutermer's house to get a drink of water to quench my thirst and rest my limbs. It being a very warm day, sir, and my being over powered with fatigue, I laid down on the lounge, and before I knew it I was curled in the arms of sleep for some two or three hours. When I awoke, I got up to take my pocket book from my pocket to pay Mrs. Mutermer for the use of her lounge during my hours of sleep, but to my great surprise I found that my pocket book had been slip out of my pocket by the slippery hand of that French girl, Mrs. Mutermer."

Esq. Maure: "Was there any one else in the house, Mr. Iverson, besides Mrs. Mutermer, while you was there?"

Answer: "Yes, sir, that young boy was there."

Question: "Well, how do you know but what he took your money?"

Answer: "Pah, there is no one took my money, sir, but that girl."

After Esq. Maure had examined Iverson, I was called on the stand as a witness against Ann Mutermer. Poor Ann, how pale she look as I took my stand. How bad she wanted to give me a sly look and a wink, but Iverson was eyeing her too sharp. Never mind, Ann, said I to myself. Don't fear. Don't let nothing trouble your mind. I know my business. There shan't one of them black curly hairs that comes tumbling down in ringlets from your head be hurt. The lying dog, Annie. I have got him just where I want him, and if the truth must be told without hurting you, Annie, here it comes, plain and plump.

"Well, Rob," said Esq. Maure with a smile on his face, "do you know yon Iverson?"

Answer: "No, sir."

Esq. Maure's question: "Well, did you ever see yon chap before?"

Answer: "Oh yes, sir, I seen that fancy looking fellow today."

Question: "Well, did you ever see him before today?"

Answer: "No, sir."

Question: "Well, where and when was the first time that ever you saw him?"

Answer: Now, Annie, you fair little rosy cheek girl, you keep your ears open and swear to just what I do and all will be right. Here I go, Annie. "Esquire, the first time and the first place that ever I seen Iverson was this morning on Clay Street, a walking up and down the walk and passing Miss Mutermer's door some fifty or sixty times, and throwing side winks at Miss Mutermer, until me and my sister happen to stop in front of Miss Mutermer's door, and she and my sister fell in a deep conversation about each other's health. Iverson then step up to me and ask me who that cherry cheek damsel was that sat in the door. I told him that I was not acquainted with her, but my sister knew her better than I did. Mr. Iverson then introduced his name to me, and ask me if I wouldn't step up with him and give him an introduction to the two girls, and we both walked up to them together, and I introduced him as Mr. Iverson from the city of Baltimore, and Miss Mutermer ask him to step in. Iverson walk in the House, took a chair and a glass of brandy, and snatch yon little flower in his hands and folded her in his arms, and less than five minutes he was promenading with her in the back room."

As I ended my story, Esq. Maure bow his head and laugh, telling Mr. Iverson that he must had spent his money on some especial business, and that this would give him a lesson hereafter how he entered the House of infame, and Esq. Maure discharged the girl without any further examination, but had officers and stool pigeons on the look out to see if they could get any sight of the lost money.

Three months passed away, and not a word was said or heard about the money, although it laid yet under the stone where I had buried it and continued my business with Mr. Hallet as a bar tender, a sinking my hands deeper and deeper in all kinds of crimes, until I got so bold in crime I wasn't afraid to commit the blackest deed that was ever committed. Yea, so harden was I in crime that I even sat down and play cards on the Sabbath from morning until midnight.

One night as I entered Mrs. Mutermer's House, she told me that there was nothing to fear, and that the stolen money had all died away. I went over where I had hid it and dug it up and brought to Mrs. M—, and she presented me with five dollars of the money and gave me the handkerchief, telling me to be very careful how I used the money. The next morning I went down to the saloon and took the same bill and staked it upon the board and began to play cards, not thinking anything about the handkerchief a sticking out of my pocket, and before I got through the game, the clumsy hand of an officer was laid upon me, and my pockets search, and the bill and the handkerchief found, and I was taken before the justice of peace, who ordered me off to jail until the appearance of court.

As I was goin' towards the jail, I slip the handcuff from my wrists and dash them with all my strength in the constable's face and made my way up Buffalo Street until I passed the grave yard where laid my father. As I passed this long remembered spot, I cast my eyes towards the grave of him that gave me his fatherly advice, although I fancied to myself that I heard his voice a speaking to me from the lonesome spot where he laid some times in soft and solemn tones, and then in a loud and a terrible voice saying to me, "Is this the road I told you to tread when I closed my eyes in death? Is this the hard path you are treading? Is that the path I hoed out to you before my body was sunk low in the grave?" Such was the tender feelings of my heart when I passed the hallowed spot where lays my father, but so hard and so degraded and so sunken in vice and crimes, I ran on without shedding or dropping a tear. I can remember the days when, if the very word of my father's name was mention, all the caresses from a fond mother and all the affection of a sister couldn't keep me from a flood of tears.

Passing the grave yard, I ran across the meadow that led directly to Mrs. Mutermer's House. On gaining the door, I told Ann to sink the money low and be careful of the constables, for I was betrayed and had just made my escape. "You need not be afraid, Ann," said I, "of being betrayed if you will only hide the money and keep it out of the way." After making my arrangements right with her, I went back to the saloon and played cards till nine o'clock that night and was taken by the constable and brought to jail and shoved in with some fifteen or twenty criminals who was waiting for their trials, expecting to get clear or to come to a state prison.

Among the crowd of prisoners that was waiting trials was a poor old man who expected to end the rest of his life in a state prison, but through the mercy of the court the old man was discharged and sent Home. This old man had fought several bloody battles with the Indians, and it was pleasing to sit and hear him tell the feats and the adventures he had gone through with the Indians. The old man was relating a tale about a duel him and an Indian had one day, and just as the old fellow was getting deep into the adventure—I was called to the jail door to see an old inmate of mine.

Good God, who could it be, as I stood in front of the door? Who could that young English gent be, with his hair curled and his hat cocked one side, and a heavy gold chain a swinging from his watch pocket, and with both hands in his pocket a jingling his money? Who could it be? Reader, it was Strongman, who had just come from St. Louis and was returning back to the city of New York. Yes, it was the very little English boy that suffered with me in the House of Refuge and had made his escape with me. Before I could get a chance to call his name, he threw two shillings in the turnkey's hands and told him to shove open the door and let him in to see me. The turnkey open the door, and Strongman and me had a long talk together about my case, and how much money he had won since he had been gone, and he lent me his assistance.

"Sorry, Rob. Sorry to see you here. I suppose they will send you back to the House of Refuge, eh?" said Strongman.

"I don't know," I replied.

"Well, what can I do for you? Let me know, Rob, and if it cost me five hundred dols. or my life, I will do it for you. Let me know by tomorrow. I stop down here at the Eagle Hotel,[57] and day after tomorrow I am goin' to start for New York with five hundred in my pocket, and am goin' to luff her over in the bank and go up to the Navy yard and hire out as a sailor and play the drop game on some of them sailors until I win about seven hundred, and then I shall go off to England and set up a sporting House. Be careful, Rob, how you call my name, for I have change it, and if ever you live to get clear, don't fail to come down to York, and be sure to come to the Navy yard and ask for Jim Hawkins, for that is my name now to which I am goin' by. Give a call to Mrs. Flinn House. I leave the directions with her for you. If the judge only sends you back to the Reff., you may be sure, Rob, that I will be there with a rope less than twenty-four hours after you get there, and help you away."

"Yes, Hawkins," said I. "After Terry has had a few more cracks on my back with the cats, then you will come and help me away, will you?"

"Let him ever raise his hand to you again and put the weight of the cats on your back, and if I swing the halter the next minute, I will sink one of these bullets in his heart"—showing me his horse pistol at the same time. "Don't fail to write to me after you get your sentence and let me know whether they sent you back to the Reff., so as I can be in time to give you my assistance and help you away. Don't forget the name, Rob. Jim Hawkins."

"Ah, Strongman," said I. "I am afraid that we both will come to some bad end yet."

"Don't give way to grief, Rob, but keep up a good heart. You know what the sailor says, a short life and a merry one. Never bow yourself at no man's feet no more. Take courage and spunk, and the first one that insults you, let your pistol crack his heart. Don't forget my new name, Jim Hawkins, and slip me a letter and I will respond to it. Here, take this ten dollar note, and make good use of it. Don't forget the name, Rob. Jim Hawkins. Good bye, boy. May God bless you"—and the English chap turned suddenly around on the heel of his boot, and said a second thought had struck him. "Where is that son of a ___ that took you up? Where does he live? Tell me, and before the morning dawn I will sink his body low beneath the rolling waves. Where is he, or who is he, and where does he live?"

Thinking that my friend might do him some secret harm, I told him that I did not know where he lived or where he could be found.

"Well, good bye, boy. Don't forget Jim Hawkins."

"Hold there, old fellow. I think you have learnt to drink deep in the intoxicating cup since we met together last, eh?"

"Not much, Rob, only a little now and then."

"Be careful, Hawkins. Don't drink too deep, or it will sink you lower than Hell. Mind what I tell you. Be careful."

"Well, good bye, Rob. Don't forget to write to me after you get your sentence, and I will respond back to it."

"Good bye, Hawkins, and may God be with you if ever you have the bad luck to plough the foaming sea."

"God," said Hawkins as he gave the bell a jerk for the turnkey to come and let him out. "God, Rob? Why, I have become so harden that I don't believe there is any God."

"I say, young chap, you will believe that there is a God when you are riding upon his heavy billows, and a north wester comes a sweeping o'er your pate, and the waves is rocking your little craft like a cradle, and the tempest a swinging you among the riggings and in the mast, then, my good fellow, you will believe that there is a God. Better take them words back, Hawkins, or you will see the day when them very words will come playing and mingling with fire before your eyes like a flash of fire."

"Better take them words back, eh? No, sir, take nothing back," said Hawkins, and he press his way out through the heavy iron door, and I saw him no more.

Reader, let me leave Hawkins or Strongman a tramping the high roads of vice and crime, until he plunges his hand in the blood of his fellow and he is swinging between the heavens and the earth. Let me leave him here in this condition, and I will introduce my Reader to him in the following chapters and the awful end he came to at last.

THE TIME HAD now arrived that I, in company with twelve other prisoners, was to be brought out before the court and hear my indictment read and the charge that was laid against me. There I stood, a boy only at the age of thirteen, arraigned before the judge and jury to hear what my doom would be, and to hear the angry sentence of the judge a sealing up my doom and consigning me away to a dark and a gloomy prison, there to become the inmate of hard and rash treatment, and often times to be loaded down with balls and chains and heavy shackles.

As I entered the court House, the people stared and gazed upon me and my unhappy comrades as though we were a mere show of animals. The court being called to order, our indictments was read, and the district attorney orders us to be ready for our trials on the following day, and sent us back to jail. There was thirteen of us in the whole to be tried, and I knew that it would take a whole week to try us, and I sent for Miss Mutermer to come down to the jail and see me before the expiration of the week and before my doom would be forever sealed. On the following day, Miss Mutermer made her appearance at the jail door and ask me if there was anything that laid in her power that she could do for me. As she put that question to me, I began to reflect a little and to see if I stood in need of her assistance. Yes, Reader, though it was through the means of Miss Mutermer that I was standing between an iron grated door and her, yet I stood in need of her help and assistance.

"See, Robert, that you don't bring me out and mention my name, and I will do all that lays in my power for you. I suppose you have no lawyer, Robert."

"No, Miss Mutermer," I replied, after a little reflection of what I had gone through at the House of Refuge, and that I wasn't a mite too old to be sent back there to answer for the escape that I had made, and to receive Miller's and Strongman's punishments upon my own (for that was the rule in the House of Refuge in them days: if three made their escape and one got catch, he had to bear his own punishments and the other two). "No, Mrs. Mutermer," I replied, "I have no lawyer to stand and plead my case, no lawyer to stand between me and Mr. Iverson, who has sworn to be a witness against me, no lawyer to speak one kind word to me or to set any encouragements before me."

"Then," said Mrs. Mutermer, "I will go and engage a lawyer for you, but mind and say nothing to any living person where you got the money from, or from whose hands you received the handkerchief." As she said these words, she turned to go away and seek for a lawyer who would take my case in hand and, if possible, rescue and save me from becoming the inmate of the House of Refuge.

"Mrs. Mutermer," said I as she turned to go way, "if there is any possible means of your saving me from goin' back to the House of Refuge, I wish you would do it, for it will save me from a severe punishment."

She inquired my age, and taking it down on a piece of paper, she tramp her way directly towards Lawyer Hastings'[58] office and employed him as my counsel. Two hours passed away before the girl returned, and at the hour of one, Mr. Hastings and Miss Murtermer appeared at the jail door. Mr. Hastings asking me a few questions and my age, he gave me the following advice.

"Boy," said he, "you are nothing but a mere boy, and as the money and handkerchief was found in your possession and can have no clear evidence where you got the said property, my best advice is for you to plead guilty, and that will be the end of it, and I will put my best influence before the court to have a light sentence pronounced upon you."

"But Mr. Hastings," I replied, "I want this case taken into hand so as not to bring Miss Mutermer into any trouble."

"Very well, Robert," said the lawyer. "Just follow the direction which I laid out to you, and that will put an end to the whole case, and make your sentence a great deal lighter."

Throwing Mr. Hastings ten dols., which Strongman had left me, I begged him with tears—yes, Reader, with mercies from heaven—to keep me from being sent back to the House of Refuge, where I would have to suffer under the burning heats of the cats if I returned back. Mr. Hastings ask me my age and put it down on a piece of paper, giving me his word and assurance that I should not become the inmate of the House of Refuge, and he and Miss Mutermer pressed their way out of a dark and a gloomy jail into the fresh air, where the voice of mirth and music was once more struck upon their ears.

———

LET ME LEAVE Miss Mutermer here, a treading the high roads of vice and crime, and I will introduce the reader to her in the following chapters and the awful end and death she suffered within two years, after to which my story begins—

'Twas a Wednesday morning, just as the town clock was striking the hour of eight, that thirteen prisoners' names was called to get ready to go to the court House. I was one of the number that belong to that hard, rough looking crew. Yes, Reader, I was numbered among the transgressors of that day. With handcuffs on my wrists I made my way to the court House, where sat loafers and idlers, gentlemen and peasants, judges and juries, constables and sheriffs, farmers and merchants, thieves and robbers, night prowlers and murders, who had committed the darkest and blackest deeds under the cover of midnight, yet they sat there with their freedom and liberty, and went unpunished. Yes, there I sat in a box, gazed and stared at by these black hearted law breakers who was allowed to go unpunished and ramble where they was might to, while I for one small crime was to become a dog, a fugitive and a vagabond and the inmate of a dark and a gloomy prison. Yes, Reader, there I sat, confined case in the box, look upon by these infernal scamps who had dipped their hands deeper in crime than ever I had dared to, and yet without punishment—and among them was my prosecutor, Iverson, who was committing the most horrible and blackest deeds under the shades of midnight than my pen is able to describe, and which I will unfold to the Reader in the following chapters.

My indictment being read again before the assembled crowd, to which I have just described above, I plead guilty to the whole charge, and sat there awaiting to hear my doom, what and where my lot would be. While I sat there, I heard the trials of thieves, robbers, burglars, forgers, counterfeiters, and horse thieves, and so forth. Trials all being over, we were handcuffed together again and sent back to the jail till the next morning, and then we was to come and hear our sentences pronounced and our future prospects blasted and withered forever. Ah, the sorrowful morning came which brought many a doneful cry and sorrowful tears from the eyes of my companions, who was to suffer with me and pass under the same treatment. On our entering the court House, we had hard work to press our way through the crowd who had gathered there to hear our sentences pronounced. As I entered the door, there I saw Iverson with a cigar in his mouth, and his hat cock on one side, looking independent as though he was the son of some lord or duke.

Court being called to order, the judge called my name and told me stand up. He then ask me if I had anything to say why the sentence of the law should not be pronounced upon me. I told him that I had nothing to say, and he said that I was yet young and tender in years, and by the influence of older persons I had been brought into vice and crime, and that I look to him as a smart intelligent boy. Judge Samson then ask me my age, and bowing my head low in the

sink of shame, I was afraid to give him my right age, which was thirteen, for fear of being sent back to New York, and I told him that I
was fifteen years old.[59]

"Your sentence," said he, "will be two years hard labor in the
Auburn State Prison," and he sealed up my doom by saying that he
hope that the two years of my sentence would bring around a solid
reformation in my heart and character. After passing all of our sentences, we were ushered back to the jail to be ready to take the boat
the next morning and make our march onward to our long and lonesome Homes.

"Blast that cursed and infernal white French bitch," said Iverson
as I passed him, "she is the dirty little w— that took my money out
of my pocket, and that poor little innocent darkie has got to suffer
for her deeds."

I casted my eye on Iverson without saying one word and left the
court House with tears streaming from my eyes. As soon as I entered
my cell, I sat down and wrote the following letter to Strongman—

Rochester—May 1st—1840—
    My Dear and honest friend I have only time to drop you a few
lines—I rec— my sentence yesterday from Judge Samson for the
term of two years across the long bridge—and if I ever live to get
out I will ceartainly come down to york and see you—what think
you now—old hawk—think there is a God yet—be careful ere his
all vengful hand may come down upon you so heavey some day
that you will feel evry boane in your frame crack—me thinks old
chap—that we twain have felt some of his heavey strokes already—
and that so hard as to convince us that there is a God—what think
you—ye mortal worm of a day what think ye—you may think this
to be a strange letter—you sporting little fool but let me tell you
that there is somthing in it which you will recollect some day or
another—and I want you to respond back to it—better Direct
your letter to auburn in care of the principal keeper of the prison

and perhaps I may get it—this is all at present—and I have the honor Sir with great Respect to be your most Humble and obedient Servant—From Rob—your friend—

After writing this letter and fulfilling my promise, I closed it and sealed it and directed it to Mrs. Flinn in the City of New York, and handed it to Mrs. Mutermer, who came down to see me in the afternoon and who promised to post it the same day.

The next morning, on the second day of May in 1840, thirteen of us in number, bound down in irons strong,[60] was put aboard the canal boat called *James Savage* and began our journey. See, Reader, look— thirteen of us in number, all pressing and making our way to a dark and a gloomy. Look at me, nothing but a boy at the age of thirteen, loaded down with chains, marching off to become the inmate of a dark, rough, and gloomy looking prison. Here I sit, stowed away in one corner of the boat, looking and hearing the pitiful sighs and groans of Peter Nicks' wife and little children. Poor Peter, how my heart beats in sorrow for you, as I sit a gazing here upon them six little children of yours, who perhaps you may never see again. Ere before the expiration of ten years shall roll over them white locks of yours, yon little female of your loins may be tramping over the graves of the dead and looking for the fresh turf that covers her father's remains. The feet of your wife may be seen a treading over the sleeping dead, and her voice may be mingling with tears, but all of this you cannot heed.

What, John Elsworth, you broken hearted looking sinner you— you are sitting alone, eh, a reading that little testament which Henry A. Brewster[61] gave you before you left, and which you promised with a solemn oath to read and study carefully during the two years you have to pass with me? Read on, John, and though I am a sinner, yet from the very bottom of my heart I say may God bless you. Look at that hard, rough looking face, old Jones there, laugh and grin and cut up his shines. Laugh on, grin on, you hard hearted old devil you, Jones, and ere before five long years drops over your fate, your laughter will be turned into weeping. What, how happy John Elsworth feels! He got religion before he left the jail and made his promise to Henry A. Brewster that he would live for God during the rest of his days and die for God. How happy poor John feels, and there he sits a cheering us with his beautiful voice and singing—

Oh tell me no more of this world's vain store,
For the time for such trifles with me now is o'er.[62]

Thus did we press our way on until we came to the weigh lock, and Nicks, who was doomed to a gloomy prison for ten years, gave his wife and six little bright eyed children each a kiss and a shake of the hand, i.e., and a father's advice. They got off the boat and stood upon the weigh lock until the boat was ready to start. I shall never forget the looks of that bleeding heart woman, as she stood there a weeping and wailing the loss of her husband and holding a little infant in her arms, and five more[63] little children a hanging and clinging ahold of her dress. As the boat shoved out of the dock, she took us each by the hand, and from her throbbing heart, she said, "May God be with each one of you and spare your lives, to come from yon gloomy prison better men than you are now."

Thus passing slowly along, we reach Montezuma[64] in three days, just as the sun was throwing her last glittering ray over the tops of the trees. Getting off at Montezuma, the sheriff hired two wagons the same night, and at the hour of nine we found ourselves enclosed within the walls of a gloomy prison.

As we entered the office, the guard who was on night duty went up stairs, and in a few moments made his return, followed by an elderly looking gentleman whose locks was white as the drifting snow. This gentleman was Esq. Cook,[65] the principal Keeper of the prison. Esq. Cook order the guard to search our pockets and take us below and have our irons cut off. After getting our irons pluck off, the guard in a rough and harsh way orders us to follow him. In we march, until we came to a halt in front of a dark, gloomy, lonesome looking dungeon. Unlocking the door, he jerked it open and order us to go in and lay down on the hard oak floor, without a bed or a blanket to cover us. Locking the door, he put his hand on the lever to see if all was right and safe. He ordered us not to make the least stir or noise through the night, nor not to speak one word. If we did, we should hear from it with sorrow in the morning.

Reader, could you but witness the tears, the groans, and the sighs that went from that gloomy dungeon that night, it would melted your heart. The night wore slowly away, and at the hour of half past six, the bell rung for the prisoners to get up and get ready for to do that big heavy day's works that laid ready for them to do. After the convicts had all got their breakfast, the keeper of the kitchen, whose name I shall call Mr. Ritchardson, came with the key, and unlock us, and ordered us to follow him out into the kitchen, where we was to be shaved, have our hair crop close to our heads, and change our clothes and have the real uniform state prison mark on. Thus rigged and equipped in the robes of disgrace, we are ready to enter the hall with the hospital keeper and stand before the clerk, who puts the following questions to the convict, which he must answer—

How old are you? Where was you born? What county did you come from? And what's the crime that you are charged with? Are your parents living, and are you a married man? How many children have you? And what kind of an education have you? Are you a temperance man or intemperance? Are your parents religious, and did you ever attend a Sabbath school? How many times have you ever been in a county jail, or how many times have you ever been fined?

Poor convict, how low he hangs his head in the ditch of shame as the clerk put the question to him and ask him if he is a temperance man. How shame the rascal looks, and how he hates to answer the question. How the thought strikes his hearts like a dagger as he stands there and thinks that only a few nights since, when he had returned from one of his drunken sprees, that his clumsy and heavy old hand struck the wife of his bosom in the face and made her carry a pair of black eyes for a long time, and the impudent villain had the heart to up lift his cruel hand at his mother—at that old mother who had watch over him night and day—and no wonder, Reader, that he bows his head in shame, when the clerk puts that question to him.

———

THE READER WILL understand that I am now introducing him to the prison and the rules and regulations and modes of punishments as they were in 1840, when I first entered the prison—and as I have just entered the prison, let me leave the reader here, and give him an introduction to a faithful and a dutiful old soldier who stand upon the prison, a keeping watch night and day. He is a fine old fellow. I have been acquainted with him ever since I was so high, ever since I was a boy of thirteen years old, and I was acquainted with Mr. Cray[66] his founder, and I am able to give the reader a history of this old soldier's life and his adventures, his feats and his character, together with his career and down fall and his everlasting ruin and destruction. When this old fellow first entered the prison, the Warden and the inspectors took so much interest and delight into him that they placed him higher above any of the officers of the prison, and though it was strictly against the rule of the prison in those days for either convict or officer to smoke within the walls of the prison, yet they broke over their strictest rules themselves and allowed this old chap to have his pipe and use it when ever he chooses. What think you, Reader, of an officer who lays down rules for the inmates of the prison to keep and live up to, and they themselves are the very first ones to break over them? What think you of such an officer? As I can't answer the question myself, I will leave it to the candid reader as a mystery to find out.

Well, after this old fellow had received such due respects, he shouldered his musket and stood like a brave soldier upon his throne to meet the stormy battles and the midnight air that would come a hurling their stormy darts and their frosty nights at him. How my heart has yearned and almost melted within me when I have been standing for a long time a looking at this poor old fellow and the sad condition to which he is place in, and the sufferings to which he will have to endure until the almighty sends a thunder bolt and knocks him from the high and lofty position to which he now stands. Many has been the cold and stormy nights, when both keeper and guard has been wrapped sweetly in the arms of sleep, that this dutiful old fellow has stood his watch like a brave man. The midnight air and the stormy winds have swept and howled over his head. Thunder bolts and lightnings has played before his face. Snow flakes and beating rain has come a pelting down on him. The glittering sun has throwed his melting rays on him. The shadow of the almighty's hand has passed over his face. Yet the old fellow heeds them not. Neither does he pay any respects to them. Why, the old bachelor looks to me like a proud, haughty old fellow, and if it wasn't for that devilish old pipe in his mouth, I should respect and like him very much. Look, Reader, how straight and firm he stands. See how he holds up his head and defies the sun to scorch him, or the northern blast to hurl him from his throne.

Every time I think of this old chap, he puts me in mind of an old drunkard which I once knew, and had made himself so low and so degraded that he was hated by every one. But by and by the old fellow got sick of liquor, and looking at himself all dressed in rags, and thinking of the poverty that he was bringing upon his family, he dash the cup from his quivering hand, stripped himself of his rags, wash the deep stain of drunkardness from his character, and in the course of a few years he received a high station in life. Reader, I like this dutiful and brave old soldier for one thing—that is because he is a temperance man. I believe he hates a drunkard, for he won't look at a drunkard. Neither can he bear the smell of liquor, nor is he one of those that jeers and sneers at poverty, nor mixes or mingles with riches.

One cold frosty morning, just as the keepers was coming in all bundled up in their over coats, twisting and turning their heads at a small blow of a southwester, I had to shear off in one corner where no officer could see me and laugh heartily. What a fuss they made at a little breeze of wind that came a fanning their faces, while this poor old fellow had been a standing the cold watches of the night. Dutiful old soldier, said I to myself, one winter's day you have outrode many a wintery storm and stuck to your duty like a faithful guard, and yet they have never supplied you with an over coat. See how clean he keeps his musket, and how strict he is to be right on the spot at the precise hour of duty. I don't believe the sergeant ever had to speak a word to him about keeping his musket clean or about being on duty at the precise hour.

There is one bad trick about this fellow which I don't like much, and that is he hates to work. He won't look at it. I believe the old chap would rather cut the buttons off of his coat and sell them than to work. Why, Reader, if you spoke to him about work, he wouldn't listen to you. Nay, he wouldn't look at you. Now he puts me in mind of some of these contractors, who comes in the shops a puffing and blowing as though they had done a heavy day's work, to lay heavy and tedious burdens upon the convicts' shoulders to do, but they themselves won't so much as dirty their little fingers with it.

As I stood a gazing at this old soldier one day, the Warden happen to pass me, and I had a good notion to put the question to him and ask him if he thought that yon old soldier would stand so firmly and bold upon the field of battle and face a deadly enemy, if duty called him forth—but being a little afraid of insulting and hurting the old soldier's dignity, I did not put the question to the Warden. How many more years this honorable old soldier has got to stay up there with his musket at his shoulder I am unable to tell, but Reader, many will be the cold winter nights, and many the hot bleaching days, many will be the loud thunders that will clap and rap over his head, and many will be the forked lightnings that will play before his face, before he drops from his lofty white throne.

When I cast my eyes on the old chap, he puts me in mind of a song which a little shepherd boy struck up and sung one day, when he was out on the green plains attending his father's flock. His song was about one of these very old fellows, and Reader, this was the shepherd boy's song—

> They have ears, but they hear not.
> They have feet, but they walk not.
> Hands have they, but they handle not.
> Nose but they smell not, mouths but they speak not
> And the very man that made them is like unto them.[67]

Ye brave and proud and haughty old fellow, though you might stand firm and bold upon the field of battle, and meet the deadly enemy face to face, and never dodge at the crack of a musket, nor flinch at the loud roar of the cannon when she was playing her balls and throwing her hot bomb shells in your face—yet, you brave old fellow you, let me tell you that the terrible day is coming when you will fall from the position in which you now stand, and though you have faced the stormy winds and stood the cold blast of the nights, yet a hand stronger than the winds, and colder than the midnight air, will know you from where you now stand, and dash you to the ground, and you will melt away like wax before the burning blaze, and your everlasting destruction and destination will be sealed up forever.

I HAVE NOW introduced the reader to this venerable old soldier, Copper John, who stands upon the top of the prison. Let me now take you politely by the hand and lead you through this dark and gloomy old castle. Look on the left as you enter the front gate, and your eyes will be dazzled with a garden of rich flowers. Cast your eyes on the right as you come in, and you will see three or four cherry and pear trees that are beginning to fall and decay away. Keep straight along until you reach the hall, and cast your eyes up over the door on your left hand side, where you will see a little board up over the door in large capital letters, which says clerk's office. Step in and thrust your hand into your pocket, and pull out a quarter and hand it to him, and he will present you a ticket which you must hand to the sergeant, and he will provide you with a guard who will conduct you through the prison.

The reader will remember that I am conducting the visitor through the prison as it was in the year 1840. The sergeant has now provided you with a guard. He lays his hand on the iron lever, and the old iron door swings upon its hinges and lets you out into the north wing. Passing along a few steps, you pass those dark and gloomy cabins where the prisoner has to take up his silent and solitary abode at night. Leaving this dark and lonesome wing, where everything looks dismal, silent, and cold, the guard brings you out into the cooper shop, where you may see men rigged in striped clothes of shame and disgrace, a toiling and laboring and bearing the heavy burdens of a hot summer's day. From the cooper shop, he leads you into the tool shop, which stands in a slanting position against the wall, with sky light windows fix in the roof, that the prisoner may have light enough to do his work. In this shop they make planes, chisels, and so forth. From this dusty old shop, he leads you out into the open air, where you have a chance to brush a little of the dust off of your nice silk dresses.

Crossing the road, the guard leads you into the weave shop, where you may see some twenty hands to work, a weaving carpets. From this noisy old shop, you strike out into the open air again, and before you have time to take one puff of fresh air, you find yourself into the machine shop, where the loud clap of the smith's hammer comes sounding heavy in your ears. Leaving this noisy and smoky old work shop, the guard conducts you into the comb shop, which you are glad to get out of as quick as you can, on the account of the filthy smell. In this shop they make combs of every description. Leaving this filthy shop, you soon find yourself a passing through the cabinet shop, where your eyes will be dazzled with furniture of every description, and with a puzzled mind which piece you would choose to sit into your parlor if you was goin' to buy. From the cabinet shop, your conductor leads you into the hame shop amidst dust and smoke, and you are a lucky gent or a lady if you get out into the open air without having your throat choke up with smoke and dust. In this shop they make hames and carry on silver plating.

From the hame shop, the guard leads you into the south wing, where everything looks black and dark as midnight, and the convict have to take up his solitary abode and snooze out the long and lonesome nights of his time. Leaving these dark and chilly looking cabins, the guard leads you into the dining room, where you see the tables all set with seven or eight hundred wooden plates. As you pass on, you soon find yourself into the kitchen, where the guard politely shows you a kettle of soup and a pot of mush, a junk of beef, and a piece of brown bread.

If you are a particular friend of the guard's, he will take time to search for the Warden and get his permission to conduct you up into the hospital. Mind, you have got to be his very identical and particular friend, or you can't get a peep at the face of yon dying youth, who is just a wrestling and fighting hard with the enemy of death. Reader, are you his friend? Have you hummed a long yarn in his ears as you have been passing through the shops? Have you talk sweet to him and tried to bring back to his mind the happy days of your boyhood and youth? Have you brought to his remembrance some well remembered tale which you use to sit and spin in your father's log cabin during the long winter nights? Does the old guard remember the tale yet? Does he recognize you yet? Has he forgot the song which you and him use to be a humming over as you both stroll along together up yon shady lane? Well then, Reader, as the guard has not forgot them happy hours and those gone by days, he returns to you with a heavy, clumsy looking key in his hand and conducts you to the hospital.

Onward, onward, you press your way through a dark and a gloomy wing, until your feet enters the threshold of the hospital door. How black and dismal everything looks. How still and silent is everything around you. Not a word or a lisp is heard through out the room. Not a smile hangs on your face as you stand between the living and the dead. Everything looks neat and clean. Every man that is able to sit up is hanging back in his chair, with his hand under his chin and his elbow a leaning on the bed, and seems to be a doleing over his hard allotment and the condition which he is placed in. Casting your eyes at the further end of the room, you see a young man a pining away under the awful and dreadful disease of masturbation, and ere before yon sun sets in the west, he must pay the debt of nature, without a friend in the world to shed a tear at his destination. Poor fellow, you says to yourself as you turn from this dark cavel with a heart of pity and compassion, and as you skip down the stairs and through the wing, your mind is thrown back to yon dying boy, with no sister to wipe the cold sweat from his brow, nor no mother to smooth the pillow for his drooping head, no father to come and cheer his heart.

All looks black, doneful and dismal, and with a sicken heart you turn from the dark scene which you have just witness, and with a revel of thoughts a swimming into your mind, the guard conducts you back to the hall, from whence you first started from, and before you know where you are, you are bounding and skipping through the hall out into the open streets, where you begin to snuff the fresh air and brush off some of the state prison dirt that still hangs and clings to your clothes, which you got on you as you passed through the shops to inspect the work and to gaze at the unhappy harden inmate of a dark and a gloomy prison.

I HAVE NOW conducted my reader as a visitor through this gloomy looking old castle, and took the pains to conduct him through every department of it as it was in the year 1840. I shall now lay out the rules and the regulations of the prison as it was in 1840, and continue on with my History and the improvements that has been made within the prison from that time up to the present time, which is 1858, and I hope as I lay these rules out to the reader, that he won't be astonish when I come to tell him that the rules in 1840 were more stricter and severe and lived up to than they are now, for I must confess with an open and an honest heart that the Auburn State Prison is a paradise today than what it was then, as the reader shall see in the following chapters.

In the first place, the convict must not swing his hammock and go to bed until the bell rings at eight o'clock. He must then strip off his clothes, swing his hammock, and go right to bed, and not be seen up by the guard through the night until the bell rings for him to get up in the morning at half past five. He must then be up and dressed and be standing at his door in readiness, so as when the Keeper comes along and raises the lever of his door, he may push it open and come out. He must not have a knife or a fork either in his cell or about his person. He must have no book slate, arithmetic, nor nothing in his cell but his bible and tract and spoon in his cell, to eat his mush with. He must hang up his bed clothes every morning when he first gets up and not let them be seen on his bed, or the number of his cell is taken down and handed to the Keeper, and the convict may think himself a lucky adventure if he gets off with a dozen scratches on his back with the old cat's paws.

When marching, we must keep close together, with our arms folded and our heads to the right, our heads bowed and our eyes a looking down upon the ground. When sitting at the table, we must keep our arms folded, our head bowed, with our eyes directly down on our dishes before us, not allowed to touch a knife or a fork or to unfold our arms until the bell rings as a signal for us to eat. Must not pass a piece of bread or meat or a potato from one man to another, either behind you or before you, at your right hand or at your left hand. It makes no odds how bad your companion may want it, you must not hand it to him, for if you do, off comes your shirt, and less than a minute's time you are suffering under the pains of the cats, and you are paying the penalties for breaking over the rules. If you have more than you want to eat, hand it to the waiter, and he will give it to the next man that wants it.

Must not take no provisions out from the table with you to the shop. Must not swing your hammock on Sundays without a direct written order from the Doctor. Must not be seen a running through the yard when sent from one shop to another on some errand. When goin' through the yard on any particular business, you must keep your arms folded and your head bowed towards the ground until you reach the place of your destination. Must not be seen a tinkering in your cell. Must not be seen with a pocket in your pants, coat, or vest. Must not look up off of your work and cast an uplifted eye at spectators. (I like that rule. It's a good rule. How does it look for convicts to be staring and gazing spectators and strangers in the face as they are passing through the shops? It looks to me like shame and misery. They came through to gaze and stare at us, and not we at them.) No, Reader, we are not allow to look up at that old aged mother or father, who perhaps are passing through the shops, and who peradventure we may never see again on this side of the grave. Their very foot prints which they have left behind them seem to be sacred to us. When in church, we must keep our eyes directly on the chaplain and not be a gazing around us. Must not speak a word or look up at the inspectors as they are passing through the shops, without they first speak to the convict. Must not talk, without it is in the presence of the Keeper. No trafficking or trading with each other. No smoking without a written order from the Doctor. Must not use or be seen with any tobacco.

I say, old chap, over whose head fifty winters has already swept its blasted winds into your face, what are you goin' to do now for tobac? Been a chewing the old cud for more than fifty years, and now you have got to throw the old soldier one side, eh? It comes down hard upon you, don't it, old man? Ain't you sorry you come here, old fellow, eh? Been up to see the Doctor yet, old chap, about your cud? Did you tell him that you couldn't do without, eh? Did you put on a long face and tell him that you was continually sick to your stomach? Well, what did he say? Ha-ha, told you to put a piece of stick into your mouth and chew it, eh? Ain't you sorry you come, old man? They have played a sharp game upon you here, old fellow. Sorry you come at last, eh? God bless you, old fellow. I feel sorry for you and sympathize with you in your lone condition and your hard allotment, but let me tell you, old man, that you will see tighter and harder times than these a rolling and rushing over them silvery locks of yours before the expiration of your time.

Reader, do you want to know how these old fellows use to do when they was hard up for tobacco? Methinks I hear you say yes. Well then, when one of these old fellows would be a strolling along from the hospital, with his arms folded, he would take good care to keep his eyes directly down on the ground until he came across an old cud of tobacco, which perhaps had been laying under the snow all winter and had been thrown away by some of the contractors or officers of the prison. As soon as the old chap would see one of these old soldiers, he would make a full halt and stand and look all around him to see if any of the officers was looking at him. The old fellow being satisfied that no one was seeing him, he would bend over and pretend he was tying his shoe, and pick the old cud up, and straighten himself up. He would then give another side look to see if any one was a watching him, and seeing no one, the old chap would unbutton his coat and thrust his hand into his bosom and pull out a dirty looking piece of rag, where he had a dozen more of the same kind of old soldiers, and wrap it up as careful as though it was pure gold, and stow it away in his bosom, button up his coat, pass on with his head down and his arms folded as though nothing had happened, a looking for more of the same kind.

I will now lay out the regulations of the prison as it was in 1840. There were then ten shops again, which had been let out on a contract, to which I here give the reader a list of—

A list and the names of the different shops in 1840

The Cooper Shop.
Tool—do.
Weave—do.

Hame—do.
Cabinet—do.
Shoe—do.
Tailor—do.
Machine—do.
Comb—do.
Spin—do.

These shops was built against the wall in a slanting position, with sky lights fix in the roofs of them, and in a very bad condition, letting the water down through the roofs on the convict's work in stormy weather. They had been standing for many years, and had began to decay already,[68] and a few more years would brought them a falling and crumbling to the ground. The whole prison took up five acres of ground.

THE READER WILL remember that it was one of them mild and beautiful evenings in the month of May that I entered this gloomy looking prison, in company with twelve others, who was to be my companions and inmates until the expiration of our sentences, and on the fourth day of that beautiful and soft month, we was ushered in the presence of the clerk to go through our prison examination. After the clerk had ask us a different number questions, the Keeper brought us before the Doctor, who ask us the following questions—

Where are you from? What is the crime that you are charged with? How old are you? Are your parents a living? Where was you born? Was you ever under a religious education? Was you ever sick? Did you ever have the small pox? Did you ever have any of your bones broken? Did you ever have any bad disorders about you? Are you a well and a healthy man? Have you a wife and children? How many times have you ever been in a county jail? How many fines have you ever had laid upon you? Ah, are you a temperance man? Look, Reader, see the hoary head old scamp bow his head. See that big tear that stands a glistening in his eyes, and almost ready to drop, as the Doctor puts the question to him and asks him if he was a temperance man.

After the Doctor had gone through this exercise and examination, we was separated from each other and taken off to the shops, where we wasn't allowed hardly to look at each other for fear of a severe punishment. I was fortunate enough to get in one of the best shops in the prison, where we had a good, kind, open hearted contractor, whose looks bespoke good nature. I had not been in the shop no more than two minutes before the Keeper called me up to the desk, and in a rough and an ugly manner ask me what my name was, and where I was from, and how long I came for. He then told me that he was goin' to lay out some rules to me, which he expected I should live up to and obey. After giving out these rules to me, he showed me the cat of nine tails and told me that if I broke over his rules, I might expect to take a dozen of them on my back. He then pointed his cane to a stool that stood hard by, and told me to sit down on it and fold my arms and hold down my head and not to look up until the foreman or contractor put me to work.

Pah, you old tyrant you, said I to myself, as I sat there in this doneful condition, pah, you old villain you, who cares for you or your rules? Who cares for you or your cats? Why, you old pimp you, said I to myself, I have gone under them little fellows many a day. I have gone under the treatment of them little cat's paws many a time. I have had them sunken deeper into my back than ever you dare to sink them. I have had a worse punishment with them than ever you dare to give me. Pah, you old tyrant, who cares for you or your cats? Who cares for you or your rules?

While I was sitting in this deep reverie of thoughts, I heard the heavy tramp of footsteps a treading behind me, and in a moment's time the heavy weight of a man's hand was laid upon my shoulder. "Here, get up here youngster, and take off your cap," said one of the officer in a rough tone of a voice. I stood up before Capt. Tylor,[69] and taking off my cap, I made a low bow to him.

"Where are you from?" said he.

"I am from Rochester, sir," I replied.

"How long have you come for?"

"Two years, sir," said I.

"Pah," said he, "that's nothing. We will make a man of you before that time. How old are you?"

"Thirteen, sir," said I.

"Well," said he, "you must be a good boy and behave yourself well, and try to be as good and as smart a man as your father was. I was acquainted with your father. Be careful, now," said he, "that none of these older inmates don't get the upper hand of you and lead you astray. Look out," said Mr. Tylor, "that they don't play their skillful influence over you, and you yield yourself to their bad examples. There many a dare face scoundrel in here that will lead you into trouble and laugh at you in the end. Look out for them." As he said these words to me and gave me such a lesson of good advice, he thrust his hands into his pocket and made his way out of door.

Oh, how I cried. How I sob. How my lips quivered when Mr. Tylor mention my father's name. A convulsive sobs and tears came rushing down my dark cheeks as I heard the sacred name of my father mentioned. Taking my seat again, I covered my face with both hands and gave way to a full flood of tears, and sat in this condition until the bell rung for dinner.

The men all fell in their respected places, formed into a single file, folded their arms, and at the word go, on they marched, off to the dining room to refresh themselves with coarse rough grub. Now as I passed through the dining room, I had a sly chance of looking some of the convicts in the face, to see if ever I had ever seen any of them before—but I hardly seen a new face which was strange to me. I recognized some blooming little faces which I had seen in the House of Refuge. I received winks from many an eye that had witness the punishments I received when a boy in the House of Refuge. Many was the dark and blooming eyes that I saw in that gloomy prison that had witness that awful and cruel punishment to which

Strongman and I got through the means of that black hearted Thom King. Among eight hundred prisoners, there were over one hundred and fifty that I was well acquainted with and had been boys with me in the House of Refuge. There I saw Jack Williams and Thom Payne, Joe Coutler and Harry Williams, Willie Jones and Charlie Kendell, Jim Edwards and Aleainor Mills.[70] All, once little villains and scamps with me in the House of Refuge, had gone through the same treatment that I had gone through, had played in the same yard that I had played in, had ate under the same old roof, and under the same old timbers had heard many a solemn prayer and blessing, and now had come forth into the world and followed the high roads of vice and crime, and was now inmates with me in a dark and a gloomy prison.

In the afternoon Mr. Hewson,[71] the contractor, put me to work aside a black man that was all the time full of his devilment, and told him to learn me how to make chair bottoms. Every little chance that this nig could get, he would come to my bench and pretend that he was showing me something about my work, when at the same time he would be a talking about something else, which would make me burst out and laugh. One day this nig had said something to me which made me laugh very much and caused the tears to rush from my eyes. The Keeper happen to see this piece of fun a goin' on, and he called us both down and wanted to know what it was that tickled us so. The nig confessed what it was, and the Keeper ordered him to pull off his shirt, and he gave him a dozen on his bare back. He then called me and ask me if his rules was so hard that I couldn't live up to them, or if I honestly meant to tread and trample them under my feet. I gave him no answer, and he ordered me to pull off my coat and vest and leave my shirt on. I took off my coat and vest, and raising the lid of his desk, he drew out a blue raw hide, told me to stand around, fold my arms, which I did. He then gave me seven cuts on the back and told me to put on my coat and vest, and the next act he caught me in, he would put something else on my back which would make me buldge.

No, you won't, you old tyrant you, I said to myself as I slung my coat across my arm and went off to my work. No, you won't. You nor your cats nor raw hide can't make me flinch. I won't flinch for you. I'll show the boys that I can stand them little pusses just as good as a man can. So off I went to my work, a muttering over something to myself. What it was I don't remember, for my bosom was burning with madness and my eye a flashing like fire.

It was only the next day when I sat at the table that Mills unfolded his arms and put his hand under the table and passed me a note, which I was lucky enough to get without the Keeper a seeing me, which after I got to my cell at night I opened it and read it, and this was the contents of that note—

> Well old Hawk cross the long bridge at last eh—been a looking for you a long time—come at last Eh—well look out now for hard times and rough useage—for they take delight in swinging the old cat here—look so as you have had a scratch of the old paw already. How they feel old boy Eh—worse then them down to the Reffuge they show no respects to persons here—rich or poor black or white they serve them all a like—look out—How long did they throw you for—spose you come from Rochester Eh—dont fail to give me answer to this.
>
> yours Respects—Aleainor Mills—

After looking and reading over the contents of this note, I took the pencil which Mills had wrapped up in his note for me and sat down and tore a clean white leaf out of my bible and gave him the following answer—

The Author's Answer to Mills' Note

> Spose I'll have to see hard times here Eh—old boy—have to rush through iltreatment—and plough through rough and hard useage—have to eat corse rough grub—and obey the point of

evry cane and finger that comes a pointing into my face—and fall down on my marrows at evry blow the tyrantical hand gives me with the cats—Eh ye blooming looking youth you—

The next morning while at breakfast, I under took to pass this note to Mills, but the sharp eye of the Keeper got a glance of it and come and took it away from me, and when I got back to the shop, the Keeper open it and read it. He then called me up and ask me concerning the note, and who this Mills was and what shop he work in. There I was, caught far and squire on the spot, and how to get out of it I knew not—but a second thought struck me at once, which seemed to tell me that there was one way opened in which I could make my escape from this punishment, or at least make it a thousand fold lighter, and that was to tell the truth. So I took courage, stepped right up to the captain's office, told the truth, paid my bill by explaining the truth to him, and the account was settled with seventeen light blows on my bare back with the cats.

How firm I stood, with my arms folded, during that sorrowful moment. Never flinch, never buldge, never shed a tear, but stood my ground and took it like a man. I must confess that the little fellows did burn and sting me, and I felt the pangs of their sharp cuts, but to flinch would been madness to me. I knew what scorns and sneers I should had to met with if I played the part of a boy and bursted out and cried, then again I knew the praises that I would have if I stood still and never flinch at a dozen small blows. Now I am no man that makes light of suffering humanity. No, Reader, I am no joker over pain and misery. It isn't a thing to be joked with. God bless you, you poor sons of sufferings, wherever you may be, or wherever your lot may be casted. I sympathize with you. I have suffered enough to know what it is, and they who suffer are the only ones that can feel it. But I could not help to stick my face away in one corner one day and laugh heartily to see Lundy, a great tall six footer, jump and fall down on his marrows, then give a loud scream at every blow the Keeper gave him, while I, nothing but a boy at the age of thirteen, stood before the old tyrant and never flinch under the strongest blow that he gave me.

After I had put on my shirt and gone back to my work, one of the inmates pretended that he was showing me something about my work, and at the same time began to encourage me and praise me up, how well I had stood the cats, and to be careful of that nig that work aside of me, or he would get me into trouble every day, and that the Keeper was a foul old fiend and such like, to which I told him that I didn't care for the Keeper nor his cats neither. Reader, will you believe me? The convict went right down and told the Keeper what I had said, and again was I called up to answer for what I had said to that convict. Then with tears in my eyes I began to remember what Mr. Tylor had said to me, and I fell in a deep thoughts of reflection.

'TWAS A BEAUTIFUL fourth of July's morning that the golden rays of the sun came a shooting through our iron grated windows, that I sat at the table in deep and melancholy thoughts and reflections, that the weight of a big heavy hickory cane came plump across my knuckles, for handing the man next to me a piece of meat which I did not want. After I got back to the shop, the Keeper called me up before him (which I did no more care about than if I had never stood before him before, for I began to get use to his calls) and ask me if I certainly meant to break over and run through those bright and golden rules of his. I tried to make some excuse for breaking over that rule. I tried to find a mantle to cover the deed, but all in vain. I had broken the rule and forgotten the advice of Mr. Tylor, and now I was arraigned and stood convicted and must suffer the penalty of it, by suffering under the bending and biting galls of the old cat, and be lock up in the dungeon until the next morning.

Never will I forget that bright and palmy day of July as I was strolling to the hospital that I over took Mills, who had been an inmate with me in the House of Refuge, and fell in a conversation with him until one of the relief officers stepped up to us and ask us our names and the name of the shops that we belong to. On my returning back to the shop from the hospital, I found that the Relief Keeper had caught us a talking and had reported us to our respected keepers for talking.

The Keeper called me up to his desk and ask me who that young chap was that I was talking to, and what we was talking about. "I see," said the officer, "that you don't try nor mean to get along here without suffering under the lash every day. What to do with you I know not, without it is to whip you to death right on the spot."

While the Keeper was talking to me, Esq. Cook, the Warden of the prison, came through the shop, and the Keeper took him one side and whispered something into his ear about me. They held a long conversation about me for some minutes while I stood with my face towards the desk.

After they had got through with there their conversation, Esq. Cook took his seat behind the Keeper's desk, and in a rash and an ugly tone, the Keeper called me in the presence of Esq. Cook and said, "This boy, Esq., is becoming a harden convict. He is listening to the silly tales and counsels of the older inmates, and following their devilish vices, and learning all the iniquities and miseries that is prevailing within the prison. He is letting these older inmates have their influence over him, and learning to play their mean and devilish tricks, and what to do with him I know not. I have whip him until the blood came streaming from his back, and it appears to have no effect upon the boy at all. What to do with him, sir, I cannot tell. I am tired of throwing the lash upon his back. He is a smart boy and seems to be endown with good reasons and factualities, and if I let him lead the course that he is now a leading, he will surely become an harden convict, and one day or another will be loaded down with heavy balls and chains and become the inmate of a dark and a gloomy dungeon. What shall I do with him, Esq.? I know no other way to do, only to put him over into your hands, and into your hands I now place the harden youth. Take him and act out your own pleasure with him."

The reader must have some idea of the feelings of my mind during that conversation of the Warden's and the Keeper. There I stood, a nothing but a mere boy, before two officers, a weeping and crying. Horrors, horrors, horrors, eternal horror of horrors came beating and pealting upon my mind.

"You say," said Esq. Cook to the officer, who stood with the cats in his hand, "that you don't know what to do with yon boy."

"No, sir," the officer replied. "It was only yesterday that I gave him a severe punishment, and now I give the youth over into your hands, that he may pass through hard and rough treatment."

As the officer said these words, Esq. Cook ask him what kind of treatment I had been through besides the cats. "Have you consign him in solitary confinement yet?"

"Yes, sir," said the officer. "I have consign him away to a dark and a gloomy dungeon and fed him on bread and water once a day, and it has had no effect upon the boy at all, and if he is allowed to go on in the path which he is now treading, he will be the ringleader of all the vices and crimes that are prevailing within the walls of a gloomy prison."

"Into your hands," said Esq. Cook, "will I commend yon boy. See that you go under a hard and rough treatment with him first with the cats. Then, after that, give him over into my hands, and I'll see what virtue there is in the stocks. Then, if he keeps on leading the career that he now leads, the crack of the pistol shall prove his destiny."

As Esq. Cook said these words, the officer ordered me to pull off my shirt. I obeyed his authority and took off my shirt, and he sunk forty and two blows into my back with the cats. After I had put on my shirt, Esq. Cook ordered me to follow him. Like a dog with his tail hanging down to the ground did I follow this venerable gentleman, whose gray hairs I honor and respect to this very day. Pressing his way onward, he led me to the south wing and enclosed me in a large box which they called the stocks, and made my hands feet and head fast so as I could not stir my body at all. These stocks when closed and made fast are as dark and black as midnight. It benumbs the hands and feet and stops the circulation of the blood for a long time. Not a spark or one single ray of light is there to be seen until the officer sees fit to open the door and let his captive free.

It was late in the afternoon when I heard the heavy tramp of two officers making their way to the box where I was consign. The heavy weights of their canes coming down upon the floor seemed to tell me that they was the very ones who had consign me to the stocks. As they approach this box of torture, they unlock the door, and made my hands and feet free from torture and pain, and ordered me back to the shop. Slowly and sadly did I pace my way back to the shop, in a pensive manner, while the Keeper kept close up at my heels, with a big hickory cane in his hand.

The reader must imagine to himself how I felt, and the pain I was under goin' and bearing after goin' through this treatment of punishment. You must remember that I felt weary and faint, and was glad enough to lay my head down upon the cold floor as soon as I entered my cell, and though it was strictly against the rule for the convict to swing his hammock before the bell rung at eight o'clock for him to turn in, yet so faint and exhausted was I that I swung my bed just as soon as I entered my cell.

The night guard came along and look into my cell and found me covered up in bed. "Haloo. Here," said he, "come up here to the door, sir."

I got up on my hands and knees and creep to the door as well as I could, suffering with pain at every inch I moved.

"Who told you to go to bed, sir?" said the guard. "Who gave you permission, sir? Don't you know that it is against the rules for you to swing your hammock?"

"Sir," said I, "the pains and sufferings which I have endured this day has caused me to break over this rule."

"Don't care," said he, "if a man is breathing his last breath of life, he is no business to break over the rules and go to bed without permission. Get up, sir, and put on your clothes."

In vain did I try to reason and expostulate with the hard and cold hearted devil, but all of my tears and begging and reasoning and rough and cruel treatment couldn't make any effect on this cold hearted devil's heart, but went right off and got the key of my cell door and unlock it and ordered me to follow him down stairs.

Pensively and slowly did I follow the demon down stairs, while the cold clods of blood still clung to my back, groping my way down the stairs. He led me out into the kitchen and order me to pull off my shirt. I strip myself and turned my back around towards the cruel hearted guard, and all the marks and blood that came oozing from my back couldn't soften the heart of that guard, and he laid four light lashes upon my back with the cats.

ON THAT DARK and lonesome night, as I sat pensive and lonely in one corner of my cell, with both hands up to my face, and weeping and givin' my mind to a few thoughts of serious reflection, I was aroused from this reverie of reflections by a kind and a sweet voice that struck upon my ears like a band of music proceeding from the white milk throne of heaven.

"Good evening, good evening," said the venerable old gentleman as he approach my cell and extended his hand through my iron grated door.

"Good evening, sir," said I as I extend my black paw into his milk white hand.

"You look very pensive and sad this evening," said the chaplain. "You look so as you have passed through trouble today."

"Yes, sir," I replied. "I have been drinking out of the cup of sorrow today, and now tonight I'll have to taste the bitter bread of pain."

Talking with me on the subject of religion for a few moments, the Rev. Gentleman ask me how old I was, and if my father and mother was yet alive.

"Sir," said I, "I am thirteen years of age, and the green grass is now waving o'er the grave of my father, and many has been the midwinter snows that has blown over his grave. The green turf has been a singing place for birds, and the spot has always been sacred to me, and no time nor distance can mar or scratch from my memory. And as for my mother," said I, "she was alive when I left the land of my nativity." Oh how I wept and how I cried, when I heard the sacred name of my father and mother mention. As the chaplain stood in front of my iron grated door, he seemed to me like a new born angel, sent from the portals of the sky to come and unlock the prisoner's door, unbind his chains, and let the prisoner free.

He comes—yes, Reader, he comes to my dark and gloom cell where I am consigned and brings words of peace and joy. He comes to buoy up the down, broken heart of the prisoner and smooth his soft hand over his stricken brow. He is my friend, and to him I can unfold all of my sorrows and griefs, and on his shoulders can I lay my heavy weight of sorrows, and it is him that will bear them away to the bleeding cross. He is the best friend the convict ever haves around this dark and gloomy prison. He is the one that tries to make our burdens lighter and our situation more pleasant. He is the one that comes from the cottage to the prisoner's tomb like cell and mixes and mingles with us in a friendly manner, speaking kind and soft words which seem new to the convict. (The reader must re-member that the convict haves to hear hard rash words spoken to him while in prison, and a kind word from the chaplain and a kind look and the shake of the hand which he doesn't very often meet with softens the old devil's heart some and makes him weep and shed many a sorrowful tear.) He is the one that tries to point that harden old gray head convict to the bleeding cross—i.e., he is the one that tries to bring back to that cherry cheek young youth's mind the days of his childhood, when the mother printed a prayer with a kiss upon his cursed lips.

Reader, if you are so unfortunate to become the inmate of a gloomy prison, never, oh never, give a cross or an angry look at the chaplain. Never curse him in your heart, for if you do, the birds of the air will carry the curse Home at eve tide. Never speak a cross or an angry word to him, but use him well. Treat him kindly, and he will visit your lonely cell and try to buoy up your down casted spir-its and delight to do you good during the time you stay in prison, and when you leave yon gloomy old palace, you will find in him a confidential friend who will sympathize with you for what you have already passed through, and his soft hand will try to wipe away the dropping tears from your eyes, and the same warm hand will smooth the trouble that comes mingling down your brow. How often, oh how often have I stood with my ears up to the iron grated door of my cell and listen to hear the tramp of the chaplain's feet as he left my lonely cell. The tread of his very feet seemed to sound like music upon my ears. How lonesome, sad, and pensive I'd feel again when he was gone. No wonder the old prophet struck up a song and said, How beautiful are the feet of those that brings glad tiding upon the end of their tongues?[72] Thus have I stood and listen at my door till the last tread of the chaplain's feet died away in the distance. . . .

IT WAS A bright mid summer's day, as I was marching from the table, that I casted my eyes on three young men who had just come in. Taking a close side look at the middle man, whose face I had recognized before, I found that it was Iverson, the man who had been the means of sending me to a dark and a gloomy prison. With a burning passion I long to get a chance to speak to him, but I found it impossible on account of the relief keepers, who was sneaking and peering around to catch every convict they could a talking. Four months had passed away before I got my opportunity to speak to Iverson. We were then both patients in the hospital, and as my bed was right next to his, we both had a good opportunity of talking to each other.

"My God, Iverson," said I, "is this you?"

"Yes, my boy, this is me," said Iverson. "For heaven sake, Rob, don't betray my right name. You must now call me by the fictitious name which I came here by."

"And what name is that?" said I.

"Halsey Thomas,"[73] said Iverson.

Hell and damnation, said I to my self. I remember the youth now. He was once a boy with me in the House of Refuge. By the Heavens, why didn't I betray the scoundrel in the court House and have his oath rejected? The scamp, I have known him to be a thief and a burglary from his boyhood. Fool, fool, accursed fool that I was. Why didn't I betray the scamp, and I wouldn't been here a mingling with the young villain today. But as it was forever too late to betray you now, Iverson, to the policeman, let us have a little chat together, for now is our time, and the curtain of darkness is covering the land.

"Well, Rob, didn't know me when we sat together in Miss Mutermer's House, eh? Didn't know that you and me had both eaten at one table and work in one shop down to the House of Ref, eh? Didn't know that when you sat in the court House? I knew you, Rob, but you didn't know me. But pawn my old coat, Rob," said Iverson, "if ever I thought they'd set you a sailing down here. Cursed fool you was, Rob, to take the blame of that dam infernal little w— and come down here to prison to pass a poor, miserable life. Why didn't you let the trial go on, and I would throwed the dirty little bitch in a dark and a gloomy prison and cleared you from the scrape altogether?"

"Never mind, Iverson," said I. "I have only a few more months to stay, then I rush out into the world again to mix and mingle with old companions."

"Well, Rob, God help you, boy. I wish I was goin' with you," said Iverson, "for I know where I can make a crack of ten thousand all in gold—but my complaint is so bad that I am afraid that I shall never see the outside of them walls again."

There Iverson and I laid, a talking till the late hour of midnight. The scoundrel unfolded to me the cracks and burglaries he had made, and the pistols he had loaded and discharged at travelers, and bodies he had laid cold and sunken with stones beneath the watery waves, and closed up his dark catalogue of crimes by telling me how he came to get here in prison. Iverson was about the age of eighteen and in good circumstances when I last saw him. He had been up to Buffalo and spent his money in the House of infame, and frequenting those places of hell until he became the prey of a deadly disease— lost his gold watch, his character, his reputation—committed a crime which brought him to a gloomy prison, and there he stood with me right smack upon the platform of misery and an inmate with me in a dark and a gloomy prison.

THE DEEP PRINT of shame and misery was stamped deep into my face, and I bore the shameful marks of Cain upon my forehead, and the curse of a fugitive and a vagabond was printed deep upon my brow, and I was yet the inmate of a gloomy prison.

"Pick up that piece of meat, sir. Do you hear me? Pick that piece of meat off of the floor," said an officer to me one day, as I sat at the table and threw a piece of meat on the floor which I did not like. As he said them words, he brought the heavy weight of his cane across my head, which caused my head to hum for some minutes after.

"Take that boy and consign him away to the dungeon," said one of the officers.

"Yes, you dam black hearted curse," said I. "Does the inspectors allow you to rap men over their heads with your canes and break their skulls in?"

"Do you hear me?" echoed the hoarse voice of the Keeper again. "Do you hear me? Take yon boy and lock him up." Two officers stepped up to me and took me by the coat collar and led me away to the dungeon.

"I have suffered enough through your tyrannical hands," said I, "and I am not a goin' to stand it any longer."

"Shut up, sir. Shut up, or I'll knock your brains out with my cane," said one of the officers.

"You darest, you dare face looking devil you? You daren't," said I, as I drew a knife from my bosom, which I had concealed.

"I'll tend you by and by, young boy," said a heavy looking tyrant.

"This dungeon, sir, is lighter than your black hearts," said I, in madness—"and your hearts and cruel deeds is darker than this dungeon, and your characters is blacker than your hearts."

"Present that knife, sir, into my hands," said the officer.

"I won't, sir," I replied. "I will present it to your heart, you black hearted villain," said I, while madness came flashing in my breast like a flame of fire and took possession of my whole soul and body.

"Unlock yon dungeon door," said Esq. Cook as he approach my dungeon door, with the chaplain at his side.

"The knife," said the officer.

"I won't, by the Heavens, I won't give it up."

"The knife, or I'll strike you dead on the spot," said the officer, as he raised his cane to strike me.

"Stand back," said I, "or I'll plunge you to the heart."

"Close in on him," said Esq. Cook, and as he said these words, one of the officers made his way towards me—and I stood my ground, with my knife drawn in my hand, refusing to give it up.

"The pistol," said one of the officers. Esq. Cook presented the pistol into the under officer's hand, who cock it and threaten to blow my brains out in two minutes if I didn't deliver the knife into his hand.

"Hold. Hold. Stand back," said the chaplain as he rush forwards and stood between me and the officer. "I ask you, in the authority of these officers," said the chaplain, "for that knife, and I hope that you will deliver it into my hands."

The kind and tender words of the chaplain brought the knife from my hands into his. Esq. Cook ordered the officer to take me from the dungeon and consign me away to my cell, where I might have a chance to see the chaplain, and reflect on my past conduct, until he got ready to tend to me.

"What did I tell you, Esq.?" said the officer, as he slammed my door to and turn the key on me. "What did I tell you? Didn't I tell you that yon boy would become an harden convict if he was left to himself? It those cursed and infernal inmates," said the officer, "that have been a blowing their silly tales in his ears, and their cunning influences have been playing and shadowing over his mind."

As the officer said these words to Esq. Cook, the Esq. ordered me to take my bible down from off my shelf and sit down in one corner of my cell and reflect on my past conduct until he had time to take my case in hand. I took my bible from my shelf, and with all my might I dash it to the floor and pick it up and tore it in a thousand pieces and tramp the leaves under my feet. Ah, thou precious old book, how often have I thought of thee. I tremble with fear every time I think of thee, and fear that every rag of thy contents which I trod under foot will rise up in the judgment day and condemn me.

Having nothing more to do, and no more injury to commit on the state, I sat in one corner of my cell and covered my face with both hands and gave way to a full flood of tears and silent reflections, and these was my reflection—that I entered the prison with my mother's prayer printed upon my lips and my father's blessings upon my head, endown with good reason and an ample store of good education, but you, ye dare face looking devils, have whip my mother's prayers from my lips into curses, and beaten my father's blessing from my head with a heavy hickory club, and took away from me all the good reason which God had endowed me with.

"Oh, cruel and wicked wretch of a boy," said the chaplain, as he approach my iron grated door, and saw the leaves of my bible torn and scattered on the cell floor. "Oh, cruel wretch," he echoed the second time. "How could you be so wicked and cruel to tear up your bible, and to destroy the richest treasure that is given you here within the walls of a dark and a gloomy prison? Wicked wretch, the day is a coming when you will have to answer for every word of that sacred book which you have trodden under your feet."

As the chaplain said these words, I bursted in a flood of tears, and with a quivering lip I told the chaplain that it was those hard hearted officers that had made me hard and cruel, and that they was preparing me for higher crimes and making me to become the fit subject of the gallows.

Givin' me a few words of good advice, he turned from my dark and gloomy cell and left me to reflect over the scene that laid scattered at my feet. Oh, the horrors of that day came heaving in my breast as I paced my cell backwards and forth, with large drops of tears a dripping from my eyes. Cruel and wicked wretch of a devil, said I to myself in a burning rage of anger, after I had mused over my folly. Wicked and infernal scamp of a boy, you have destroyed that humble old monitor that learnt you A, B, C, torn and trampled under your feet the good counsels it has given, and thrown away your day of grace. Humble and precious old book, said I to myself, with tears dropping from my eyes. Humble old fellow, thou pled and counseled with me under the roof of that humble old cottage of my childhood and birth, and when I left the land of my nativity, thou followed me to a dark and a gloomy prison, and now I have rendered the evil for good. Wretched and wicked, cruel and black hearted wretch, when thou closes thine eyes in sleep the contents and the counsels of that precious book shall haunt thee like a thief in the night. When thou art toiling and laboring under the burning heats of the sun, the thoughts of thy bible shall pierce thy heart like a dagger. When the cold night of death shall over take you, and the messenger of death shall extend his frosty hand to lead thee up to judgment, then the leaves of thy bible will be there as a witness against thee, and a voice louder than ten thousand peals of thunders will say, Where is that book you threw away?

The prisoner confined in his cold gloomy cell
far, far from the friends that hath love'd him so well
he sits thinking in silence on scenes of the past
His heart full of grief and the tears falling fast.

Alone in his sorrows with none to condole
How sad the regrets that embitters his soul
he mourns on the Hour that he first went astray
and yielded his heart to the tempter's vile sway.

oh now is the time to extend him your hand
to snatch from extinction the still burning brand

yes, now is the time while his heart is yet warm
to list to his yearnings and whisper reform.

ah, could you have thought that when kindness was soft
that neglect and illtreatment would harden too oft
that cut off from all virtue a man will in time,
Sit brooding on vice and preparing for crime.[74]

'Twas a fine beautiful mid summer's Sabbath morn, when the
town clock was striking the hour of eleven, that an ugly, dare face
looking officer came up to my cell, and unlocking my door, he ordered me to follow him to the south wing. Keeping close behind the
officer, with my hands tied in front of me, I followed him until we
reach the south wing, where stood Esq. Cook and another dare face
looking villain, with pistols in their hands. Untying my hands, the
officers ordered me to pull off my cap and stand two spaces back and
give an account of my misbehavior at the table.

I stood a trembling boy before them, not knowing where to commence or what to say.

"You have nothing to say," said the second officer, "nor no reason
to give why this pistol shouldn't be discharged at your heart, and
send you across that vast ocean whither no mortal is ever permitted
to return again?"

As he said these word, he presented the pistol at my breast, and
was about ready to fire, when the voice of the third officer ordered
him to hold a moment. "You," said the officer, "are a bad boy, and
leading a poor and a miserable life. You are listening to the silly
yarns of the older inmates and following their devilish deeds and
learning their bad examples. You are bringing pain and misery upon
yourself and preparing for the gallows as fast as time can let you. You
have learnt the miseries and the iniquities of the prison, and you are
the ring leader of every vice and crime that prevails within the prison.
You tore your bible to pieces and tramp the leaves of it under your

feet. You put forth words out of your mouth which will rise up in the judgment day and condemn you. You are bringing sorrow upon yourself, and the gray hairs of your mother down to her grave. The crack of this pistol will end your career forever, and will send you to that land where you will never see no more trouble.

"Are you ready to resign yourself in the hands of dissolving nature?" said Esq. Cook.

"No, sir," I replied, as a deluge of tears came streaming and flowing from my eyes.

"Be ready," said the third officer, "for in five minutes thy soul shall be a sailing across that vast sea of eternity which you will never cross again."

"Three minutes more, sir, is allotted you, and thy mortal soul shall take its everlasting flight. Are you ready, sir?"

"One moment, sir, if you please," said I, as I threw my arms around Esq. Cook's neck, and with tears and loud sobs begged him to spare my life.

"Your life, sir, is in the hands of yon officers, and it is for them to decide the question."

"Stand back, and the crack of this pistol shall decide the question, and ere two minutes shall roll o'er thy head the death tale shall be told."

Again did I fall down upon my knees and clasp my hands together, and begged Esq. Cook to save my life, for I knew it was in his power. As I arose from my knees, the three officers stepped one side and held a long conversation and concluded to give me a severe punishment with the cats. After consulting together for more than an half hour, the officers ordered me to follow them to the kitchen. On my arriving in the kitchen, I saw several officers a standing on the desk awaiting my arrival, and among them was Mr. Hard Heart, Mr. No Feelings. Mr. Cruel Heart, Mr. Demon, Mr. Fiend, Mr. Love Torture, Mr. Tyrant, and Mr. Cat Bearer, all consulting together to see whose duty it should be to inflict a punishment upon me with the cats, according to the decree of the Warden. After consulting the matter over, the bloody duty fell upon Mr. Cat Bearer, while Mr. Love Torture stood by to keep count of how many heavy blows I got.

"Off with your shirt, sir," said Mr. Cat Bearer in a rough and an ugly tone of voice. "Off with it, sir," said he. "I am goin' to kill or cure."

Stripping off my shirt, the tyrannical curse bounded my hands fast in front of me and ordered me to stand around, turning my back towards him. He threw sixty-seven lashes on me, according to the orders of Esq. Cook. I was then to stand over the drain while one of the inmates wash my back in a pail of salt brine. After passing through this kind of treatment, I was taken back to my cell by one of the officers and lock up.

Reader, would you like to know the feelings and the effects that those tormented little creatures haves upon the back? When throwed upon the back of the sufferer, they sting like the prick of a needle, and when sunken in very deep, the sufferer feels as though he had been bitten by the bite of a dog or been scratch by the paw of a cat. The cats are made of cat gut strings, with a little knot tied at the ends, and wounded at the ends with a small thread wire.

'Twas a pleasant day in the month of September, as I sat by the bedside of Iverson in the hospital, that the rolling of his eyes and the heavy beats of his breast seemed to tell me that the hour of his dissolution was drawing to a close, and that death couldn't be standing at a far distance. The cold shake of his hand and the quivering lips of the dying boy seemed to tell me all at once that the cold night of death was fast approaching, and there was but a step between him and death.

"Iverson," said I, "you are goin' fast, and a few moments more, and you will be sailing across that wide ocean, which you will never cross again."

"Yes, Rob," said the dying boy. "I feel the clumsy hand of death to work at my castle now, and ere the midnight hour he will have it torn to the ground, and my spirit will go a sailing down the cold streams of death, until it enters in the presence of him who gave it. How hard, how clumsy and heavy the old fellow's hand feels upon me," said the dying youth. "Hand me a drink," said Iverson, "that I may cool my parched tongue and burning lips."

I handed the youth a cup of cold water, and the threads of life began to be snapping fast.

"Iverson," said I. "How do you feel?"

"I feel," said Iverson, "the burning pains of Hell a gnawing my soul. Death, death—eternal death," said the dying boy. "Eternal death, pain and misery shall be my portion forever."

Again did I take the cold icicle hand of Iverson, and told him that the mystery of that mid day robbery that was committed under the roof of Miss Mutermer would shortly be brought out into the open day light, and that I was the innocent sufferer of that mid day's robbery.

"Wish I was dead," said Iverson with a blasphemous oath, "and sailing down the stream."

"You wicked wretch you, Iverson," said I, "how dare you utter such blasphemous oaths and wishes when you are on the very brink of that stream which lies open to you view?"

"Give me another drink, Rob," said Iverson, "and I'll drink in honor of your health."

I handed the cursed wretch another drink, and his eye balls began to roll and flash like a streak of lightning, and the signs of death stood a blazing in his face. "Hell and damnation," said Iverson, as he grasped the old companion of his boyhood up and dashed it to the floor. "Take that bible out of my sight." And the fiery looking eyes of Iverson, which was mingling with blood, gave another glance at the bible which he had dash to the floor, and the dying youth turned on his back, and a convulsive sobs and groans, bitter cries, blasphemous oaths, Hells and damnations proceeded from the lips of the dying Iverson. A heavy heave, a loud and a mournful groan, a horrible yell of murder, and the youth stretch himself out and expired, while his soul launch upon that little bark which was to buoy it in the presence of him that gave it—and his body was given into the hands of the dissectors. Thus died Iverson, within the walls of a gloomy prison, under the fictitious name of Halsey Thomas.[75]

As I STOOD a leaning against a pile of boards one day in the month of September, and bathing myself in the sun, I was accosted by two venerable looking gentlemens whose looks bespoke good nature, and whose hearts seemed to beat with pity and sympathy towards me.

"What a pity, what a pity!" shouted the silvery haired gentleman, "what a pity it is that you are leading such a hard and a miserable life, bringing cruel tortures and punishments upon yourself, and listening to the advices of those that rejoices over your punishments and illtreatments. Hast thou a father?" said Mr. Parsons.[76]

"My father," said I, "lays cold and silent in the grave."

"And thy mother?" said Mr. Hewson.[77]

"My mother," said I, a pointing with my finger toward the land of my birth, "was alive when I left the land of my childhood."

"Alas," said Mr. Hewson. "How wretched must she be, and this night perhaps she will be a weeping for thee."

As these two gents mention the parental names of my father and mother, a flood of tears gushed from my eyes, and I wept before them like a child, for I was yet young and tender in years. There I stood, before these two gentleman who appeared to befriend me and sympathize with me in my deep sorrows and distress. No whipping cats nor torturing stocks, no gloomy cells nor lonesome dungeons, no time nor distance can eradicate or mar the sorrows of that day from my heart. No dare devil nor no tyrant can make me forget the day that I stood, a trembling youth, before Mr. Parsons and Mr. Hewson.

"Be careful," said Mr. Parsons, "that you ain't led away again by the cruel hands of your inmates and have to suffer under the rod."

"Wicked little wretch," said Mr. Hewson, "you tore the companion of your youth and guide up and tramp it under your feet. Thou little black hearted devil, the voice of thy companion will cry to thee out of the ground until the day that thou goest down to thy grave."

With a quivering lips I took up the words of Cain and said, "My punishment is more than I can bear."[78]

"Ugly and hard hearted boy, hast thou not learnt that the way of the transgressor is hard?"

"And the rod," said Mr. Hewson, "was made for the fool's back."

"Yea, and the wicked," said Mr. Parsons, "shall be beaten with many stripes. Awful, awful, alas awful will be your doom, at the day of judgment," said Mr. Parsons, "if you don't lead a different life."

"I think that we have given him crumbs enough out of that sacred old volume that lays on my table at Home," said Mr. Hewson, "for I see they begin to choke him and makes the tears come out of his eyes."

As he said these words, I wipe the tears from my eyes with my coat sleeve and went into the shop with a determination to do better during the remainder of my time in the prison. As I entered the shop door, I met with just what I expected from the inmates, and nothing but scorns and sneers and derisions was my companion during the working hours of the day. Long will I remember that good old gentleman Mr. Parsons, and long will I honor the gray hairs of Daniel Hewson. Many has been the long and lonesome nights when I have woken from my sleep and thought of the good counsels that was given to me on that September's day by Mr. Hewson and Parsons, and when lock in a dark and a gloomy cell, my thoughts has wander back to the counsels of that good old man that now lays a sleeping and slumbering beneath the cold clods, and these have been my thoughts—

Wonder if the venerable old man is wearing that starry crown, and dressed in that long and white robe a coming down to his feet. Wonder if he is got the golden harp and timbrel in his hand, and striking up one of those new songs which no dare devil on earth can never learn. Wonder if the venerable old man is veiling his face and falling down with the four and twenty elders, and givin' his homage to him that sits upon the throne forever and ever. Wonder if he is walking upon that sea of glass and drinking from that crystal stream, while his bones lays bleaching beneath the sands. Rest, Mr. Parsons, rest, till thy bones shall crumble away to the last sand, and peaceful may thy slumbers be, until that last morn shall beam on the world and the last sun shall set in the west.

THE BEAUTIFUL AND bright Sabbath morn of my liberation came at last, and on the first day of May in 1842 the officer came to my cell and unlock the door and led me to the wardrobe, where I changed my streaked clothes of disgrace and appeared before the clerk in a neat suite of citizen's clothes, and a little bundle under my arm which contained one shirt and one pair of socks. Two other unfortunate devils who had come to prison with me was standing at my side,[79] a gazing out of the window into the streets, while the clerk was asking me the following questions—

"What is your name, sir? Where are you from, and what is the judge's name that sentence you? How long did you come for, and what was the crime that you was charged with? Were you guilty of the charge? Were you ever in a prison before, or in a county jail? Was you ever fined? Have you a wife and children? Have you a father or a mother a living? Did you have a trade before you came to prison? What employment did you follow when you was out, and what was you doing when you was arrested? Have you an education? Could you read or write when you first entered this dark and gloomy castle? Are you a temperate?"

"Yes, sir, Mr. Clerk, thank God, I can look you right plump in the face and eyes, and without a blush in my face to condemn me or to betray me, I can say that I am a temperate man—and I'll challenge the tallest angel in heaven to come down and swear in the presence of him that sits upon the throne forever and ever and say that he ever seen me dip my lips in the intoxicated bowl."

After the clerk had ask us the above question, he handed us a pen to sign our names on a scrip of paper and gave us the following advice—

"Be careful, boys, and don't fall into any bad company that will bring you back here to prison. Remember that you can never commit a crime without being detected, and the all piercing eye of God watches every movement you make." With these words, he pays the convict money enough to take him back to the land of his friends and Home, and the poor devil with blazing eyes and a cheerful heart rushes out into the open streets and stand there to look and to be look at. As Mr. Smith the clerk handed me the portion of money that was allotted to me,[80] he held out a little testament in his hand and bade me to take it and read it and follow its precepts and choose it as the man of my counsel.

"Hast thou a mother?" said Mr. Smith.

"My mother was alive, sir," said I, a pointing with my finger towards the scene of my childhood and birth, and with tears a streaming from my eyes, "was alive when I left my native land."

"Alas," said Mr. Smith. "How wretched must she be." He then made a long pause and added, with tears in his eyes, "Go return to thy mother, that thy mother may yet have pleasure when she sees the sun arise in the morning and the trees blossom in the spring. Go cheer the broken heart of thy mother, and wipe away the deep stain which you have stamp upon her brow."

Handing me a letter, I plunged forth into the open street, and shouldering my little bundle, I began my Homeward march. Oh, how my heart beat highly with joys and my eyes beamed with gladness as I tramp towards the land of my nativity. On the fourth day of May in the year 1842, I touch the latch of the old cottage door under whose roof I had been sheltered in the days of my infancy. The sun was just a setting in the west as I opened the cottage door, with the marks of trouble and care printed deep upon my brow and the blooming heats of boyhood and youth a glittering in my face.

"You look as though you had seen a heap of trouble, my son," said an elderly woman, as she arose from her seat and threw her arms around my neck and printed a mother's kiss on my cheek, and a flood of tears bursted forth from her eyes, and her tears came dripping down upon my shoulder. "You have fetch this punishment all upon yourself," said my mother, as I stood a weeping before her. "For the future, my son, I pray you never to forget your father's parting words, and the prayer and the advice of your afflicted mother."

As I entered the bedroom, I opened the letter which I had got at the prison and found that it was written to me shortly after I entered the prison, and had been directed in care of the chaplain. The letter had been written by my old companion Strongman, who was an inmate with me in the House of Refuge and had made his escape with me to Harvest Straw, and sign by the fictitious name of James Hawkins.

Reader, those was the dark and gloomy days when gross darkness hovered over the prison, and the prisoners sat in one total darkness of ignorance and heathenism. Those was the dark days when no prisoner was allowed to write a letter to his friends or to make one single mark with a pencil, and though the Honorable Wm. H. Seward was chief justice of the state, yet he in all of his power couldn't grant the prisoner the privilege of writing one kind word Home to his friends, though they laid at the point of death. Those was the dark and lonesome days when the convict had no library books to read, nothing but his bible and tract, and if he wanted to kill time during the long summer days, he must take his bible or tract from his shelf and wear away the long and lonesome hours that came a hanging on him like a heavy weight by reading them. The convict had no slate and pencil to kill time with, nor did he dare to have a knife in his possession to whittle time away. Ah, Reader, those was the dark and cruel days when young Plume was stripped stark naked and laid across the bench with his hands tied to the floor, and received such a severe punishment with the cats that he expired a few days after. Them was the days when the prisoners' backs was cut and lacerated with the cats till the blood came running down their backs.

Many was the nights that the prisoners returned to their cells with their backs cut and hacked up with the cats, and cursing and damning their makers and uttering hard and horrible oaths, until the bell rung for them to swing their hammocks. I have heard horrible and bitter groans ascend up from those low cabins. Painful sighs and heavy groans came beating upon my ear from some poor inmate below me or next to me. Again the loud cry of vengeance has been heard a speaking in the midnight hour, as the prisoner laid in a half dream of sleep and murmuring over to himself the illtreatment which he had passed through.

THOUGH IT MAY seem strange to the reader, yet truth is stranger than fiction, that the inmate of the prison never receives one soft word of kindness from the officers, from the day he enters the prison until the day he is discharged. His only friend and adviser is the chaplain, who welcomes him with a visit after he is shut up in his cell at night. How glad the humble old sinner feels, the morning of his sentence expires. With what joy does he hail that beautiful and delightful morning, as it comes a bursting forth from the east. Poor down cast and broken hearted devil, how his eyes glistens as he enters the hall to get his discharge.

Poor miserable old wretch you, when you first entered the prison, you thought that you would never see the outside of that front gate, eh? You thought that you must close them weeping eyes of yours in a dark and a gloomy prison, eh, old fellow? But the long wishful day has come at last, and the day has opened with a bright and a dazzling prospect before you. Your long nights of sorrow has swept away in a mid summer's sun shine. But, old fellow, let me tell you, before you go, that you have the deep print of a state prison mark stamp upon your brow, and with that mark you have got to face a cold, frosty world, for the avenger of blood will be close upon your heels, and the marks and prints of Cain will betray you wherever you go.

"Cash over, cash over, clerk, and let me be a making my tracks towards the happy Home of my boyhood and youth. Cash over, and let me leave this gloomy old palace. I say, clerk, is this all the money you give to a poor old wretch like me who has work hard for five years in a gloomy prison?"

"Yes, sir, that is all," says the clerk.

"Hardly enough to push me Home. How long before the next train goes, clerk? Ah, I hear the bell ring, so fare you well, clerk, I am bound for Home."

"Halloo there, old fellow, the chaplain wants to see you before you go."

"Can't stop now. Can't stop. Homeward bound."

"No, but come and see what he wants. May be he may say something to you that may do you some good, or he may have something for you which may give you a push out in the busy world."

"Good God, I can't stay, can't stop a minute. Been away from Home five long years, and the old woman expect to see me bounding through the gate today."

"So, old Hawk, you won't listen to what the chaplain got to say, eh?"

"Can't stay. There's the cars ready to start now. So farewell to you, and God bless you."

"You wicked old curse you, you had ought to been stretch upon the gallows with Peter years ago and hung with the same suspender that he hung himself with, for I believe that you are a hard, cruel hearted old curse."

"Well," says the old fellow, "if I am hard, I have been harden within the walls of a gloomy prison, and if I am cruel, I have learnt it within the walls of a gloomy prison, for 'sthere where cruelty, pain, shame, and misery dwells."

As the old fellow speeds his way, he touches the gate which he swung with his own hands one Sabbath morn just five years ago. He looks around and he see a deep hole in the fence where the musket ball lodged one Sabbath morn when he was firing at a mark just five years ago. Onward he tramps, towards the House, and he treads over the little mound that he dug and laid a sweet little angel in it just five years ago. He approaches the door, and his clumsy old hand gives a thrill knock, and the strange voice of a female bids him enter. He looks around and finds that strangers has taken possession of his House, and his sweet angeled wife lays covered with sods beneath the ground.

With tears in his eyes, he inquires for the spot where lays the mortal remains of the wife of his bosom. Gazing among the unfrequented knolls, he see a new made grave, with a withering turf that marks the sacred spot where lays the mortal remains of his angeled wife. Weeping over the silent spot for a moment, he sits himself down at the head of the grave, where lays all that was once fair and beautiful as an angel, and he kisses the green sod that covers all that was once sacred to him. As he leaves the sacred spot, he has the marks of grief stricken upon his brow, and the heart of the wicked wretch is ready to burst and bleed.

Looking back on the scenes of his boyhood and youth, he remembers a rich old farmer that lives a few miles up the country, that has a rich store of gold hid away in the old pine chest. With a firm resolution to grasp the glittering treasure, he presses his way on towards the lordly looking mansion until he comes within sight of the roof. He then makes his way to a patch of woods and hides himself till darkness begins to cover the land. Then he begins the cruel deed of plunder and robbery under the cover of darkness, until the heavy hand of the officers is laid upon him, and he becomes the inmate of a dark and a gloomy prison again.

Let us now follow the unfortunate wretch to his gloomy Home, where he will have to sit down in sorrow and plough through a long term of years.

"Well, old fellow, back again, eh? How long did you get this time, old man?"

"Three and half."

"Is that all, old fellow?"

"Yes, and I wouldn't got that if the court hadn't bribed the judge, and the judge bribed the jury."

"Old man, I don't understand your meaning, exactly. Suppose you explain yourself a little plainer."

"Well, sir, I mean to say that the jury was prejudice against me, and was bribed by a pack of hounds, and without judge or jury I was dispatch off to a dark and a gloomy prison, and here I am consign for three and a half."

"God bless you, old man, I feel sorry for you and sympathize with you in your sufferings, although I am goin' under the same discipline and illtreatments that you will have to go through. Well, old chap, being that we have got our galleries all swept off clean, and we are out of the sight and hearing of the officers, suppose we sit down here, and give me a little history of your adventures during the time that you was out."

"Very well, sir, I have no objections."

"Very well then, old man, begin your story—Hark, old man, I hear the footsteps of some officer. Let me see who it is. Ah, it's no one but the chaplain, a goin' around to see if each prisoner has a bible in his cell. So go on with your tale, old man."

"Well, sir, you remember the morning that I left this dismal looking old place?"

"Ah yes, old man, I do remember that bright and beautiful morn, when the sun was throwing his golden rays through our iron grated windows, and your heart, old man, beated highly with joys, and your eyes beamed with gladness, and you longed to reach the happy Home of your childhood and birth. Yes, old man, long will I remember that happy day. Proceed, old man, with your story."

"Well, sir, with only two dollars in my pocket, I rush out of the front gate and commenced my Homeward march. Between the hours of eight and nine I reach the happy cottage which I once use to own. As I gave a heavy rap at the door, I heard the strange voice of a female who bid me enter. I opened the door, and looking this female in the face, I found that strangers had taken possession of my House and lot while I had been gone from Home. The House and lot was under mortgage when I left, and after I came away the rap of the sheriff's mallet told the tale, and my wife was driven out of doors without a House or a Home or a friend in the world, and the poor creature died with a broken heart, and the affections of my bosom lays moldering away to dust. After takin' another look at the old cottage, I made my way to the grave yard, and with tears trinkling from my eyes, I saw the new made grave of my wife. Seating myself at the head of her grave, I wept like a child and moisten the green sods with my tears. Goin' along a little further, I stumbled o'er the grave of my little daughter, whose little remains has turned to dust long before this."

"Hold a little, old fellow, I must interrupt you for a moment. You say that you sat down o'er the grave of your wife and wept like a child?"

"Yes, sir, and I would have wept large drops of blood if I only could."

"Well, old man, I must confess that you have touch a soft spot in my heart now, for I remember the very day that my father was buried, that long after the sun had sunk behind the clouds that I sat all alone at the head of my father's grave and wept like a child, and I felt the effects and the lost of my father. Well, old fellow, proceed with your story."

"Well, sir, leaving those lonesome solitudes of the dead, I began to think about leaving for the distance west, where my father and mother lives, but not having one red cent in my pocket nor no means of getting to them, I was obliged to plunge hands into the treasures of a rich farmer who I knew in the days of my boyhood, and commit a crime which brought me back to this lonesome place."

"Well, old man, when the clerk ask you if you was guilty, what did you tell him?"

"Why, I told him no."

"Well, old man, was you guilty?"

"Guilty, yes, I was guilty as a dog."

"Well, old man, why didn't you stop and hear what the chaplain had to say to you that day you went out? Perhaps he might given your little craft such a push down the stream that you would never stopt till you had landed right in front of your father's door, and peradventure you wouldn't been back here today. Ah, old man, you acted the part of a fool. He called you and hollered to you to come back, but you refused his calls. Perhaps he might given you a God's blessing, old fellow, and that might been worth a hundred to you. Ain't you sorry, old fellow, that you didn't stop and hear what he had to say?"

"Indeed I am."

"Well, old man, when I leave this dismal old place again, I mean to leave it with the chaplain's blessings pronounced upon my head, and with that blessing I mean to keep as a prize and rush through this dark world with it till the day I go down to my grave. Old fellow, I believe that you are a harden old convict, for you don't seem to have any reflections about you at all."

"Reflections, sir? Why, my mind is drowned in reflections every night, when I enter yon lonesome cell."

"Well, what are those reflections?"

"Well, sir, in the first place, I remember that dark and chilly night when I had returned from a rum hole, where the song and the toast, the bowl and the midnight chorus, had been passed around. I staggered for Home. 'Twas a cold midwinter's night. The moon was throwing her silvery light in the streets. As I staggered a past the window of my House, I saw the angel form of my wife a standing at the window, and with strained eyes she was looking and waiting for my return. It was late, and the town clock had given the hour of one. There stood my wife, bathe in tears. Casting her eyes out of the window, she caught my figure, and with a scream and a shriek she plunged out into the street with her hair hanging o'er her face and with tears in her eyes. She begged me to come in the House and retire to bed, but as I entered the House, I caught her by the hair of her head and forced her from the door. Bolting the door, I staggered over chairs, tables, and stands until I reach the little crib where laid my innocent little daughter, folded in the arms of sleep. Takin' the little witch up in these clumsy hands of mine, I dash her to the floor and left her a bleeding in her gore."

"You cursed and infernal old black hearted devil you. State prison is too good for you, and now old man I believe that you have caused your wife and daughter to go down to their graves in sorrow."

Masturbation,[81] or The Demon of a Cell

I will now unfold the secrets and the habits of the prisoners and point out the man of masturbation to the reader, as he first enters the prison. Reader, enter the prison on some lovely morning between the hours of nine and ten, and you'll see some fifty or sixty fine looking young men with their hands up to their sides or up to their backs, and an old dirty piece of rag tied around their heads, strolling and making their way to the hospital to pay the Doctor their morning visits. Reader, watch them till they get at the head of the stairs, and the little devil makes a full halt and begins to examine his own pulse before he steps within the door. If he sees his pulse is in good order, he hits his elbow a hard rap against the wall, and then begins to feel of his pulse again, and with one hand up to his side and the other up to his head or back, he walks in and takes a seat near some post, where he begins to knock his elbow, till the officer calls his name to come up and be examined by the Doctor.

Watch his steps and ways, Reader, as he paces his way towards the Doctor, his head bowed and his eyes casted with shame towards the floor. With the marks and prints of masturbation printed deep under the lower brow of the eye, he takes his seat before the Doctor, who asks him the following questions:

"Well, sir, what's the trouble with you this morning? You seem to come up here every morning, and I am continually bothered with your morning visits. What's the trouble?"

"Doctor, I have a severe pain in my head and back. My head is continually dizzy, and before my eyes I see the quick flashes of stars and different shades of light. My back pains me awfully. I am continually sick at my stomach and feel very weak. Can you excuse me from labor today, Doctor?"

With a heart of feeling and an eye of pity, the Doctor examines the cursed little devil and then the dialogue commences between the Doctor and the infernal little wretch.

"How long," says the Doctor, "have you been here in prison?"

"Three months, sir."

"How long did you come for?"

"Two and a half, sir."

Looking the little devil in the eye again, he tells him that he is a boy of masturbation, and unless he stops the devilish game and practice, it will end his career in a premature grave. As the Doctor unfolds his crime and devilish deeds to him, the poor little curse denies it with an open face and declares that he has never been guilty of the deed since he has been in prison. Again the Doctor puts the question to the wicked little devil and asks him how old he is.

"Seventeen, sir."

While the Doctor is goin' through with this examination, the Warden happens to step in, and then the Dialogue begins between the two concerning this little demon who is still sitting before him. "Warden, I find that this young boy is a boy of masturbation, and if he don't stop it, he'll soon become a demon of the cell, and from thence he'll find an untimely grave."

"Doctor, are you sure that yon boy is a boy of masturbation?"

"Sir, I am just as sure of it as I am sitting here, and have the evidence of it under the lower brow of his eye."

"Well, Doctor, suppose you go on and prove to me that yon boy is a boy of masturbation."

"Very well, sir. Do you see that little blue streak under the lower brow of his eye?"

"I do, sir."

"Well, that's one sign of it, and those little shadows that comes a playing and flashing before his eyes is another sign of it, and unless he stops it, Warden, he'll become a demon of the cell, and all the doctors on earth and the tallest angels in heaven can't save him from a premature grave. I now give him over into your hands, with the hopes that he may quit the devilish crime and deed, for it takes away all of his good feelings, makes him weak and sick, takes away his reason which God has given him, and in after days he becomes crazy, and like a brute he lays down and dies. Into your hands I commit the boy, for I am tired of his every morning visits."

With sympathy the Doctor tells the demon to go down. Watch him, Reader, as he leaves his seat, and turning around to the Doctor he ask him if he won't administer a little medicine to ease his pains.

"I can't," says the Doctor, "give you anything this morning, for all the medicines on earth can't cure your disease."

With curses on the end of his tongue, he turns around and looks the Doctor in the face, and with madness he spits out his blasphemous oaths, which the poor Doctor haves to carry them on his shoulder and unload them in the street or lay them low at the foot of the bleeding cross.

I remember some years ago, as Doctor Briggs[82] stood in the center of the yard, that I step up to him, and pointing out one of these demons of a cell I ask him why yon fellow had that dirty rag continually tied around his head. The Doct. gave a smile and seemed to be taken with surprise when I put that question to him, but not knowing what I meant until I had told him the mysteries and the secret habits of the man, the Doctor bursted out in a loud laugh, which was just as much to say to me that truth is stranger than fiction. I have been the inmate of a gloomy prison for many a long year and endured hard labor, gone through all kinds of illtreatments and hard usages, and I will challenge the best Doctor on earth and the tallest angel in heaven to come and look me right plump in the eye and see if there is one single spark of masturbation a burning or beaming in my eyes, or the marks and the prints of it under my eye brow.

The Death of a Demon

"Murder, murder, murder, hell and damnation, take that devil away! Murder, murder, bring that infernal wretch to me till I lay him cold and senseless at my feet! Do you hear me? Bring him to me. He slayed my father, and with one stroke of his bloody hand he laid my sister cold at his feet, and betrayed the innocent blood of my sister. Bring the damn infernal wretch to me, that I may seek the revenge of my sister."

Reader, these are the bloody and horrible cries of the man of masturbation, who has made himself so low and practiced the devilish deed until he became a demon of the cell and suffering under the effects of insanity. Again the loud cry of "murder" goes up from his lonely cabin, and in a few moments more we find the officers a standing in front of his cell, a calling to the waiters to bring ropes, chains, handcuff, and straight jackets to bind the unfortunate wretch and make him fast, until they can get him to the hospital. Hear his bloody cries for vengeance as they are making him fast. Hear his doneful notes of pain, and see the big tears a rolling down his cheeks. Ah, see the heavy drops of sweat that comes dripping from his brow, and look at them eyes of his a flashing with blood and fire. Hear his sorrowful groans, and again his blasphemous prayers. Hear his bitter curses as he enters the hospital, and see his uplifted hand to give the Doctor a blow as he comes near to examine him.

Hark, and you hear the bloody cry of "murder" again proceeding from his mouth, while his eyes is reading over the dark catalogue that is written against him on the wall. He thinks he sees friends who has been laid in their silent graves for years, and he thinks he see a man's hand a writing down his dark character on the walls. Hark, and you'll hear him a striking up one of his old midnight airs. Hear his cursed calls for heaven to damn his soul and blast all of his future prospects. Hear him grunt and groan until you hear the heavy tramp of the

Warden's feet who has come to see what the trouble is. Reader, hear the sorrowful dialogue between the Doctor and the Warden again.

"What did I tell you, Warden, what did I tell you about yon boy? Didn't I tell you that yon boy would one day or another become a demon of a cell and go down to a premature grave? Didn't I tell you that insanity would one day or another take possession of the brain of yon boy? Ah, I remember—yes, Warden, I remember the very day that yon boy entered this prison, and his cheeks was as red and handsome as a rose. He was the fairest flower cup that ever I seen, just in the morning of life—but alas, alas, the withering hand of masturbation has snatch the blooming youth away."

"Doctor, can't you administer something that will restore him and ease his pains a little?"

"Warden, all the medicine on this side of the grave couldn't save him."

"Hark, I hear the heavy tramp of the avenger. There he comes, with the uplifted dagger in his hand, to strike the blow that never misses. How fast he wings his way. How sharp his dagger looks, and how eager he is to do the deed. Who art thou?"

"I am the angel of death."

"And what is thy errand, and who sent thee?"

"My errand is to plunge this dagger in the heart of yon demon. I was sent by Him in whose hand is the life and breath of every mortal. Stand back, give way till I enter."

"Hold, hold a moment, thou heavenly avenger."

"Nay, I cannot stop. Let me do the bloody deed and take my everlasting flight."

One stroke, and the deed is done. A heavy groan, a heave of the breast, and a curse from the mortal lips, and the dagger tells the last doneful tale, and the cursed wretch stretches himself out and dies, and his spirit goes back to him who gave it. Reader, this is the awful end of the man of masturbation, and the destiny of the demon of a cell. Ah, methinks I hear his bitter cries and his doneful notes. Methinks I hear his blasphemous prayers, and his spiteful looks. Methinks I hear his midnight songs, and in letters of gold I see the hand writing a standing against him, and on the walls I read his character and doom in large capital letters. Methinks I see the great drops of blood a dripping from the point of the dagger as the angel takes his everlasting flight. Yes, methinks I see the floor stained with the blood of a demon.

> Death has been here and borne away
> a brother from our side
> just in the morning of his bloom
> as young as me he died.
> Not long ago he fill'd his place
> and sat with us to learn
> but now he's run his mortal race
> and never can return—
> again.[83]

> I saw an unfrequented mound
> where weeds and brambles wav'd
> they said no tears had fallen there
> it was a demon's grave.[84]

Reader, I have now opened and unfolded to you the mysteries and the miseries of Auburn Prison during the year 1840, and the awful consequences of masturbation, which prevails among the inmates of the prison until this day.

The Dream

THE READER WILL remember that the glittering sun was just a setting in the west, and the curtains of darkness began to cover the globe, as I reach the happy Home of my childhood and birth. As I sat myself down by the side of my mother, I began to tell her of the pains and miseries, the hard usages and the illtreatments to which I had passed through, until the clock struck the hour of ten, and I retired to rest and fell in the arms of sleep and began to dream of the tortures and torments to which I had passed through during the two years of my confinement . . . and thus did I dream. . . .

I dreamed that I had just returned from a dark and a gloomy prison and was standing before my mother, and the tears came trinkling down her cheeks. I thought that I could not bear to see those warm tears of affection flow any longer without wreaking some revenge on him who had been the means of my long separation from my mother, although the infernal wretch's body laid cold and silent in the hands of the dissectors, who stood ready with their glittering instruments to dress the flesh from off his bones. . . . I thought that I disguised myself in the dress of a female, and taking a dagger in my hand, I thought that I opened the door and plunged my way out in the open streets. I thought that the night was very dark and cloudy and was suited to the purpose of my design.

I thought that after I had open the door and plunged into the open streets, that I pressed my way onward until I came in front of a lordly mansion and halted in front of the door. I thought, as I stood in front of that door, that I turned my face around in every direction to see if I could see the form of any humane being who might be on the watch, a watching the cruel deed to which my bloody hands was about to commit. . . .

Seeing no person, I thought that I gave a heavy rap at the door with the handle of my dagger, and a voice within said, "Who is there?"

"A female," I replied. . . .

I thought the bolt sprung and the door opened, and the form of a man stood trembling before me. I thought the man ask me what brought me to his door, so late an hour of the night. I thought, as he said them words, that I drew my dagger and plunged it to his heart, and he fell at my feet with the loud cry of "murder" proceeding from his mouth. I thought that I with drew the dagger, and pressing my foot upon his breast, I thought that I gave him another plunge, and ere before he could give the second cry of "murder," the villain laid dead at my feet.

Pressing my way through several departments of the House, I thought that I entered a bedroom where laid a female wrapped in a long white robe and folded sweetly in the arms of sleep. As I stood by her bed, with an uplifted and a drawn dagger in my hand, I thought that I look the innocent girl in the face, and she awoke and looked as pale as death.

"Who art thou?" said I as she opened her beautiful eyes.

"I am the wife of him whom you have just laid waste at your feet."

"Woman," said I, "the tale of this midnight hour shall be told in the darkest deeds of crime by the revenge of your blood." I thought as I said these words, she gave one loud shriek and scream of "murder," and I plunged the dagger to her heart, and one stroke of the cruel instrument told the lamenting tale of that midnight murder in one short hour. . . .

I thought that the smooth hand of a female passed gently o'er my brow, which caused me to wake from that tormented and cruel dream. . . .[85]

A Sequel to the Dream

TURNING OVER ON my side, I fell asleep and dreamed again. I dreamed that I made my way from that lordly mansion, with my clothes and dagger stained with the blood of an innocent female, and the blood of him who had been the cause of my separation for two years from those whom I loved, with my hands stained with innocent gore. I thought that I made my way to the police office, where I gave myself up as the murderer of two innocent beings. I thought that I was arraigned before the court and plead guilty of the horrible deed. I thought that I was taken to a prison and a gallows higher than Haman's[86] was prepared for me. . . .

I thought that I was mounted on the gallows high and was swinging between the heavens and the earth for the horrible and bloody crime which I had committed. I thought that my spirit took its everlasting flight in the presence of God and stood before his white milk throne. . . .

I thought that I saw a venerable looking man, seated upon the throne with a book in his hand. I thought that his hair was as white as the drifting snow and his face shone brighter than ten thousand suns. I thought that I saw my father a standing in front of the throne, a holding up a bible in his hand, and stood ready to be a swift witness against me, as I stood arraigned before the judgment throne of God. I thought the honorable judge ask my father if that was his son.

"Yes," said my father (a holding up a bible in his hand), "that is my son, and in his hands I gave him a price to get wisdom, and I left him a dying father's advice and prayer, and yet not withstanding all of this, he has slighted the blessing which I left him."

I thought, as my father said these words, he veiled his face and fell down before the throne with four and twenty elders, who was robed in long white dresses a coming down below their feet, and they struck up a beautiful song, saying "Thou art worthy, oh God, to receive blessings, honors, and glory."

Casting my eyes on the right side of the throne, I thought I saw one liken unto the son of God. I thought that he held both of his hands up to me and showed me the prints which the assassin had made, and pointing with his fingers towards his side, he showed me the wounds which the soldiers had made with their spears. . . .

Casting his eyes down towards his feet, me thought he showed me the marks where the murderers drove the rough spikes through his feet. Me thought I saw the tears come trinkling from his eyes as he showed me a cup mingled with vinegar and gall. Ah yes, me thought that I saw those large drops of sweat and blood come foaming from his brow as he said to me, "All this was for thee," and he turned to find a place to weep, and bowing his head he found a place under his father's throne, and there he spilt those tears for me. . . .

The honorable judge then held up a dagger and a female's dress, all stained with blood, and said that those were witnesses against me, for they was the robes and the dagger of that midnight murder. "Art thou guilty?" said he.

I thought that I told him that I was guilty and deserved the deepest ditch in hell. Me thought a cloven footed looking devil stood by my side, with a heavy chain in one hand and a large key in the other. Me thought I heard the honest judge say, "Take him, bind him hand and foot, and cast him into outer darkness."

Me thought, when the judge pronounced this sentence against me, that I said, "Amen, and amen." I thought that after my sentence had been pronounced, that this cloven footed devil bound me hand and foot and led me away through a waste and a barren land. Not a tree, not a shrub, not a rock or a stone nor one spear of grass was there to be seen through out that long journey to which we was travelling. I saw no humane beings through out that burning plain.

Onward and onward we pressed our way, while every once and a while the heavy peal of a thunder would strike upon my ears, and then a voice louder than ten thousand thunders would say, "And what, you knew your duty but did it not." Thus did that thunder like voice keep a pealing in my ears, until I reach the place of my destination.

Being tired and weary, me thought I ask the infernal wretch to let me sit down and rest. I thought, as I ask him this, that another peal of thunder struck upon mine ears and said, "And what, you knew your duty but did it not." And as the voice died away in the distance, I thought we came in front of a large hole that was dug in the ground, and I thought the old scamp pick me up and tumbled me in, head foremost. Methought I sunk some thousands of feet before I rose at the surface.

As I rose, methought I found myself in one vast burning lake of fire, mingled with brimstone and smoke. There I saw fathers and mothers, brothers and sisters, aunts and cousins, husbands and wives, parents and children, calling upon each other for one drop of water to cool their parched tongues and burning lips. I thought I saw husbands a clinging to their wives and children, and children a clinging to their parents, and calling for rocks and mountains to fall and cover their defenseless heads. . . .

Me thought I heard the doneful cry of millions upon millions, taking up the bitter words and saying, "The harvest is past, the summer is ended, and my soul is not save!" Me thought I heard another cry, mingled with pitiful cries and saying, "Oh that I had sought his favor!" And their doneful cries died away in everlasting pain and misery, and the tortures and the torments of that burning day heated me so hot that I awoke, and behold, it was nought but a dream.

The Death of Miss Mutermer, and the Journey to New York

Pause we here for a moment until I inform the reader the information which my mother gave me concerning Miss Mutermer, and what had happened to her during the two years to which I had been gone. My mother informed me that Miss Mutermer had become the inmate of the county House shortly after I had left, and there ended her days. . . .

As my mother said these words, a heavy clap of thunder came rolling over my head, and the heavens became as black as the sack cloth of hair. A gust of wind followed, and the boughs of every tree that stood around the little cottage made obeisance to every breeze that came a sweeping o'er their tops. The flash of lightning came swift across my face, and another peal of thunder brought large drops of rain a beating against the side of the little cottage and the window sashes.

"That thunder," said my mother, "puts me in mind of the voice of God a speaking to the rebellious sons of men."

As she said these words, another peal of thunder broke forth from the east and died pleasantly away in the distant west. A heavy deluge of rain descended upon the earth, and all nature seemed to be rapt in one eternal silence. For two hours did the rain continue to come down, and then a beautiful sun broke forth through the clouds and came a shining from the east, and the bow was seen in the heavens.

As my mother stood a gazing at these wonderful sights, I swung my coat across my arm, and taking the parental shake of the hand, my mother printed a kiss upon my cheek, and I started for the city of New York. As I turned down the little lane that led from the cottage, I took the last look of the roof of the little dwelling that once covered my head, and the big tears came a streaming from my eyes.

It was between the hours of nine and ten that I landed in the city of New York. As I was walking up Leonard Street, I met a slender looking youth whose countenance I thought I had recognized once before. Passing this beautiful looking youth I made a low bow to him and pressed my way up the city. The youth stopped a few moments, and casting his eyes closely upon me, he followed me some ten rods up the street. Meeting a colored man, I ask him if he could direct me to the House of one Miss Flinn who resided in the city. As I said these words, the ruby cheek looking youth came up to me, and grasping me by the hand, he shook it till I thought the very blood would spurt from my veins.

"You are a stranger to me, sir," said I.

"A stranger to you?" the youth replied.

"Yes, sir," said I.

"Have you forgotten me, Rob?" said the youth.

"I have, sir," I replied, "but your looks seems to tell me that I have seen you somewhere before. But where I cannot now tell."

"Don't you remember Mike Flinn?" said the youth.

"I do," said I.

"Well, this is me."

With a blasphemous oath upon my tongue, I ask the youth if he was the very Mike Flinn who had made his escape with Strongman, Nicholas Miller, and me from the House of Refuge.[87]

The youth swore pine and blank that he was the very boy, and went on to relate the story of our escape, and the sufferings to which we were in, the day that we made our escape. And also he related to me the kindness of Capt. Smith, who had took us on board of the steamer and conveyed us to Harvest Straw, where we was nursed by Mrs. Johnson and several other ladies. This story convinced me at once that the youth who stood before me was none other than Mike Flinn. Locking arm in arm, we strolled up the city until we reach the Sixth Avenue, and entering in a little cottage, I found myself once more under the roof of Mrs. Flinn.

As I took a chair, I ask Mrs. Flinn if she could give me any information concerning Strongman.

"Poor Strongman," said the woman, as big drops of tears stole down her cheeks. "Poor Strongman is no more."

Good God, said I to myself, what does the woman mean? Is she crazy, or what is it that causes those big drops to run from her eyes? What does the woman mean when she says he is no more? Does she mean to say that he is dead? "I do not understand what you mean, Miss Flinn," said I, "when you say he is no more. Will you please to explain yourself?"

"Yes, sir. I mean, Robert, that Strongman has kicked the bucket and is dead."

"Tell me, Mrs. Flinn," said I, "are you in earnest of what you say?"

"I am, Robert," said the woman, as she wiped the warm tears from her eyes. "He entered the Navy, and gave in his name James Hawkins, and fell in a fuss with one of the sailors, and struck him dead on the spot, and poor Strongman had to pay the penalty of that murder by swinging between the heavens and the earth."

As Mrs. Flinn said those words, I rose from my seat, and in company with Mike we pressed our way towards the Navy yard. As I entered the yard, I ask one of the sailors if there was a young chap in their crew by the name of Hawkins.

"No," said the sailor, "he has kick the bucket long ago and has gone down to David Jones' locker. And did you know Hawkins?" said the sailor.

"Yes," I replied.

"Where did you know him?"

"I knew him in the west," said I.

"And has he parents a living?"

"Yes," I replied, "he has rich parents a living somewhere in the west."

"Never came across a heartier boy in my life than Hawkins was," said the sailor. With an oath upon his lips, he swore that he would rather stretch the hemp himself than to seen Hawkins die the death he did.

Turning from this sad tale of pain and misery, I made my way out of the yard, with the painful thoughts that Strongman was now a mingling with the wretched and damned in Hell. I then began to think of the pains and miseries to which him and me had endured through the means of that black hearted Thom King, and the cursed and wicked oath which he uttered in my presence the last time I saw him. . . .

It was getting late in the afternoon, and Mike and me returned to the House of his mother's. Seating ourselves down, I began to ask Mike how the world had went with him from the day that we parted.

"Rough, Rob, I tell you it has went rough with me. I have met with many a storm, and many has been the tempest that has blown in my face, and many has been the trouble waves that has rolled o'er my head. And thank God I've bluffed through them all, and there ain't a hair in my head singed. I tell you, Rob, I've got a friend that sticks closer to me now than a brother."

"Who is that friend, Mike?" said I.

"Well, Rob, being we have got so deep in the conversation, I'll give you the whole story of my life since the day we parted."

Drawing my chair up close to him, he gave me the following narrative:

"Rob, I was a poor, miserable beggar, pinch with hunger and thirst and robed in the rags of shame and disgrace, and hadn't a place to lay my head, and I was obliged to go and hire myself out to an old farmer and feed swine, and my food was nothing but the husks which the swine did eat, and my lodging was in the hog pen with the hogs at night.[88] I thought it a very hard thing to rob the swine of their husks to satisfy my hunger, and one day as I stood in the hog pen, I examined myself from head to foot and found myself a sailing in rags. After takin' a close examination of myself, I gave a leap from that old filthy old pen and pressed my way towards my father's House. You have no idea, sir, how I look. I was covered with mud and filth and dangled in rags. I was a shame to let the old man my father see me, but I had made the resolution to return back Home to him and tell him just the truth of the whole matter and the condition which I had been place in. With this resolution, I took courage and pressed my way over hill, dale, and mountains, o'er lakes, rivers, and brooks, through muddy swamps and dark deserts. It was just about the eleventh hour of the day as I ascended the hill that look down upon the roof of my father's mansion. As I stood a gazing upon the little cottages that surrounded my father's House, I saw the hired servants a eating and drinking and having a plenty and enough to spare. There I stood, ashamed to let my father see me, but casting his eyes up towards the hill, he saw me and knew me, and with out stretch arms he flew towards me, and down the hill I ran, and the old man clasp me right in his arms, printed a deep kiss upon my cheek, and wash me with his tears."

"Well, Mike, what did he do with you then?"

"Well, he stripped me of my rags and put a new suite on me, put a ring on my hands and shoes on my feet, and we dined together. Rob, me and you have seen trouble enough, and now I bid you to arise and go and seek your father's face."

Mrs. Sibley[89] Presenting the Author with a Little Testament

'TWAS IN THE month of June 1842 that I left the city of New York and made my way Home. Stopping in Canandaigua, I entered the mansion of Mrs. Sibley, who by some means or another had found that I had been the inmate of a prison. Calling me towards her, she gave me a motherly advice and told me to shun the paths that leads to vice and crime and prepare myself to meet God in peace. As she said these words, she presented a little testament in my hand and bade me to read it night and day and keep it as the guide of my youth. Taking the little testament from this lady's hand, I put it in my pocket and bade her good bye, and commenced my way Home.

He Reaches His Home; He Sees the Tears Fall from His Mother's Eyes

'TWAS THREE O'CLOCK in the afternoon when I reach my Home, and as I entered the door, my mother flung her arms around my neck, and again she stamp the kiss upon my cheeks. "My son," said she, "I've been afraid that you had fell in with some bad company and found your way back to a gloomy prison." As she said these words, the tears came trinkling from her eyes, and a heavy load of grief laid loaded upon my heart. . . .

When in my early life and prime
I trod the paths of vice and crime
my mother's counsels I forsook
the evil road to crime I took.

When in my heart she tried to place
the gospel's truths and richer grace
the tears ran trinkling from her eyes
methinks I hear a mother's cries.

A voice from heaven to me did say,
"dear son that road's a crooked way
for sake the paths of crime and sin
and heavenly gates you'll enter in."

He Visits Nicholas Miller; He Becomes the Inmate of a Prison

'TWAS THE 27TH day of June in the year 1842 that I went up to Avon Springs, and there I saw Nicholas Miller, who had made his escape with me from the House of Refuge. Taking him by the hand, I informed him of Strongman and the horrible death which he died under. Thunder struck and amazed, the boy gave a loud cry of horror and distress which was mingled with tears.

Leaving Avon Springs, I returned Home and committed a crime which brought me back to a gloomy prison.

As I entered the prison, I found that the old shops had been all torn down, and new large brick buildings had been erected in their stead for the sole purpose of the convicts to labor in. A new library had been establish, and the convict had the chance of killing time by reading choice Histories. Every man that couldn't read or write or cipher was provided with a spelling book and slate and arithmetic and a lamp to study by during the long winter nights, and a teacher employed from the outside to teach those who couldn't read, write, or cipher. Novels had been circulated through out the prison by some means unbeknown to the officers. The convict was allowed to take down his hammock as soon as he got in his cell if he chose. The mode of punishing with the cats was abolish, and several different modes of punishments was got up. The convict was allowed to draw one plug of tobacco a week and have pockets in his clothes.[90]

For two months I lived up to the rules and regulations of the prison, and being angry one day, I took a chair and stove it to the floor. The officer called me up for it and ordered me to follow him to the dungeon. I told him that I wouldn't stir one step for him until I seen the Warden.

"The Warden has nothing to do with you, sir," said he. "I want you to go with me."

I told him plain and plump that I wouldn't go a step with him, and he drew his cane to strike me with. As he drew his cane, I sprung to my work bench and grasp a knife and told him if he laid the weight of that cane on me, I would plunge that knife through him. As I said these words, the relief officer sprang to the desk, and snatching a revolver, he presented it at me.

"Present that knife to me, sir," said he.

"I won't, sir," said I as I stood with the knife drawn in my hand.

"Present that knife to me, sir, or I'll level you to the floor with my cane."

"I won't, sir."

"Crack that pistol on him if he don't deliver that knife."

As he said these words, the relief officer demanded the knife from me, which I held on to until the Warden came. As the Warden entered the door, the relief officer said that he demanded that knife from me in the name and in the authority of the Warden.

"Warden or no Warden, sir, you can't have that knife." As I said these words, the Warden demand the knife from me, which I thought was no more than my duty to deliver into his hands, as he had the higher power in his hands. Handing the Warden the knife, he ordered me to follow him to the dungeon, which I did, and was kept there until the next morning.

The Author Is Put in Chains and Tied Up

THE NEXT MORNING, between the hours of nine and ten, three officers and the Warden came to the dungeon door, and looking in, the Warden ask me if my temper had got cool. I told him it had. He then ask me kind and gently what I thought of myself for acting in the way that I did towards my Keeper. I made no reply, for I had no good reason to give. It was that bad and devilish temper of mine which had led me astray. He then ask me if I didn't think that I deserved a severe punishment. I told him I did, and he unlock my cell and ordered me to follow him. I followed him to the state shop, and taking an heavy iron ball and chain, he made it fast to my leg and put a pair of handcuffs around my wrists and made me hold both hands up straight over my head, where he took a rope, and bringing one end through the handcuffs, he made it fast, and then drew the other end of the rope though a pulley until it brought me right firm upon my tiptoes and made the rope fast. In this tedious and tiresome condition I stood a crying with pain for two hours. At the end of two hours he unfasten the rope and let me loose, but kept the ball and chain on me for three weeks after. My hands was swollen so by the rope that I was not able to work for three weeks after. . . .

The Author Is Handcuffed and Buck upon a Barrel

"THIS WAY, SIR," said an officer to me one morning in a snapping and a snarling way. "This way, sir." I followed the gallows looking gentleman up to his desk, to see what he wanted of me so early in the morning. As I reach the desk, he ordered me to take off my cap and get upon that barrel.

"What now, sir, captain? What now, sir?" I repeated.

"Insolence to the foreman.[91] Get up there."

"Oh, well, sir," said I, "if that is all the kind of punishments that you are goin' to give me for insulting the foreman, I will give him a little of my sauce to eat every day, for he deserves it once and while."

"No words, sir. No words back," said the officer. "I won't hear no such talk as that."

As he said this, I sprung upon the barrel like a streak of lightning, and the officer put the handcuffs around my wrist and the stick under my legs, and went away and left me to condole and brood o'er my past conduct, and to become a spectacle to spectators who were passing through the shop most every hour of the day.

Look, Reader, what a pretty looking sight. That is a man buck upon a barrel, to be stared and gazed at by spectators.

For three hours I was kept in this condition, until the blood began to stop a circulating in my hands, arms, and legs, and I was forced to beg the foreman's pardon, and that settled the whole hash, and I was unloosed. . . .

The Author Is Put in an Iron Yoke

"This way, sir."

"What now, sir?"

"Come along, I tell you, and come this way."

"Can't come, sir, till the Warden comes through the shop."

"Very well, sir, stay where you are, and I bet you'll rue the day that you didn't come when I called you."

Ching a ling goes the bell for the waiter to come. In he comes, and in the twinkling of an eye the officer gives him his orders, and before the officer haves time to get the words out of his mouth, the waiter is on a run after the Warden.

Halloo, there comes the Warden, a strolling along with his heavy cane in his hand. Wonder what he'll do with me. Shower, I guess. By the infernal G—, he shan't throw a drop of water on my head till he hears my complaint. He's just as much a right to hear my complaint as he has the Keeper's, and he has got to do it, too, before he punish me.

After hearing what the officer has to say, the Warden gives a beckon with his hand for me to come to him. With the burning rage of madness I pull off my cap and dash it to the floor, and he begins to ask me what's the trouble now. I relate my story to him, and he tells me that I am reported for being very saucy to the foreman, and brings a million of other old indictments against me which I had committed two or three years ago.[92] He then orders me to submit myself to the punishments which the Keeper is ready to inflict upon me.

With the burning heat of madness I submit myself into his hands, and he loads me down with a heavy iron yoke and a fourteen weight ball attach at each end of the yoke. This I must wear until I beg the foreman's pardon and confess my faults to the Keeper and give him some good reason why I didn't come up to him when he first called me. With many tears and hard beggings, he takes the heavy burden off my neck, and I feel as weak as a child three days old.

Hear what the officer says, Reader, as he is taking that old Egyptian yoke off of my neck: "Bad fellow, sir, if you don't behave, we'll kill you here. You are the worst scamp that is in the prison. Don't know what to do with you."

And with these words and a thousand other threats he orders me back to my work. . . .

The Author in the Showering Bath

"I WANT YOU to follow me," said a rough hearted officer to me one cold winter's morning, as I stood shivering over the stove with cold. I followed the hard, cold hearted wretch, while he led me away to the showering[93] bath. I was well aware of what the officer wanted of me when he called me, and I prepared myself with a knife to plunge in his heart, the moment he under took to commit the cruelty upon me which he had intended to. He was an officer which I never liked, nor could I ever bear the sight of him when he'd be a passing through the shops.[94] I was determined to plunge a knife deep in his heart the moment I reach the showering bath, if a good opportunity was offered, and lay the cruel hearted wretch dead at my feet, and suffer in the hands and power of the law rather than to be haunted to death by this cruel and tyrannical Keeper.

As I reach the shower bath, there stood three officers with big heavy clubs in their hands, and Doctor Briggs to witness the cruel scene of treatment to which I was to pass through. Having reach the spot where the cruel deed was to be committed, the officer addressed me thus: "You are a hard, harden convict and the ringleader of every vice and crime. There's not a crime committed within the walls of the prison but what you dip your fingers into it and seem to have a part and a share of it. Now, sir, I am goin' to give you such a severe showering, here in the presence of Doctor Briggs and these other officers, that you will never forget till the day that you go down to your grave."

As the black hearted wretch said these words, he ordered me to strip off my clothes and get in the showering bath. As he ordered me thus to do, I drew a long dirk knife from my pocket, which I had concealed for the purpose of destroying his life the moment he attempt to stir a foot towards me, and told him that I was not a goin' in that showering bath to be illtreated by a G— D— set of drunken cruel hearted wretches.

Again did he order me to pull off my clothes and get in the showering bath. As he ordered me the second time, I drew the knife with all my might and made a desperate plunge at him, and would laid him cold and senseless at my feet in one moment's time, had not two heavy looking convicts sprung from one of the cells, where they had been concealed by the officers to interfere in the matter the moment I made a point. Grabbing me by the arm, the two convicts got around me, and two of the officers, and threw me down and tore the clothes off of my back and put me in the showering bath, where my hands head and feet were made fast, and then the cruel work commenced and did not stop (only at intervals for me to get breath) till I had received eleven barrels of water.

While this operation was goin' on, some dozen or more officers came down to see the cruel torture committed on me. After givin' me as much water as they thought that I could stand, they took me out of the showering bath, and made a ball and chain fast to my leg, which I had to carry for four weeks.

Reader, I hardly know what to say or what to call this little water craft. I think I must call her the *Conqueror*. I pity the passenger that ever steps on board of her, and when I see so many young men a taking passage on her, it makes me shiver and ache all over. She is a dangerous little craft to sail on, and the passenger who steps aboard of her is continually in danger of his life, or of getting his good reason lost. Woe unto the poor unfortunate passenger who steps on board of her, if has committed a heavy crime, for he will be sure to meet with a heavy tempest. But if his crime is a small one, a light gale blows up, and the poor unfortunate little scamp get off with a light showering. Glad is that poor man who is board of her, and expecting every moment to be lost in an ocean of showers, glad is he when she touches the harbor and lets her anchors drop. How his heart beats with joy, when he hears the captain give the orders to take in the sails. This little craft is conducted by the Warden of the prison, and he has the whole control of her, nor no captain darest take a passenger on board of her without his consent or without he's a standing by. . . .

The Author with an Iron Cap on his Head

"I HARDLY KNOW what to do with you," said an officer to me, as I stood by the side of another chap, a talking to him one day without the consent of the Keeper.[95] "I hardly know what to do with you. You are all the time a talking. Come this way till I put the cap on your head."

"No, sir," said I. "You can't put no iron cap on my head for talking."

"You won't put that cap on your head, sir?" said he.

"No, sir," said I, as I stood with a knife in my hand. "You can't crown me with no such royal diadems as that. I'd look well with an iron crown stuck upon my head, wouldn't I?" said I.

"You had better put it on," said the officer, "before I send for the Warden."

As he said them words, I stepped up and let him put the iron cap on my head, and I went off to my work bench a muttering over words of revenge to myself, with the knife still in my hand. Look, Reader, ain't that a handsome lookin' crown for a man to wear two or three days on a stretch. . . .

The Author in the Spread Eagle,
or Col. Lewis' Advice to Him

'TWAS A MID summer's day, when I was called by an officer to follow him over to the state shop, where hung a rope in the shape of a swing, which the convicts gave the name of a spread eagle. This spread eagle was a kind of a mode of punishing the convicts who disobeyed the rules of the shop. As I reach the state shop, the officer let down the ropes and made them fast to each wrist. He then tied one end of the rope around my ankle, and taking hold of the other end, which was made fast in a pulley, he began to hoist away until both of my arms was stretch out at full length, and then made the rope fast to a staple that was drove in the window. Taking hold of another rope, he pulled on that until it brought my leg up straight about two feet from the floor and made the rope fast, and went and sat down in a chair to watch the pain and misery to which I was to go through, goin' through this suffering and torture and tormented pain for about one hour.

Col. Lewis,[96] the principal Warden of the prison, happened to pass through the shop and see me in my painful condition, a standing on one leg, and arm stretch out in full length. He step up to me and ask me if I couldn't get along without goin' under so much torture and punishments. I told the old gentleman that I thought I could if I only tried. He then told me that I was a smart boy to work and was endowed with a good reason and knew enough to go right straight along without getting into any trouble at all. "You let your temper carry you astray, and when that gets a goin' it appears as though the very devil is working within you. I think you have suffered and gone through hardships enough to know how to behave yourself."

As the old gentleman stood a talking to me in this manner, the tears came rolling down my cheeks, and I began to think of the advice which Mr. Parsons and Mr. Hewson gave to me in former days, and the prayer and the blessing to which my father gave to me before he died. The Col. then ask me how long I had been strung up, to which I replied about one hour. He then went and interceded with the Keeper for me, and I was let loose from this tormented mode of torture, promising Col. Lewis that I would strive to do better in the future.

Look, Reader, ain't that a beautiful looking swing for a man to stand in for two or three hours on a stretch? It benumbs the whole body, and for days after the poor unfortunate wretch feels the tortures and pains of that cruel spread eagle. . . .

Col. Ritchardson Advice to the Author

IT WAS A cold winter's day as I stood in the kitchen a warming myself by the stove that Col. Ritchardson[97] step up to me and address me in the following words:

"How often I think of you when I am Home, and long after your eyes is closed in sleep I am praying for you. It makes my very heart bleed when I think what a fool you have made of yourself, and become the harden convict of a gloomy prison. You have allowed yourself to become the wretch of all kinds of punishments. Why, oh why not now, from this very cold winter's day, start and be a man? You may think what you please or say what you mind to, yet I tell you, young man, that my very heart bleeds for you, and my prayer to God is night and day that you will one day or another reform and become a man. Remember, the day is coming when you must lay your drooping head upon the pillow of death, and must dip your feet in the cold streams of Jordan. Then that soul of yours must stand in the sight of that God who will be your judge. You may laugh, scorn, and sneer as much as you please to what I now say to you, but remember that that day will surely over take you soon. You'll hear the heavy tramp of the angel's feet a treading at your door, and with a voice louder than thunder, he'll stand with one foot upon the sea and the other on the land, and with his uplifted sword will swear in the name of him that sent him, that time's no more. Then, oh then where will that soul of yours be?"

As I stood before the gentleman upon the cold stone floor, the tears came trinkling from my eyes, and I thought of the advice which my father gave me before he died. There I stood, a living mimic before him, not knowing hardly what to say as he unfolded to me the terrors of that day when I must stand with the millions before the judgment bar. With tears streaming from my eyes, I turned from the venerable old gentleman and went and sat down alone by myself and fell in a deep reflection.

Ah, thought I to myself, Mr. Ritchardson, cannot I hide myself in some rock or cave in that day? Cannot I screen myself from his all searching eye in that day, or can't I call for some rock or mountain to fall and cover my defenseless head in that day?

But the voice of this venerable old man seemed to respond back to me and say, No, no, for in that day the rocks and the mountains will fall and melt away like wax before a burning blaze. The moon will become as red as blood, and the stars of the heavens will fall and fade away. The sun will become as black as the sack cloth of hair, and all nature will be a weeping and wailing in that day, because of those things which shall fall upon the heads of men.

Listening to the good advice of this venerable old man, I made up my mind at once that I would go on and try to reform and become a better man—and from that day to this I have had no trouble nor no punishments, for the terror of that day seems to prick me still to the heart. . . .

But in that day when I shall stand before God, I'll show him my back where the tyrant has printed it with the cats, and will point him to a dark and a gloomy dungeon where I've laid my head many a cold night, without a bed or a blanket, and some days not a morsel of bread to eat, and I will point him to the showering bath and tell him of the water that has been showered on my head. I will show him the tyrants that has tortured and tormented me during my confinement within the gloomy walls of a prison.[98] Those who might have done me a heap of good turned to be my destroyers, and took away all of the good principles and reasons to which I was endowed with, and the high and noble mind which God had given to me have all been destroyed by hard usage and a heavy club. The very prayers which my mother printed upon my lips have all been wash away beneath the waters of a showering bath. . . .

The Convict's Jewelry, His Necklace, and Diet; How the Convict Kills Time

THE CONVICT'S JEWELRY consist of iron or brass. For instance his finger ring, which is made out of a piece of thick brass or iron, is highly polish up and wore on his finger until it begins to turn its color or to get a little rusty. He then pulls it off and rubs it for hours on a stretch until it begins to shine. He then puts it on his finger or wraps it up nicely in a piece of rag or cotton, and there keeps it until Sunday. He then puts it on and wears it to church as a show. His breast pin consist of the same metal, and polish in the same manner. . . .

His necklace is a piece of cloth like his shirt, which is a piece of coarse bed ticking, with a bow nicely tied in it. . . .

His diet is brown bread, beef, potatoes, and a pint of coffee once a day. This he haves for his breakfast. For his dinner he haves bread, meat, potatoes, soup, and a cup of cold water. For his supper he haves a dish of mush and molasses and a cup of cold water. This he marches off with to his lonely cell at night, and there devours it with a craving appetite. If the poor unfortunate wretch is sick with a broken down health and cannot eat this coarse, rough food, he goes and makes his complaint to the Doctor, who orders his coarse diet to be changed for finer food until he gets better. This finer food consists of fried meat, bake potatoes, white bread, crackers, coffee, and a cup of tea. Before the convict can get this kind of diet from the Doctor to eat, he's got to give a good reason why he can't eat the same kind of coarse, rough food that the rest of the convicts eats, and to go through a thorough examination by the Doctor, and if the Doctor finds that he is a man of masturbation and of secret habits, who is bringing a premature disease and death upon himself, or if he sees the least spark of masturbation a playing and blooming in the wicked wretch's eye, he turns him away with a scorn of pity and haves nothing to do with the wretched devil, but leaves him to gripple and grovel out the remainder of his days in pain and misery. But if he finds him a poor sickly being who has not brought his own disease upon himself, he changes his diet, and the poor sickly man is allowed to eat it till he gets well or till he goes down to his grave, or into the cruel hands of the dissectors. . . .

Hard to tell, yet it is true, the way in which the convict kills time. Those long and lonesome hours in summer, and during the long Sabbath days, when he is consign all day long in his lonesome cell, he sits down and pulls an old jack knife from his pocket, and he begins to whittle out a cane and carve it, or tinker at a tooth pick, or perhaps to finish an old jack knife which he has been to work on for more than two months, which after he gets it done he trades it off for a plug of tobacco or a finger ring.

Thus does he sit in his lonely cell, a tinkering and killing time, until the bell rings for him to get ready for church. The Keeper then unlocks his door, and he marches off to church, where he hears a good sermon preach by the chaplain, and then return back to his lonely cell the same wicked and harden convict as he was when he left his cell. He then sits down and begins to hum over some old song to himself, or curses and damns the day that ever he was sent to a dark and a gloomy prison. Getting into one corner of his cell, he sits down and devours the humble meal which he brought up to his cell with him, and there begins to brood upon vice and crime and over his hard fate.

With these thoughts a swimming in his mind, he swings his hammock and throws himself down upon it, folds his arms across his breast, and gives way to sleep. He then awakes, and in a mournful manner he says aloud, "I wish I was Home with my wife and children. . . ."

He then arises from his cold, rough bed and begins to pace his cell to and fro until he is tired. With tears in his eyes, he sits down in one corner of his gloomy cell, and covering his face with both hands, he gives way to a full flood of tears, and again we hear the mournful sigh resounding from his lonely cabin—"that I wish I was . . ."

As he says these words over in a doneful way, he falls in a deep reverie of meditations and reflections and says, "What is it that has brought me here to this dark and dismal prison, where I must spend the best of my days in illtreatment and hard usage? What is it that has hurled me from my peaceful Home, and from the side of my wife and children, and from the society of my father and mother?" With a fountain of tears in his eyes he says, "Ah, I see the cause of my down fall now. I see why I have been torn from under the parental roof and brought here to pass a term of years in this gloomy prison. . . ."

And he says, "It was for the early vices and crimes which I practiced and followed in my early childhood and youth, and breaking through the parental restraints of a kind and a fond mother. This is what has brought me here to become the inmate of a cold and a gloomy prison, and the harden convict of a demon's cell, and the infernal wretch of a gloomy dungeon."

With these sober and silent reflections, he throws himself down upon his bed again and falls to sleep, a dreaming of the pains and miseries to which he'll have to pass through while confined within the walls of a gloomy prison. . . .

Reader, this is the way and the manner in which the convict kills time, until the long rolling years of his sentence expires, and the day breaks forth for him to rush out into the open world again, where he may go and enjoy the happy comforts of his wife and children. . . .

The New Comer; Dialogue Between the New Comer and an Old Inmate

Hark, methinks I hear the heavy rattling of chains, and with them the loud cries of some new prisoner who has just entered the prison. Grief and sorrow seems to be mingled with those tears. Ah, there he is. What a fine looking young man he appears to be. He must be the son of some rich gentleman. He seems to be endowed with high and lofty principles and polish manners.

A rough voice of an officer, which seems to speak in thunder like tone, orders the young man to strip himself and get in that tub of hot water and wash himself all over clean. This done, the same harsh voice of the Keeper orders him to get out of the tub and put on a uniform of streaked clothes, and to have his hair bobbed off close to his head. After passing through this operation of cleansing and dressing, the officer in a harsh way orders the poor broken hearted wretch to follow him.

With a down casted look and a face as pale as death, the poor unfortunate exile follows the officer until he reaches the clerk's office, where he must pass through an examination, and answer the many questions which the clerk will put to him. After passing through this examination, he follows the officer back to the kitchen, where he sits down and bows his head down toward the cold stone floor, and covering his face with both hands, he falls to a weeping. An old inmate happens to be a sitting aside of the unhappy youth, and casting his eyes up towards the officer to see if he can get a good chance to speak to the new comer, the Dialogue then commences between the two:

"God bless you, young man, don't cry."

"I can't help it," says the new comer.

"Well, I feel sorry for you, young man, and sympathize with you in your hard and cold allotment. How long did the judge throw you for?"

"Four and a half, sir."

"Well, my good friend, let me tell you that those four and a half years will hang as heavy as a mill stone upon you, and they'll seem like ten long years to you. But let me tell you one thing. You must keep up good courage and don't give way to grief and sorrow, for that has proved the ruination of many young men within the walls of this prison, and they have gone down to an untimely grave. So, young man, take my advice and keep up your courage until the expiration of sentence."

"I suppose that I'll have to pass through a good many hardships here."

"Yes indeed, young man, you will. You'll have to meet with the sneers and scorns of the older inmates and yield yourself to their bad habits and influences. You'll have to learn and follow their devilish devices until you learn the mysteries and the miseries of the prison and become the demon of a cell. You'll have to listen to their silly tales and yield yourself to the different modes of punishments that prevails within the walls of a gloomy prison. My heart bleeds for you, young man, when I think of the hard treatments to which you'll have to endure here in prison. You'll have to hear rash and ugly words from your Keeper and obey the point of his cane or finger in the direction that he points you in. You'll have to be the unfortunate wretch of an iron yoke or the miserable wretch of a ball and chain, and if you cast an ugly look at those torturers which tortures and pains your body, or if you give a side look at that cold hearted tyrant that caused you to suffer in this manner, he'll take you off to the showering bath and there shower you till your reason is taken away from you. Nor is this all, young man. You'll be taken off to the shop where there will be a heavy day's work given to you for to do, and if you don't put in and do it . . .

"You must go to the dungeon
and there you must stay
and eat bread and water
for many along day. . . ."

"This is hard, rough looking food. I don't believe I can eat it. My constitution won't bear it."

"Yes, young man, it is very coarse looking nutriment, but we've got to eat it or go without. You must eat a little to a time until you get use to it."

"How bad I feel. How sorry I am that I never took the good advice of my mother."

"Yes, young man, it makes my heart ache every time I see so many young men a rushing within the walls of a gloomy prison, where in the course of time he will become the harden inmate of a gloomy prison. . . ."

Again the new comer bows his head and covers his face with both hands and falls to a weeping. His tears, his sighs, his bitter groans and loud sobs is heard until he enters his lonesome cell. Then, oh then is the time to stand at his gloomy cell door and hear the awful and bitter wailings which he takes up. Watch him there for a few moments, as he stands bathe in tears and casting his fiery looking eyes around those cold walls that holds him so tight. Watch him as he lays his paws upon the bible that lays on his shelf, and with a heavy grasp he pulls it from his shelf and opens it and begins to fumble the leaves over and over until the bell rings him to bed.

It was a cold midwinter's day when Jack B., our new comer, had entered a dark and a gloomy cell for the first time in his life, and there with a firm resolution resolved to set out from that time forward to lead and live a better life. But alas, alas, ere three months rolled o'er his head, he had learnt all the mysteries, the miseries, and the iniquities of the prison and had become a man of masturbation and the tormented demon of a cell, and a deadly disease and a premature death is now waiting to convey his body to the tomb or into the cruel hands of the dissectors. . . .

What They Do with an Old Man That Is Stricken in Years When He First Enters the Prison, and What the Convict Does When He Is Sick

WHEN AN OLD man first enters the prison who is bowed down beneath the weight of old age, he is taken by one of the officers to the state shop, where he is allowed to sit and lounge about just as he pleases. If it is cold and stormy weather, he is allowed to take his library book or bible and sit down by the stove and pass away his lonesome hours in reading. If the weather proves to be warm and cheerful, the officers allows him to stroll about the yard, where the old man regales himself by laying down upon the green grass and refreshes himself with a little sleep. . . .

When a convict is sick, he goes before the Doctor and makes his complaint to him. The Doctor then examines him, and if he finds that the man is sick, he gives him some medicine to take, and if the man is not able to work, the Doct. hand him a written order of excuse from labor until he is well, which the convict hands to his regular Shop Keeper. The Keeper then takes the written order of excuse and reads it and orders the convict to go away and sit down until he feels better.

Here let us pause for a moment while I bring before the Reader's mind the many little tricks and games which the convict plays upon the Doctor. Every convict who is really sick or diseased is allowed to visit the Doctor every morning between the hours of nine and ten. Among the seven and eight hundred convicts that are in the prison, some sixty or seventy make it a rule to visit him every morning whether there is anything the matter with them or not, so it makes it hard for him to tell whether this man or that man is able to work or too sick to be sent back to his shop without any medicine. For instance, one man works in the cabinet shop and another man works in the cooper shop. They perhaps want to see each other or to strike up some trading game. They make a sign to each other with their hands or fingers to meet each other at the hospital on the following morning, and there they'll sit aside of each, a discussing their matters over until the officer happens to cast his eye upon them, and catches them both a talking, and orders them back to their respected shops, where they are reported and punished. The reader will see that it makes it hard for the Doctor to tell whether the convict is really sick and not able to work or whether he came up there to talk and traffic with his companion. Sundays appears to be the most proper time for this kind of business to go on with the inmates. During the chapel service, many of the convicts goes to the hospital to get rid of hearing a sermon preach or for the sole purpose to traffic and trade.

The Words of Horace C. Cook

'TWAS THE TWENTY-SEVENTH day of May in the year 1857, as I stood within the walls of a dark and a gloomy prison, that I stood before Mr. Horace C. Cook,[99] dressed in my streaked clothes of shame and disgrace. Making a low bow of respects to this gentleman, I addressed him thus: "Mr. Cook," said I, "you don't visit this gloomy place very often."

With a tear in his eye he answered me in the following manner:

"Sir," said he, "it almost breaks my very heart every time I pass through this dismal place. When I see so many young men a rushing and pressing their way here to this gloomy prison, it makes my heart bleed, and my bowels yearns every time I pass these gloomy walls."

Drawing his handkerchief from his coat pocket, he wipe the big tear from his eye and the perspiration from his brow.

"Within these walls," said Mr. Cook, "are some of the smartest and intellectual young men that are in this country, young men endowed with a good education and a good reason, and who might have done a good deal of good and might been bright and shining ornaments in the world and angels in heaven—but instead of that," said Mr. Cook, "they are spending the best of their days in a dark and a gloomy prison."

With tears in my eyes, I turned from this gentleman and went off to my lonesome cell and gave way to a deluge of tears, repeating his words over to myself and saying, "Young men, young men, who are endowed with a good reason and with a good education." Could he had been alluding to me when he uttered those last syllables, or could he have been alluding to some rich man's son who had once been a college boy with him? Methinks, Reader, he must have been a mixing me in with the number to whom he was alluding to. Yes, Mr. Cook, ah yes, when I first entered this prison in the days of my boyhood, the cheerful respects and good manners bloomed and shined in my face like a mid summer's day. I was endowed with a good reason and had a good education given to me, and had good manners of respects, and my father's prayer was printed upon my lips, and his dying advice was stamped upon my heart—but these hard and cruel hearted tyrants has beaten me with many stripes and taken my education, my good reason which God had given me, all away, and made me to become the harden convict of a gloomy prison. In that day when God shall send his holy angel, who shall swear in his name louder than a bellow of thunder that time is no more, then will I haunt the tyrants before the throne of God who has lock me in a gloomy dungeon. I will point the same tyrant out to God who oppressed me with pain and misery during my confinement within the walls of a gloomy prison.

Many has been the cold winter nights, when the winds has been a howling through my iron grated door, have I laid awake in silence and thought of the words of that Hon. man, which he said to me within the walls of a prison, and the words of Mr. Horace C. Cook still remains in my memory, and they will there stand and stick until the day that I go down to my grave, and they will be sealed up in the judgment day before the throne of God. . . .

To The Reader

Reader, I have now unfolded to you the secrets and the habits of the convicts, with the mysteries and miseries of Auburn Prison, together with the rules and regulations of the prison, from the year 1840 up to the year 1858.

I will now give you the names of the different shops as they are at the present time:

Names of the Different Shops in 1858

Cooper - Shop
Tool - do.
Weave - do.
Hame - do.

Lace - do.
State - do.
Cabinet - do.
Shoe - do.
Machine - do.
Rug - do.
Spin - do.
Taylor - do.

Conclusion

READER, MANY HAS been the sad and doneful cry which I have heard ascending up from those lonesome cabins within the walls of a gloomy prison, and in the sighing notes of pity the loud cry of some young man has said, that I wish I was Home, and the still midnight cry comes a bursting upon my ear from another quarter of the prison which says, I am sorry I come. Many has been the long Sabbath day and the cold chilly nights as I have laid on my coarse and humble couch that these doneful echoes has broke forth upon my hearing. God bless you, my dear companions of solitude and sorrow. From the very bottom of my heart I wish you was Home and encircled around the hearth of your wife and children, of your fathers and mothers, and was enfolded in the slender arms of your sisters.

Hard, hard indeed is the convict's allotment. Hard is his food, and hard and rough is his bed, and cold is his cell when he returns to it on a cold winter's night. Ill is his treatment, and hard is his usage. Black and dismal is his prospects, and gloomy is his hours. In silence he sits and thinks on the scenes of his boyhood, or in misery he paces his lonely cell, a brooding on vice and crime. With a broken heart he lays his drooping head down on his pillow at night, a thinking whether he'll ever return from those gloomy walls back Home to his friends alive.

Discouraged and heart broken, he stretches himself out on his couch and gives way to the secret habits of the convicts. Months rolls away, and he becomes the young man of masturbation and the demon of a cell. Weeks rushes on, and he dies the death of demon. He haves no knell to give the signal of his departure or to toll his body away to the grave. He has no friend to carry the sad and doneful news Home to his friends or to tell of the fatal catastrophe that had befallen him. No friends but the rough hands of the convicts to sink his bleaching bones beneath the cold clods. Not a friend in all of God's world to drop a warm tear o'er the green grass that covers his mortal remains. All is dark, cold, chilly, and dismal. Reader, be careful and take warning from one who has passed through the iron gates of sorrow and trouble. Take warning, lest you also come to this place of torment and become the inmate of a dark and a gloomy prison.

The End
by Rob Reed,
the inmate of a gloomy prison

Acknowledgments

———

Privately held for about 150 years, Austin Reed's manuscript for *The Life and the Adventures of a Haunted Convict* was discovered at a Rochester, New York, estate sale and acquired by Yale's Beinecke Rare Book Library in 2009. The original seller declined to reveal anything about the document's provenance, so little is known about who may have possessed or read it before that date. The first published research was conducted for Jeffrey H. Marks Rare Books and Between the Covers Rare Books by Jennifer Larson, who identified some of the historical figures named in the memoir and speculated that the author might have been related to Burrell and Maria Reed. A Beinecke curator, Louise Bernard, made important preliminary inquiries into the text and its contexts, then invited David Blight, Robert Stepto, and me to consult with the library's staff about its authenticity and its scholarly significance. The Beinecke's director, the late Frank Turner, supported our work with grace and with a helpful skepticism, and curators Nancy Kuhl, George Miles, and Melissa Barton were immensely generous with their time and knowledge. Marie-France Lemay, a Yale conservationist, examined the paper and ink and had the patience to teach me how to understand the results. Cathleen A. Baker of the University of Michigan's libraries expanded our understanding of the paper and its origins. Diane Ducharme, the Beinecke's paleography expert, analyzed the manuscript, the 1833 indenture agreement, and the 1895 letters to the House of Refuge to verify that all were composed by the same hand.

About those letters—they and several other crucial pieces of evidence were unearthed by the amazing Christine McKay, a freelance researcher and archivist based in New York City, who worked with me from the very beginning. Chris established the history of the Reed family, recovering Burrell and Maria's property records from the Monroe County Clerk and Surrogate Court, and verified the names of Austin's brothers, Charles and Edward, using census data and other documents. Chris also located many of Reed's prison records, and just when we thought there was nothing else to be found, she came up with the pardon records, too. Her work on this book was indispensable. Jessika Brasseaux prepared a raw transcription of Reed's text. Stephen Krewson investigated the history of Haverstraw and the American Hotel. McKenzie Granata looked into the death of Halsey Thomas and the lives of forgotten prison contractors, then served as a sharp-eyed proofreader.

I researched Reed's life and world at the American Antiquarian Society, the Burke Library at the Union Theological Seminary, the New-York Historical Society, the New York Public Library, the New York State Archives, the University of Texas's Harry Ransom Center, and the Rare Book Room of Yale Law School's Lillian Goldman Library. At each of these institutions, I was reminded that librarians are angels. As I considered how to edit Reed's prose, I benefited from conversations with Hazel Carby, Ian Cornelius, Jacqueline Goldsby, Leon Jackson, David Kastan, Robert Levine, Anthony Reed, Jonathan Senchyne, Michael Warner, and others. As I wrote my introduction and notes, I got valuable suggestions from Edward Ball, Hester Blum, Peter Coviello, Richard Deming, Leslie Jamison, Aaron Ritzenberg, and Lauren Berlant and the University of Chicago's Americanist Working Group. Wesleyan University's Center for Prison Education was kind enough to organize a workshop on my manuscript with a group of incarcerated students, who posed serious questions about both ethics and style. My own students at Yale University and at Connecticut's Cheshire Correctional Institution have been model readers, and it was a special honor to collaborate with my colleagues David Blight and Robert Stepto on this project. Many thanks to Wendy Strothman, David Ebershoff, and Caitlin McKenna, true professionals who enabled this manuscript to become a book, at last.

Some of my favorite pieces of Reed's story are about how people build homes together after the homes they were born into have fallen apart. I would like to dedicate my research and writing for this edition to the women in my family—Margaret Smith, Carolyn Madison, Lindsley Smith, Francine Mellon, Nancy Marsh, Maggie Smith, Macy Madison, Natalie Madison, and Jenny Mellon. No scholarly work has ever touched my heart with such intensities of fury or of joy.

CALEB SMITH
New Haven, CT, winter 2015

Appendix A:
Chronology of Austin Reed's Life

Using legal documents, newspaper reports, and other sources, this chronology has been prepared for readers who may wish to compare Reed's "Life and Adventures" to the information about Austin (alias Robert) Reed that became a part of the public record. This information and the sources are also included in the editor's notes to the Introduction and to Reed's text.

1823

Austin Reed is born in or near Rochester, New York, according to House of Refuge and New York State Prison records. (According to the "Life and Adventures," Reed may have been born a few years later, between 1825 and 1827.)

1827

May 17: Burrell and Maria Reed buy a house on Hunter Street in Rochester.

Burrell Reed pledges twenty-five dollars toward the founding of the African Methodist Episcopal Church, organized by Austin Steward.

1828

February 4: Burrell Reed dies. Supported by Austin Steward and Basley Baker, trustees of the AME Church, Maria Reed administers his estate. Maria and her children remain in the family home on Hunter Street.

1832

June or July (estimated): Austin Reed is indentured to the Ladd family in Avon Springs, New York. (Reed's House of Refuge case file indicates that he was an apprentice for "nearly a year.")

1833

July 19: Austin Reed is arrested for arson against the property of the Ladd family. In September, a local attorney, A. A. Bennett, represents Austin Reed at trial before a court of Oyer and Terminer. The defense calls no witnesses. Reed is convicted and sentenced to a term of ten years in the House of Refuge in New York. He is admitted to the Refuge on September 19.

1834

May 2: Thomas King, seventeen years old, dies at the House of Refuge.

1835

The House of Refuge opens a separate dormitory for "colored" inmates.

1838

David Terry succeeds Nathaniel Hart as superintendent of the Refuge. William H. Seward becomes governor of New York.

1839

May 22–23: The House of Refuge is destroyed by fire (probably arson).
June 1: Austin Reed is released from the Refuge and indentured to Abraham A. Haring, a farmer in Rockland County, New York.

1840

January 23: Staff at the House of Refuge notes that Austin Reed has "left his master" in Rockland County.

May: Austin Reed is convicted of larceny in Rochester and sentenced to two years at Auburn State Prison.

1842

May 1: Austin Reed is released from Auburn. He receives three dollars to pay for his travel home to Rochester.

December: Austin Reed is convicted of larceny and returns to Auburn for a term of five years.

1843

June 14: The first documented instance (in Auburn's daily punishment reports) of Austin Reed being subjected to the showering bath: "One pail of water for showing temper in presence of the Keeper."

August 28: According to Auburn's daily punishment reports, Austin Reed sets a fire in a prison workshop, burning two sets of matting and caning tools. He is punished with twelve lashes.

1844

Reformers found the New York Prison Association.

July 11: The prison physician records the death of Auburn inmate Halsey Thomas. On the same day, Austin Reed is punished with six lashes for quarreling with another inmate, John Lashop.

1845

February 15: The first documented instance of Austin Reed being punished in the dungeon and restricted to bread and water "for obtaining ivory from the cutlery shop under false pretences."

1847

After an inquiry into the death of inmate Charles Plumb, New York abolishes the use of the whip in state prisons.

1848

January: Austin Reed is released from Auburn.

December: Austin Reed is convicted of larceny after felony and returns to Auburn for a term of four years and four months. He
signs a quitclaim deed to sell his quarter share in the family house
to Joseph A. Eastman of Rochester.

1853

April: Austin Reed is released from Auburn. The state refunds his
"convict deposit" of $4.13.

1854

March: Austin Reed is convicted of larceny after felony and returns
to Auburn for a term of four years and three months.

1856

Benoni I. Ives is appointed chaplain at Auburn.

1858

July: Austin Reed is released from Auburn.

November: Austin Reed is convicted of larceny after felony and sentenced to a term of four years and six months at Auburn.

November–December (estimated): Reed completes the manuscript
of the "Life and Adventures."

December: Samuel Moore, an African American inmate at Auburn,
is killed in the showering bath, leading to an investigation into
punishments in the prison.

1859

May: Austin Reed is transferred from Auburn to Clinton State
Prison in Dannemora. At a meeting of the prison inspectors on
July 1, William C. Rhodes proposes that officials make an in-

quiry into Reed's "condition" at the time of his transfer from Auburn. The motion is "laid aside."

1860

September 15: Reed receives permission to write to "Mr. Pomeroy" (probably Theodore Medad Pomeroy, a prominent attorney and Republican politician from Auburn) about a possible pardon.

1862

August 3: Benoni I. Ives of Auburn State Prison visits Clinton, preaches a service in the prison chapel, and spends the afternoon talking with the inmates.

August 7: Austin Reed receives permission to write to J. D. Kingsland, a prison contractor at Clinton, about a possible pardon.

1863

May: Austin Reed is released from Clinton.

A Rochester city directory lists "Robert Reed" as a boarder at the National Hotel, a Temperance House, employed as an "artificial leg maker."

1864

January 30: "Robert Reed" is convicted of larceny after felony in Rochester and sentenced to a term of three years and three months at Auburn.

1865

February: Maria Reed dies in the family home on Hunter Street in Rochester.

1866

December 14: "Robert Reed alias Austin Reed" is released from Auburn.

1876

August 26: Governor Samuel J. Tilden pardons Austin Reed for his 1858 larceny conviction, restoring Reed's citizenship rights.

1895

April: Austin Reed writes to the superintendent of the House of Refuge in New York, inquiring about his file.

Appendix B: Austin Reed House of Refuge Case File, Indenture Agreement, and Letters from Austin Reed to the Superintendent

Note: These documents have been transcribed from microfilm records held at the New York State Archives. Because the file and letters were not intended for print, the transcriptions have not been edited.

I. House of Refuge Case File

1833 *1221*
Sept. 19

Austin Reed a boy of colour from a Court of Oyer + Terminer, held in Livingston Co. Aged 10 years born in Rochester, his father is dead, his Mother now resides in Rochester + supports her family by Washing + other work—this bright looking little negro says that he never stole any thing but a Mr. Whitmore in Rochester whipped some boys— + they were determined to set his house on fire, so they persuaded this one to go along with them—they made the attempt, this boy looked on—the other boys were put in jail, this one whipped and let go—so his Mother put him to live with a Mr. Ladd farmer in Avon Livingston Co, where he remained nearly a year and got dissatisfyed because he had to draw so much water + pull so many weeds from the Garden so he made an attempt to set his Masters house on fire by placing chips against the out side of the house & fireing them—which was soon discovered—for this he was sent here. Charged with the 2d degree of arson.—

1833
Sept. 19

122

Austin Reed a boy of colour from a Court of Oyer & Terminer. held in Livingston Co. Aged 10 Years born in Rochester, his father is dead, his Mother now resides in Rochester & supports her family by Washing & other work. this bright looking little negro says that he never stole any thing but a Mr Whitmore in Rochester whipped some boys – & they were determined to set his house on fire, so they persuaded this one to go along with them – they made the attempt. this boy looked on – the other boys were put in Jail. this one whipped and let go – so his Mother put him to live with a Mr Ladd farmer in Avon Livingston Co. where he remained nearly a year and got dissatisfied because he had to draw so much water & pull so many weeds from the Garden so he made an attempt to set his Masters house on fire by placing chips against the out side of the house & firing them – which was soon discovered – for this he was sent here. charged with the 2d degree of arson. –

Enters 1st Class

Remarks.

1835
Jan. 21.   A very unpromising child – possesses few if any good qualities

Nov. 12   Remains about the same. is very dishonest

1836
Oct 18   Austin is a deep knowing impudent and brazen faced boy, will tell an untruth and stick to equal to any boy we know of, is we think rather a dangerous boy to any where out of our reach

1837
March   A most notorious liar. –

First page of Austin Reed's House of Refuge case file.

Enters 1st Class
Remarks.

[1835 June 21] A very unpromising child—possesses few if any good
    qualities

[Nov. 12] Remaining about the same, is very dishonest

[1836 Oct 18] Austin is a deep knowing impudent brazen faced boy,
    will tell an untruth and stick to equal to any boy we know of, is
    we think rather a dangerous boy to any where out of our reach

[1837 March] A most notorious liar.—

[1839 June 1st.] Austin has had a longer probation than ever a boy
    has had before—he was this day Indentured to an excellent Man
    a Mr. Abraham A Haring of Ramapo Scotland Pell. Rockland Co
    N.Y. Farmer + Miller—

[1840 Jany 23.] We have since learned that he left his Master.—

2. Austin Reed Indenture Agreement

This Indenture, witnesseth that Austin Reed (a color'd boy aged sixteen years and three months Hath put himself and by these Presents,
with the consent and approbabion of the Managers of the Society for
the Reformation of Juvenile Delinquents of the city of New York,
doth voluntarily and of his own free will and accord, put himself
Apprentice to Mr. Abraham A. Haring of the town of Ramipo Scot-
land P.D. Rockland County and State of New York and after the
manner of an Apprentice to serve from the date hereof, for, and during the full end and term of Four years and nine months next ensu-
ing: During all which time, the said Apprentice his Master faithfully
shall serve, his secrets keep, his lawful commands every where read-
ily obey; he shall do no damage to his said Master, nor see it done by
others, without preventing the same so far as he lawfully may, and
giving notice thereof to his said Master: he shall not waste his said
Master's goods, nor lend unlawfully to any: he shall not absent himself day nor night from said Master's service, without his leave; Nor
frequent Ale-Houses, Taverns, nor Play-Houses: but in all things

behave himself as a faithful Apprentice ought to do, during the said term. And the said Master shall use the utmost of his endeavor to teach, or cause to be instructed, the said Apprentice in the trade and mystery of Farming and Milling—procure and provide for him sufficient Meat, Drink, Apparel, Lodging, and Washing, fitting for an Apprentice, and cause him to be instructed in reading, writing, and arithmetic, during the said term; and at the experation thereof, shall give a new bible to the said apprentice, and a suit of new clothing in addition to his old ones in wear.

And for the true performance of all and singular covenants agreements aforesaid, the said parties bind themselvs unto the other firmly by these presents. In Witness Whereof, the said parties have interchangably set their hands and seals hereunto:

Dated, the Thirty-first day of May in the Sixty-third year of the independence of the united States of America, and in the year of our Lord one thousand eighte hundred and thirty-nine.

SEALED AND DELIVERED
IN THE PRESENCE OF
[Signed: David Terry Jr.]   [Signed: Abraham A
    Haring]   [Signed: Austin Reed]

3. First Letter from Austin Reed to the House of Refuge

Rochester N.Y. April 4th 1895.
Mr. Supertendant (Dear Sir-
    I am a colord man and live in the city of Rochester, N.Y there I was born. I was sent to N. York House of Reffuge from Geneseo Livenston county the time the Reffuge placed up in the Bowery. my No. was 1221. Mr. Nathanel Hart was then supertendant, and Mr Samuel S Wood was the assistince. Mr. Williams was School teacher. I was the first colord boy that was bound out after the old Reffuge burnt down. I was bound out in a little village calld

Rochester N.Y april 9ᵗʰ 18 95

Mr. Superintendent — Dear Sir.

I am a colored man and live in the city of Rochester. N.Y there I was born. I was sent to N. York House of Refuge from Geneseo Livingston county the time the Reffuge burned up in the Bowery. my No. was 1221. Mr. Nathanel Hart was then superintendent. and mr Samuel S. Wood was the assistant. Mr. Williams was School teacher I was the first colored boy that was bound out after the ofe Reffuge burnt down I was bound out in a little village called Nyack down on the banks of the Hudson River. Now then dear Sir I have give you some idea about my case I am Nait given a history of my life and what I have been through since I left the Reffuge will you please. to do me the kindness as to look over some of your old record books and See if you can find my name in any of them and what year and the date of month I was sent the Reffuge my name is austin Reed. you will have find one of the books that dates way back at the time the old Reffuge burnt down the whole institution was distrayed by fire except the female department and the office. well then if the office was Saved of course the record books must been saved with it. am very desire to find out the year. and the date of the month. and How old I was when I went there. and by what judge I was sentence by as I am to leave Rochester in a few days for a long time will you please to send me answer between now and Saturday. morning please to direct your answer to —

First page of one of Reed's two 1895 letters to the superintendent of the House of Refuge.

Nyack down on the banks of the Hudson River. Now then dear Sir—I Have given you some idea about my case. I am Now given a History of my life and what I have been through since I left the Reffuge. will you please to do me the kindness as to look over some of your old record books and See if you can find my name in any of them and what year and the date of month I was sent the Reffuge my name is Austin Reed. you will Have find one of the books that dates way back at the time the old Reffuge burnt down the whole institution was distroyed by fire except the female department and the office. well then if the office was saved of course the record books must been Saved with it. am very desires to find out the year and the date of the month, and How old I was when I went there, and by what judge I was sentence by as I am to leave Rochester in a few days for a long time will you please to send me answers Between now and Saturday morning please to direct your answer to—

Austin Reed. to No 70. Frankford St
Rochester city. N.Y.
Yours Respectfully
Austin Reed

4. Second Letter from Austin Reed to the House of Refuge

Rochester N.Y April 14th 1895.

Mr. Master (Dear Sir

I am ever so much oblige to you for the trouble you put your self to in looking over the record and finding the information I required. can it be possiable that it has been 60 years ago Since I was a inmate of the refuge. oh my Dear friend if you only knew the troubles and trials I have been through since I left the old reffuge it would make your heart bleed. after I left the reffuge I ran away from the farmer I was bound out to and came Home to Rochester my own native Home. I had not been Home long before I fell into vice and crime again and sent to the auburn prison for two years. I served the time out. and went Home again and comtted another crime and was sent back to auburn for five years. Served my time our there and was sent back again on an old inditement the auburn prison was over crowed and I was transferd with fifty other prisoners to Danamora prison. live my time out there and went to albany where I got six months in the penitentiary on a United States crime. went to cleaveland and was Sent to the penitentiary for Six years Served my time out there. went and enlisted in the army and served there untill the war broke up. got an Honorable discharge while in the war I seen thousand of my countrymen fall in the battle field one night while laying in camp, my camp mate said to me. Reed I am in earnest with you. none of us knows the day nor the Hour when we to will be shot down and be calld before the judgment seat of God now look over your past life and aks your self if you are ready. if not get ready. for in such an Hour as you think not the Son of man will come. I did look over my past life. and oh such a dark life it I bursted on in tears. Then Said Jones for that was His name. let us both Kneel down before God and ask him to be merciful to us sinners and for Jesuses sake to have mercy upon our Souls and forgive us all of our Sins and iniquities and Save us from all Sin we did So prayd till the sweat and tears roll'd down our faces like like great drops of due and I Have prayd and tryd Hard to serve my God with all my Heart mind and strength. Depending on His good promise that who so ever will call upon the name of God in sincerity and from there Hearts shall be saved and today my dear brother I feel that I Have been made clean in the blood of the lamb. that was slain from the foundation of the earth goin all over the union and telling sinners. the troubles and trials that I Have been through and How I came to be a christian man and the life I am now leading. Hoping some day when I Shall gather up my cold feet in death. I may mount the air with Eagle wings. and enter the golden Gates of Heaven. Seated on the white milk Horse with the golden Halter in my Hand and riding through the courts of Heaven Singing the new song of moses and the lamb. oh my dear dear friend may you be like Mr Hart the suptendant of the old reffuge pray and take these you Have under your care and try Hard to reform them. but not like Mr. Terry abuse them and tie them Hand foot and throw the cat of nine tails on them till you could not see a white spot on there poor backs. and lock them up in dark dungen on bread and water one a day. oh no Mr. Master dont do Such a thing for if do there blood will be required of your Hands. but talk and pray with them, and for them. I Have Started two or three times to come to N. York and Speak to the children there but I. Have been calld away to other place my Having my expences payd and a collection made up for me where ever I was. calld Now then Mr. Master I shall close this letter Hoping that God will bless you and all your under officers also and may His blessing follow you and your good work till the day of your death. and that you may Have a Seat in Heaven with all the redeemd in Heaven. Here is a few verses I composed my-self—

the prisoner confind in His cold gloom cell
far—far from the friends that once loved Him so well
He Sits thinking in Silence on the sceanes of the past
His Heart full of greif and the tears falling fast

He is alone in His sorrows with none to condole
How sad the regret that embitters His Soul
He mourns on the Hours he first went astray
and yeilded His Heart to the tempters vile sway

Oh now is the time so extend Him your Hand
to snatch from extinction the still burning brand
yes now is the time while his Heart is yet warm
to listen to yearnings and whisper reform

oh could you Have thought that when kindness would soften
what neglect and illtreatment would Harden to often
that cut off from all virtue the man may in time
Sit brooding on vice and preparing for crime[1]—

yours Respectfully, Austin Reed

Appendix C:
Textual Emendations

p. xxxiii, line 7	missing word *it* inserted for consistency with previous sentence
p. 3, line 5	*angle* changed to *angel* here and elsewhere
p. 5, line 3	Apparently a combination of *scalding* and *scolding*
p. 6, line 17	*Spring* changed to *Springs*
p. 6, line 18	Missing word *I* inserted by ed. for consistency with surrounding phrases.
p. 7, line 29	*bath* changed to *bathe* for consistency with the author's usage, above
p. 10, line 22	*one them* changed to *one of them*
p. 11, line 4	*sever* changed to *severe*
p. 11, line 18	*Orsband* changed to *Osborne* here and for the remainder of this chapter. Reed spells the name *Osborne* in the following chapter.
p. 12, line 9	*slep* changed to *slept*
p. 12, line 22	*wrapt* changed to *wrapped*
p. 12, line 22	*ice sickel* changed to *icicle* here and throughout the text
p. 12, line 25	*seem'd echo* changed to *seemed to echo*
p. 13, line 17	*Schrouldren*, and below, *Schouldren*, changed to *Scoundrel*
p. 13, line 30	*oozen* changed to *oozin'*
p. 15, line 9	*dam'd* changed to *damned*
p. 16, line 16	*bath* changed to *bathe*
p. 16, line 22	*wrapt* changed to *wrapped*
p. 16, line 26	*lighting* changed to *lightning* here and elsewhere
p. 17, line 24	*on ravel'd* changed to *unraveled*
p. 18, line 28	*throw'd* changed to *throwed*
p. 18, line 29	*on tieing* changed to *untying*
p. 19, line 15	*hallowd* changed to *hollered* here and elsewhere
p. 20, line 13	Missing word *the* inserted by ed.
p. 20, line 14	Missing word *be* inserted by ed.
p. 20, line 16	Missing word *with* inserted by ed.

p. 20, line 23	*risk* changed to *wrists*
p. 20, line 27	*sheded* changed to *shed*
p. 21, line 12	*nices* changed to *nicest*
p. 22, line 25	*crowed* changed to *crowded*
p. 22, line 31	*labour* changed to *labor* here and elsewhere in the manuscript
p. 25, line 9	*stept* changed to *stepped*
p. 25, line 31	*conquor* changed to *conqueror*
p. 26, line 29	*Chatam* changed to *Chatham*
p. 27, line 4	*Kimble* changed to *Kimbell* here and elsewhere
p. 27, line 5	*develity* changed to *devilry*
p. 27, lines 6–7	*int* changed to *in it*
p. 27, line 27	*blooming dale road* changed to *Bloomingdale Road*
p. 27, line 28	Missing word *of* inserted by ed.
p. 28, line 4	*brooklyne* changed to *Brooklyn*
p. 28, line 7	*past* changed to *passed*
p. 28, line 33	*lofering* changed to *loafing*
p. 29, line 14	*wood Swayer* changed to *wood sawyer*
p. 30, line 5	*nessary* changed to *necessary*
p. 31, line 3	*duch* changed to *Dutch*
p. 33, line 2	*road* changed to *rode*
p. 33, line 30	*bring* changed to *bringing*
p. 34, line 14	*crehole* changed to *creole*
p. 34, line 25	*far* changed to *fare*
p. 35, line 32	*baitous* or *bactous* changed to *bounteous*
p. 35, line 34	*toosting* changed to *tossing*
p. 36, line 16	Missing word *him* added by ed.
p. 37, line 2	Stray words *of the* deleted by ed.
p. 37, lines 13–14	*on lock* changed to *unlock* here and elsewhere
p. 37, line 22	Here and elsewhere Reed capitalizes *Robbing*, perhaps playing on his pseudonym, Rob Reed.
p. 37, line 31	*taken* changed to *Takin'*
p. 39, line 2	*eaten* changed to *eatin'*
p. 39, line 19	*I was in kept in* changed to *I kept in*
p. 40, line 23	*angle* changed to *angel*
p. 40, line 26	*forbiden* changed to *forbiddin'*
p. 41, line 7	Missing word *or* inserted by ed.
p. 41, line 11	*Irishmans* changed to *Irishmen*
p. 41, line 33	*drean* changed to *drain*
p. 42, line 34	*rapt* changed to *wrapped*
p. 43, line 4	*there on bed* changed to *their own bed*
p. 44, lines 17–18	*presents* changed to *presence* here and elsewhere

p. 44, line 19	Missing word *for* inserted by ed.
p. 44, line 23	*rapt* changed to *wrapped*
p. 46, line 2	Missing word *father* inserted by ed.
p. 46, line 6	*feeling* changed to *feelings*
p. 48, line 15	*missen* changed to *missing*
p. 48, line 30	*scralling* changed to *crawling*
p. 49, line 1	Missing word *the* inserted by ed.
p. 49, line 9	Missing word *not* inserted by ed.
p. 49, line 21	*east india's* changed to *East Indies*
p. 49, line 27	*taken* changed to *takin'*
p. 49, line 31	*he* changed to *her*
p. 49, line 32	*riches* changed to *richest*
p. 50, line 2	Missing word *me* inserted by ed.
p. 51, lines 19–20	*supertendent* changed to *superintendence*
p. 51, line 33	Missing word *be* inserted by ed.
p. 52, lines 6–7	*well fair* changed to *welfare*
p. 52, line 12	Missing word *hard* inserted by ed.
p. 52, line 15	*eaten* changed to *eatin'*
p. 53, line 21	*wood* changed to *would*
p. 53, line 23	*pawn* changed to *upon*
p. 53, line 28	Missing word *me* inserted by ed.
p. 54, line 27	Missing word *the* inserted by ed.
p. 55, line 6	*nices* changed to *nicest*
p. 55, line 10	*eaten* changed to *eatin'*
p. 55, line 16	Missing word *to* inserted by ed.
p. 55, line 17	*The* changed to *They*
p. 56, line 7	*suits* changed to *suites* for consistency with the author's usage elsewhere in the memoir
p. 56, line 15	*policeman* changed to *policemen*
p. 57, line 1	*foremans* changed to *foremen*
p. 57, line 12	*nuckel* changed to *knuckle*
p. 57, line 22	*of* changed to *off*
p. 57, line 29	*on loosed* changed to *unloosed*
p. 58, line 15	*lodgen* changed to *lodging*
p. 58, line 25	*faultshood* changed to *falsehood* here and elsewhere
p. 59, line 10	*niger* changed to *nigger* here and elsewhere
p. 60, line 19	*striped* changed to *stripped*
p. 60, line 26	Missing word *it* inserted by ed.
p. 60, line 30	Missing word *not* inserted by ed.
p. 61, line 18	*stript* changed to *striped*
p. 62, line 1	Missing word *and* inserted by ed.
p. 62, line 3	*rite* changed to *right*

p. 62, line 24	*whole* changed to *hole*
p. 63, line 13	Missing word *eyes* inserted by ed.
p. 63, line 27	Missing word *way* inserted by ed.
p. 64, line 33	Missing word *eyes* inserted by ed.
p. 65, line 11	*the* changed to *they*
p. 65, line 24	*deprerations* changed to *desperations*
p. 65, line 26	Missing word *of* inserted by ed.
p. 66, line 3	Missing word *is* inserted by ed.
p. 66, line 7	*taken* changed to *taking*
p. 66, line 14	Missing word *not* inserted by ed.
p. 66, line 22	*taken* changed to *taking*
p. 66, lines 22–23	*we plank it firm against the and made my escape* changed to *we plank it firm against the wall, and I made my escape.* Missing words *wall* and *I* inserted by ed.
p. 67, line 9	Missing word *his* inserted by ed.
p. 67, line 32	Missing word *his* inserted by ed.
p. 67, line 34	*ravious* changed to *ravenous*
p. 69, line 2	Reed introduces the term *doneful* several times in the memoir. It seems to mean something like *doleful* or *mournful*, but there is no obvious equivalent, so it has been preserved in the text.
p. 69, line 26	*rolets* changed to *roulettes*
p. 69, line 29	Missing word *he* inserted by ed.
p. 69, line 32	*was* changed to *washed*
p. 70, line 20	*pated* changed to *patted*
p. 71, line 9	*steam* changed to *steamer*
p. 71, line 23	Author's parentheses.
p. 72, line 1	*feel* changed to *fell*
p. 72, line 21	*thrushd* changed to *thrust*
p. 72, line 28	*bath* changed to *bathe*
p. 73, line 9	*a listen* changed to *a listening*
p. 73, lines 15–16	*polters* changed to *poultice*
p. 73, line 25	*soarer* changed to *sorer*
p. 74, line 5	*close* changed to *clothes*
p. 74, line 31	*suits* changed to *suites* for consistency
p. 76, line 19	*plauge* changed to *plague*
p. 76, line 29	*lighten* changed to *lightin'*
p. 77, line 11	*pock* changed to *pocket*
p. 77, line 13	Here and elsewhere Reed seems to blend the words *hunting* and *haunting*.
p. 77, line 20	Missing word *he* inserted by ed.
p. 77, line 27	*advise* changed to *advice*

p. 78, line 14	*a* changed to *and*
p. 78, line 16	Missing word *to* inserted by ed.
p. 78, line 18	Missing word *to* inserted by ed.
p. 81, line 4	*walling* changed to *wallowing*
p. 81, line 5	*pawn* changed to *'pon*
p. 81, line 17	*Rober* changed to *robber*
p. 82, line 23	The word *by* is repeated in the ms.
p. 83, line 1	*cause* changed to *caused* for consistency with the surrounding paragraph
p. 83, line 2	Missing word *it* inserted for consistency with previous sentence
p. 83, line 6	*phesant* changed to *peasant*
p. 84, line 11	Missing word *ready* inserted by ed.
p. 85, line 32	Missing word *room* inserted by ed.
p. 86, line 6	Missing word *I* inserted by ed.
p. 86, line 31	Missing word *my* inserted by ed.
p. 88, line 6	The word *my* is repeated in the manuscript.
p. 88, line 31	The word *make* is repeated in the manuscript.
p. 89, line 9	*Poses* changed to *possess*
p. 89, line 9	The word *was* is repeated in the manuscript.
p. 91, line 1	Missing word *to* inserted by ed.
p. 91, line 13	Word left unchanged to preserve the irony that Reed may have intended. In the passages of dialogue that follow, Judge Smith continues to speak in awkward and grammatically irregular ways.
p. 91, line 29	Missing word *I* inserted by ed.
p. 91, line 31	*rath* changed to *wrath*
p. 91, line 33	Missing word *from* inserted by ed.
p. 92, line 13	The word *with* is repeated in the manuscript.
p. 92, line 19	*disgusting* changed to *discussing*
p. 92, line 25	*ting* changed to *tingling*
p. 93, lines 1–2	*traudging* changed to *trudging*
p. 93, line 4	Missing word *up* inserted by ed.
p. 93, line 7	*feticious* changed to *fictitious*
p. 94, line 8	*you* changed to *your*
p. 94, line 9	*during* changed to *doing*
p. 95, line 18	*secrete* changed to *secret*
p. 95, line 26	*some* changed to *someone*
p. 96, line 20	*dalling* changed to *dallying*
p. 97, line 9	*donful* changed to *doneful* for consistency with the author's use of this invented word elsewhere
p. 97, line 26	*hollow* changed to *holler* here and elsewhere

p. 97, line 31	*he* changed to *his*
p. 98, line 28	Missing word *have* inserted by ed.
p. 101, line 8	*presents of angle* changed to *presence of angels*
p. 101, line 11	Missing word *won't* inserted by ed.
p. 101, line 20	Missing word *her* inserted by ed.
p. 102, line 19	Missing word *I* inserted by ed.
p. 102, line 25	*toal* changed to *toll*
p. 103, line 10	*a* changed to *an*
p. 103, line 20	*rive* changed to *river*
p. 103, line 23	*word* changed to *words*
p. 104, line 3	Missing word *on* inserted by ed.
p. 104, line 6	Missing word *to* inserted by ed.
p. 106, line 8	The word *and* is repeated in the manuscript.
p. 106, line 18	Missing word *not* inserted by ed.
p. 106, line 31	*quiet* changed to *quite*
p. 106, line 33	*gropple* is apparently a combination of *grope* and *grapple*
p. 107, line 12	Missing word *hour* inserted by ed.
p. 109, line 2	The word *what* is repeated in the manuscript.
p. 109, line 17	*away* changed to *a way*
p. 109, line 22	Missing word *court* inserted by ed.
p. 109, line 24	*an* changed to *a*
p. 109, line 30	Missing word *up* inserted by ed.
p. 110, line 5	The word *not* is repeated in the manuscript.
p. 110, line 14	*the* changed to *they*
p. 110, line 33	*heavely* changed to *heavily*
p. 110, line 34	*for get* (space break between two words) changed to *forget*
p. 112, line 2	Missing word *man* inserted by ed.
p. 113, line 16	*covet* changed to *cover*
p. 114, line 17	*was was* changed to *way was*
p. 114, line 27	Missing word *of* inserted by ed.
p. 114, line 29	*decoutments* changed to *documents*
p. 115, line 2	*faults* changed to *false*
p. 115, line 15	*taken* changed to *takin'*
p. 115, line 33	Missing word *me* inserted by ed.
p. 116, lines 11–12	*Palskie* changed to *Pulaski*
p. 116, lines 25–26	*on lock my trunk with a faults key* changed to *unlock my trunk with a false key*
p. 117, line 8	*actly* changed to *actually*
p. 117, line 13	*taken* changed to *take*
p. 117, line 19	*wrapt* changed to *rapt*
p. 118, lines 6–7	*I am now listen to my mother as she trying* changed to *I am now listening to my mother as she is trying*

p. 119, line 12	*seluding*, apparently a combination of *seducing* and *deluding*
p. 119, line 14	*an* changed to *a*
p. 119, line 24	*an* changed to *a*
p. 120, line 19	*accompliments* changed to *compliments*
p. 120, line 24	Missing word *on* inserted by ed.
p. 121, line 11	*hous* (uncapitalized) changed to *House*
p. 122, line 9	Missing word *in* inserted by ed.
p. 122, line 12	*an* changed to *a*
p. 122, line 17	*while he iverson was gone* changed to *While Iverson was gone*
p. 124, line 3	*plane* changed to *plain*
p. 124, line 26	Missing word *of* inserted by ed.
p. 125, line 7	*blod* changed to *bold*
p. 125, line 22	*risks* changed to *wrists* here and elsewhere
p. 125, line 24	*past* changed to *passed*
p. 125, line 28	Missing word *he* inserted by ed.
p. 126, line 29	*N* changed to *New*
p. 127, line 2	Missing word *he* inserted by ed.
p. 127, line 6	*coast* changed to *cost*
p. 128, line 27	The word *and* is repeated in the manuscript.
p. 129, line 4	Missing word *in* inserted by ed.
p. 129, line 5	Missing words *heavens and* inserted by ed. where the manuscript is faded and illegible
p. 129, line 11	*arrange* changed to *arraigned*
p. 130, lines 33–34	*to you for to* changed to *for you to*
p. 131, line 19	*with* changed to *within*
p. 131, line 27	*pheasants* changed to *peasants*
p. 132, line 1	*punished* changed to *unpunished*
p. 132, line 21	*past* changed to *pass*
p. 133, line 18	Because Reed includes the letter as an instance of a private communication, not intended for publication, the text has been left unedited.
p. 135, line 14	*lost* changed to *loss*
p. 136, line 1	*on locking* changed to *Unlocking*
p. 136, line 22	*may* changed to *many*
p. 136, line 25	*may* changed to *many*
p. 136, line 33	*he* changed to *her*
p. 137, line 21	*choses* changed to *chooses*
p. 138, line 9	*flanks* changed to *flakes*
p. 139, line 4	*out road* changed to *outrode*
p. 140, line 2	*shepherds boy* changed to *shepherd boy's*
p. 140, line 11	*he* changed to *her*

p. 140, line 17   Reed's use of this word may suggest a combination of *knock* and *throw* as well as a divine knowledge.

p. 140, line 29   Missing word *see* inserted by ed.

p. 141, line 9   *haves* changed to *has*

p. 141, line 18   *plains* changed to *planes*

p. 142, line 8   Missing word *see* inserted by ed.

p. 142, line 18   *yearn* changed to *yarn*

p. 143, line 10   The term *cavel* seems to combine *cave* and *hovel*.

p. 143, line 27   *hall* changed to *shall*

p. 144, line 11   *for* changed to *fork*

p. 145, line 7   *you* changed to *your*

p. 145, line 25   *they* changed to *than*

p. 146, line 7   Missing word *fellows* inserted by ed.

p. 146, line 18   *on button* changed to *unbutton*

p. 147, line 12   *allready* changed to *already*

p. 147, line 27   *boanes* changed to *bones*

p. 148, line 14   *given* changed to *giving*

p. 148, line 15   *tales* changed to *tails*

p. 148, line 30   *trading* changed to *treading*

p. 149, line 14   *her* changed to *here*

p. 149, line 16   *advise* changed to *advice*

p. 149, line 26   *course* changed to *coarse*

p. 150, line 25   *of* changed to *off*

p. 150, line 34   Perhaps a combination of *budge* and *bulge*.

p. 151, line 1   Missing word *I* inserted by ed.

p. 152, line 25   Missing word *I* inserted by ed.

p. 153, line 8   *fowl* changed to *foul*

p. 153, line 13   The word *in* is repeated in the manuscript.

p. 153, line 14   *forth* changed to *fourth*

p. 153, line 21   *us* changed to *use*

p. 153, line 32   *releave* changed to *relief*

p. 153, line 32   *as* changed to *ask*

p. 154, lines 11–12   *along* changed to *a long*

p. 154, line 30   Missing word *him* inserted by ed.

p. 154, line 34   *mus* changed to *must*

p. 155, line 4   Perhaps a combination of *pelting* and *pealing*.

p. 155, line 10   The phrase *these words* is repeated in the manuscript.

p. 155, line 22   *careerer* changed to *career*

p. 155, line 24   *of* changed to *off*

p. 156, line 2   *see fits* changed to *sees fit*

p. 156, line 3   The word *when* is repeated in the manuscript.

p. 157, line 5   *grouping* changed to *groping*

p. 157, line 7	*to towards* changed to *towards*
p. 157, line 13	*given* changed to *givin'*
p. 158, line 6	*on bind* changed to *unbind*
p. 158, line 8	*consing* changed to *consigned*
p. 158, line 20	Missing word *in* inserted by ed.
p. 161, line 26	*darslent* changed to *daren't.*
p. 163, line 6	*the* changed to *thee*
p. 163, line 22	*riches* changed to *richest*
p. 163, line 31	*given* changed to *Givin'*
p. 164, line 12	*thin* changed to *thine*
p. 165, line 19	*on locking* changed to *unlocking*
p. 165, line 23	*on tying* changed to *Untying*
p. 166, line 13	Missing word *soul* inserted by ed.
p. 166, line 34	*degree* changed to *decree*
p. 167, line 3	*an* changed to *a*
p. 170, line 10	The word *said* is repeated in the manuscript.
p. 171, line 1	*given* changed to *givin'*
p. 171, line 10	*ward robe* changed to *wardrobe*
p. 172, line 6	*peirceing* changed to *piercing* (could suggest either *piercing* or *perceiving*).
p. 172, line 20	*paused* changed to *pause*
p. 174, line 9	*assleep* changed to *sleep*
p. 174, line 9	*murming* changed to *murmuring*
p. 174, line 12	*prisoner* changed to *prison*
p. 174, line 16	*feels whe the morning* changed to *feels, the morning* (fragment *whe* deleted by ed.).
p. 174, line 24	*wish for full day* changed to *wishful day*
p. 175, line 6	*far* changed to *fare*
p. 176, line 4	*Haus* changed to *House*
p. 176, line 4	*angled* changed to *angeled*
p. 176, line 8	*nolds* changed to *knolls*
p. 176, line 11	*far* changed to *fair*
p. 176, line 23	*covet* changed to *cover*
p. 178, line 3	*died a broken hearted* changed to *died with a broken heart*
p. 178, line 4	*taken* changed to *takin'*
p. 179, line 12	*prise* changed to *prize*
p. 179, line 21	*chours* changed to *chorus*
p. 179, line 27	*bath* changed to *bathe*
p. 179, line 34	*taken* changed to *Takin'*
p. 180, line 15	*devil's* changed to *devil*
p. 181, line 23	*tow* changed to *two*
p. 181, line 28	*Sir's* changed to *Sir*

p. 182, line 19	*on load* changed to *unload*
p. 183, line 14	Missing word *cell* inserted by ed.
p. 183, line 29	Missing word *hear* inserted by ed.
p. 184, line 21	*earnd* changed to *errand*
p. 185, line 3	*capitol* changed to *capital*
p. 185, line 24	Missing word *reader* inserted by ed.
p. 187, line 6	*wrapt* changed to *wrapped*
p. 187, line 8	*an* changed to *a*
p. 188, line 20	*vail'd* changed to *veiled*
p. 189, line 9	*cloveing* changed to *cloven* here and in the subsequent paragraph
p. 189, line 17	Missing word *a* inserted by ed.
p. 189, line 17	*sphere* changed to *spear*
p. 190, line 20	*Miss Mutermer I had* changed to *Miss Mutermer had*
p. 191, line 8	*wrapt* changed to *rapt*
p. 191, line 24	*coulourd* changed to *colored*
p. 191, line 24	Missing word *if* inserted by ed.
p. 191, line 28	*spirt from my vains* changed to *spurt from my veins*
p. 193, line 27	*get* changed to *getting*
p. 194, line 13	*Rob* changed to *rob*
p. 194, line 16	*taken* changed to *takin'*
p. 197, line 23	*waite* changed to *weight*
p. 197, line 25	*releave* changed to *relief* here and in subsequent paragraphs
p. 198, line 26	*on fasten* changed to *unfasten*
p. 199, line 16	*lighten* changed to *lightning*
p. 201, line 1	*beggins* changed to *beggings*
p. 201, line 9	*showing* changed to *showering*
p. 202, line 20	Missing word *in* inserted by ed.
p. 202, line 25	*given* changed to *givin'*
p. 202, lines 31–32	*taken* changed to *taking*
p. 203, line 3	Missing word *he* inserted by ed.
p. 204, line 3	*ware tow* changed to *wear two*
p. 204, line 13	Missing word *my* inserted by ed.
p. 204, line 22	Missing word *to* inserted by ed.
p. 204, line 23	*pain full* changed to *painful*
p. 204, line 28	*endown'd* changed to *endowed*
p. 205, line 9	*sung* changed to *strung*
p. 206, line 4	*joydon* changed to *Jordan*
p. 206, line 8	*angles* changed to *angel's*
p. 206, line 9	*and* changed to *on*
p. 207, line 16	*showing* changed to *showering*
p. 207, line 20	Missing word *of* inserted by ed.

p. 207, line 29	*course* changed to *coarse* here and in subsequent paragraph
p. 208, line 11	Missing word *the* inserted by ed.
p. 208, line 16	*bring* changed to *bringing*
p. 210, line 12	*commer* changed to *Comer*
p. 210, line 24	*bob'd* changed to *bobbed*
p. 212, line 31	*bath* changed to *bathe*
p. 213, line 1	The word *he* is repeated in the manuscript.
p. 214, line 15	*the* changed to *They*
p. 214, line 17	*disgusting* changed to *discussing*
p. 215, line 6	*Sir's* changed to *Sir*
p. 216, line 11	*with in* changed to *within*
p. 218, line 10	*catasphe* changed to *catastrophe*
p. 218, line 16	changed *least* to *lest*

Notes

Editor's Introduction

1. A transcription of the House of Refuge file, including Reed's letters, is included as Appendix B of this edition. This crucial piece of evidence was uncarthed by Christine McKay, a researcher and archivist whose work has been essential to the reconstruction of Reed's life.

2. According to a Rochester City Directory, the house at 70 Frankfort Street was occupied by Alfredo Mancuso in 1895 (and by other Italian laborers in the surrounding years). Reed may have taken a room in the house as a temporary boarder.

3. Records from the House of Refuge and New York's prisons indicate that Austin Reed was born in 1823. According to Reed's memoir, he may have been born a few years earlier or later; his age in the memoir does not always correspond to the official records, and he mentions falsifying his age in order to avoid being sent to the Refuge as a juvenile. An advertisement in the *Rochester Gazette* (Tuesday, October 14, 1817) indicates that Burrell Reed opened his shop in Carol Street in August 1817.

4. Austin Steward, *Twenty-Two Years a Slave, and Forty Years a Freeman* (Rochester, NY: William Alling, 1857). Burrell Reed's pledge of twenty-five dollars is recorded in the *Report of the Trustees of the African Church in the Village of Rochester* (Rochester, NY: Marshall & Dean, 1828). After Burrell Reed's death, Steward and another of the trustees, Basley Baker, cosigned the bond that enabled Maria Reed to serve as administrator of his will.

5. The deed for Burrell Reed's purchase of the property on Hunter Street on May 17, 1827, is held by the Monroe County clerk. Documents relating to Burrell Reed's death, including an inventory of property prepared by Maria Reed and a bond in the amount of $300, signed by Maria Reed and cosigned by Austin Steward and Basley Baker (both of whom were trustees of the African Methodist Episcopal Church), are held by the Monroe County Surrogate Court. The account of Maria Reed's death was printed under the title "Suffering among the Poor," *Rochester Daily Union and Advertiser*, February 13,

1865. Census records suggest that Maria Reed might have been slightly younger, between sixty-five and seventy years old, at the time of her death. The Reed family's history was shaped not only by the hard lines of racial segregation in New York State but also by the class dynamics that had already begun to divide African American communities in the North. On these dynamics, see Leslie M. Harris, *In the Shadow of Slavery: African Americans in New York City, 1626–1823* (Chicago: University of Chicago Press, 2003).

6. David Daggett, *Sketches of the Life of Joseph Mountain, A Negro* (New Haven, CT: Green, 1790) and A. D. Eddy, *"Black Jacob," A Monument of Grace* (Philadelphia: American Sunday School Union, 1842). On the history of the confession and other popular crime genres in early America, see David Brion Davis, *Homicide in American Fiction, 1798–1865: A Study in Social Values* (Ithaca, NY: Cornell University Press, 1957); Daniel E. Williams, *Pillars of Salt: An Anthology of Early American Criminal Narratives* (Madison, WI: Madison House, 1992); Daniel A. Cohen, *Pillars of Salt, Monuments of Grace: New England Crime Literature and the Birth of American Popular Culture, 1674–1860* (Amherst: University of Massachusetts Press, 1993; 2006); Karen Halttunen, *Murder Most Foul: The Killer and the American Gothic Imagination* (Cambridge, MA: Harvard University Press, 1998); Jeannine Marie DeLombard, *In the Shadow of the Gallows: Race, Crime, and American Civic Identity* (Philadelphia: University of Pennsylvania Press, 2012); Caleb Smith, *The Oracle and the Curse: A Poetics of Justice from the Revolution to the Civil War* (Cambridge, MA: Harvard University Press, 2013); and Jodi Schorb, *Reading Prisoners: Literature, Literacy, and the Transformation of American Punishment, 1700–1845* (New Brunswick, NJ: Rutgers University Press, 2014).

7. Solomon Northup, *Twelve Years a Slave* (Auburn, NY: Derby & Miller, 1853).

8. Society for the Reformation of Juvenile Delinquents in the City of New York (hereafter SRJD), *Tenth Annual Report* (New York: Mahlon Day, 1835), 16. Harriet Wilson, *Our Nig*, ed. Henry Louis Gates, Jr., and Richard J. Ellis (New York: Random House, 2011). (The full title of Wilson's book, originally published in 1859, was *Our Nig; or, Sketches from the Life of a Free Black, in a Two-Story White House, North. Showing that Slavery's Shadows Fall Even There.*) Review of Wellers Jessen, *Incendiarism in Mental Affectations and Diseases in New York State Lunatic Asylum, American Journal of Insanity*, no. 18 (1861–62), especially 174–79. Jonathan Schroeder introduced me to the historical connection between arson and the diagnosis of homesickness among child servants. My account of apprenticeship in the nineteenth century draws from Ruth Wallis Herndon and John E. Murray, eds., *Children Bound to Labor: The Pauper Apprentice System in Early America* (Ithaca, NY: Cornell University Press, 2009).

9. Austin Reed's indictment, trial, and conviction for arson in the second degree in September 1833 are recorded in the minutes book of the Livingston

County Court of Oyer and Terminer. A copy was provided by Livingston County historian Amie Alden.

10. On the history of the House of Refuge, the classic source is Robert S. Pickett, *House of Refuge: Origins of Juvenile Reform in New York State, 1815–1857* (Syracuse, NY: Syracuse University Press, 1969). See also B. K. Peirce, *A Half Century with Juvenile Delinquents, or The New York House of Refuge and Its Times* (New York: D. Appleton & Co., 1869); Anthony M. Platt, *The Child Savers: The Invention of Delinquency* (1969; 40th anniv. ed., New Brunswick, NJ: Rutgers University Press, 2009); Joseph M. Hawes, *Children in Urban Society: Juvenile Delinquency in Nineteenth-Century America* (New York: Oxford University Press, 1971); Robert M. Mennel, *Thorns and Thistles: Juvenile Delinquents in the United States, 1825–1940* (Hanover, NH: published for the University of New Hampshire by the University Press of New England, 1973); Harold Finestone, *Victims of Change: Juvenile Delinquents in American Society* (Westport, CT: Greenwood Press, 1976); Steven L. Schlossman, *Love and the American Delinquent: The Theory and Practice of "Progressive" Juvenile Justice, 1825–1920* (Chicago: University of Chicago Press, 1977); Alexander William Pisciotta, "The Theory and Practice of the New York House of Refuge, 1857–1935," PhD diss., Florida State University, 1979; John R. Sutton, *Stubborn Children: Controlling Delinquency in the United States, 1640–1981* (Berkeley: University of California Press, 1988); and Margaret K. Rosenheim, Franklin E. Zimring, David S. Tanenhaus, and Bernardine Dohrn, eds., *A Century of Juvenile Justice* (Chicago: University of Chicago Press, 2002). Of special interest to readers of Reed's memoir is Geoff K. Ward's revisionary account of race in the history of juvenile corrections, *The Black Child-Savers: Racial Democracy and Juvenile Justice* (Chicago: University of Chicago Press, 2012).

11. SRJD, *Tenth Annual Report* (1835), 17.

12. SRJD, *Ninth Annual Report* (1834), 13. On immigration and the Refuge, see Pickett, *House of Refuge*, and Sanford J. Fox, "Juvenile Justice Reform: An Historical Perspective," *Stanford Law Review* 22, no. 5 (June 1970): 1187–1239.

13. Edward S. Abdy, *Journal of a Residence and Tour in the United States of America* (London: John Murray, 1835), 5. On Abdy and racial segregation at the Refuge, see also Pickett, *House of Refuge*, 170; Mennel, *Thorns and Thistles*, 17–18; and Pisciotta, "Theory and Practice," 46. On the motives behind the construction of the Refuge's dormitory for "colored" inmates, see Hart to Stephen Allen, December 17, 1834, Stephen Allen Papers, New-York Historical Society. (An edited version appears in SRJD, *Ninth Annual Report* [1834], 15–16.) The SRJD's *Eleventh Annual Report* (1836) refers to "the completion of a new building designed for, and now occupied by, the colored inmates of the Refuge" (7). On racism in the early reformatories and in the history of juvenile justice more generally, see Ward, *Black Child-Savers*.

14. On the relations between African Americans and Irish immigrants in the nineteenth century, see Noel Ignatiev, *How the Irish Became White* (New York: Routledge, 1995). On the racialization of crime, see Khalil Gibran Muhammad, *The Condemnation of Blackness: Race, Crime, and the Making of Modern Urban America* (Cambridge, MA: Harvard University Press, 2011).

15. On the doctrine of *parens patriae* at the Refuge, see Finestone, *Victims of Change*, 28; Hawes, *Children in Urban Society*, 41; Fox, "Juvenile Justice Reform," 1188–207; and Schlossman, *Love and the American Delinquent*, 8–17.

16. SRJD, *Rules and Regulations for the Government of the House of Refuge* (New York: Mahlon Day, 1825), 3. In 1827 parents protested that work on an assembly line was not teaching their sons a useful trade. In 1826 two girls reported that they had been the victims of "seduction" by a shoemaker with a contract at the House. Hawes, *Children in Urban Society*, 50. During the Depression that began in 1837, toward the end of Austin Reed's time in the Refuge, the managers were not able to attract any contractors, and the workshops were closed for most of a year. Mennel, *Thorns and Thistles*, 16.

17. On moral instruction as heresy, see Fox, "Juvenile Justice Reform," 1195.

18. SRJD, *Ninth Annual Report* (1834), 42. The schoolteacher's report from 1838 suggests an effort to integrate education in the Refuge: "I have watched with attention the improvement of the colored children, and carefully compared their progress with that of the *other children*; and I deem it my duty to say, that it is my opinion that where equal advantages are offered to each, equal improvement may be expected. Some of the colored children are among our best readers in school." SRJD, *Thirteenth Annual Report* (1838), 31. On the Lancastrian system of instruction at the Refuge, see Pisciotta, "Theory and Practice," 40–41. New York officials had tried the same methods at Newgate Prison, in Manhattan, and upstate at Auburn; see Schorb, *Reading Prisoners*. Lindley Murray's *English Reader* went through many editions, revisions, and pirated reprintings in the early nineteenth century. See, for example, Jeremiah Goodrich, *Murray's English Reader, or Pieces in Prose and Poetry, Selected from the Best Writers* (Albany, NY: S. Shaw, 1829). The reformer who donated *Robinson Crusoe* was Isaac Collins, a founding member of the society. Hawes, *Children in Urban Society*, 45.

19. Harriet Jacobs, *Incidents in the Life of a Slave Girl* (1861; facsimile edition, New York: Oxford University Press, 1988), 31; Joseph Curtis, quoted in Pickett, *House of Refuge*, 82–83. On the movement against flogging, see Myra C. Glenn, *Campaigns Against Corporal Punishment: Prisoners, Sailors, Women, and Children in Antebellum America* (Albany: SUNY Press, 1984), and Michael Meranze, "A Criminal Is Being Beaten: The Politics of Punishment and the History of the Body," in *Possible Pasts: Becoming Colonial in Early America*, ed. Robert Blair St. George (Ithaca, NY: Cornell University Press, 2000), 302–23.

20. Elijah Devoe, *The Refuge System, or Prison Discipline Applied to Juvenile Delinquents* (New York: John R. M'Gown, 1848), 11–12.

21. Ibid., 12.

22. William Grimes, *Life of William Grimes, the Runaway Slave* (New York, 1825); Frederick Douglass, *Narrative of the Life of Frederick Douglass, an American Slave* (Boston: Anti-Slavery Office, 1845); and Ann Carson, *The Memoirs of the Celebrated and Beautiful Mrs. Ann Carson*, 2nd ed. (Philadelphia, 1838). To reconstruct the lives of inmates in the House of Refuge, even Pickett's definitive study had to rely, for the most part, on the society's own account of its efforts, because "the Refuge files represent the institution as its officials wanted it represented."

23. On the SRJD's quarrel with Seward during Terry's administration, see Pickett, *House of Refuge*, 149–55.

24. Indenture agreement between Austin Reed and Abraham Haring, May 31, 1839, New York State Archives. My discussion of the contract is informed by Amy Dru Stanley, *From Bondage to Contract: Wage Labor, Marriage, and the Market in the Age of Slave Emancipation* (Cambridge, UK: Cambridge University Press, 1998), and Saidiya Hartman, *Scenes of Subjection: Terror, Slavery, and Self-Making in Nineteenth-Century America* (New York: Oxford University Press, 1997).

25. The play may be an adaptation of John Augustus Stone's *Metamora* (1829), a historical melodrama about the war between Puritan settlers and Wampanoags in colonial times, or it may be one of the many imitations and parodies that were produced to capitalize on the huge success of Stone's work. I am grateful to Joseph Roach, Marc Robinson, and Don Wilmeth for their consultation about this scene.

26. Details on Thomas King are drawn from his House of Refuge inmate case history and the superintendent's daily journal, both held in the New York State Archives.

27. Quitclaim deed signed by Austin Reed and Joseph A. Eastman, December 1, 1848, Monroe County Clerk's Office. Maria Reed and Austin's two brothers, Charles and Edward, retained their shares until July 7, 1858, when they sold them to Eastman. Maria Reed was apparently permitted to live there until her death in 1865.

28. Stephen Allen, a merchant and politician who helped to establish the state prison at Auburn, would go on to serve as president of the SRJD from 1832 until 1852; he brought along his administrative knowledge of contract labor and his commitment to the whip. See David Lewis, *From Newgate to Dannemora: The Rise of the Penitentiary in New York, 1796–1848* (Ithaca, NY: Cornell University Press, 1965), 81–83. Throughout this section of the Introduction, my account of Auburn draws from Lewis's research.

29. On the Philadelphia system, see Negley K. Teeters and John D. Shearer, *The*

Prison at Philadelphia, Cherry Hill: The Separate System of Prison Discipline, 1829–1913 (New York: Columbia University Press, 1957); David J. Rothman, *The Discovery of the Asylum: Social Order and Disorder in the New Republic* (Boston: Little, Brown, 1971); Michael Meranze, *Laboratories of Virtue: Punishment, Revolution, and Authority in Philadelphia, 1760–1835* (Chapel Hill: University of North Carolina Press, 1996); Norman Johnston, *Eastern State Penitentiary: Crucible of Good Intentions* (Philadelphia: Philadelphia Museum of Art for the Eastern State Penitentiary Historic Site, 1994); and Caleb Smith, *The Prison and the American Imagination* (New Haven, CT: Yale University Press, 2009). Reformers in New York also experimented with an extreme form of solitary confinement. On Christmas Day 1821 the staff moved eighteen inmates into isolation cells in Auburn's north wing. The men in the north wing were assigned no labor and were required to stand all day, alone. Entombed alive, they began to deteriorate. Some were diagnosed with consumption. Some lost the use of their limbs. One smashed his head against the walls and lost an eye. Another gouged away at his veins with a shard of tin. When the news got out, New York officials abandoned their experiment before the end of the year. They did not give up on their ambitions for the penitentiary, but they looked for alternatives to solitude. See Lewis, *Newgate to Dannemora*, 68–70.

30. See Rebecca M. McLennan, *The Crisis of Imprisonment: Protest, Politics, and the Making of the American Penal State, 1776–1941* (Cambridge, UK: Cambridge University Press, 2008).

31. Auburn Prison, Daily Punishment Reports, 1836–1846, New York State Archives.

32. Dorothea Dix, *Remarks on Prisons and Prison Discipline in the United States* (Boston: Munroe & Francis, 1845), 7, 15. The frequent use of the whip at Auburn was "the most controversial feature of the entire system," according to Lewis, *Newgate to Dannemora* (93).

33. John Maroney, *Narrative of the Imprisonment of John Maroney: in the Prisons of New-York and Auburn, from 1821 until 1831; or, Maroney's Meditations, While in the School of Wisdom* (Newburgh, NY: Charles U. Cushman, 1832); Levi S. Burr, *A Voice from Sing-Sing: Giving a General Description of the State Prison* (Albany, NY: 1833); James R. Brice, *Secrets of the Mount-Pleasant State Prison, Revealed and Exposed* (Albany, NY: 1839); Isaac E. Clark, *A Voice from the Prison* (Rochester, NY: A. Strong, 1859); Horace Lane, *Five Years in State's Prison* (New York: L. Pratt, 1835) and *The Question, What Did You Do to Get There? Answered: or, Five Years in State's Prison, Revised* (New York: 1836). On early inmate narratives from New York prisons, see Jennifer Graber, "Engaging the Trope of Redemptive Suffering: Inmate Voices in the Antebellum Prison Debates," *Pennsylvania History* 79, no. 2 (Spring 2012): 209–33; and Jodi Schorb, "Written by One Who Knows: Congregate Literacy in New York

Prisons," in *Reading Prisoners*. On Horace Lane's life and writings, see also Myra C. Glenn, "Troubled Manhood in the Early Republic: The Life and Autobiography of Sailor Horace Lane," *Journal of the Early Republic* 26, no. 1 (2006): 59–93.

34. On reform in New York in the 1840s, see Lewis, *Newgate to Dannemora*, especially 201–29. On the founding of the New York Prison Association, see M. J. Heale, "The Formative Years of the New York Prison Association, 1844–1862: A Case Study in Antebellum Reform," *New-York Historical Society Quarterly* 59, no. 3 (July 1975): 320–47; and Graber, *Furnace of Affliction*, 135–56. On the relations between secular and spiritualist currents in the reform movement, see John Lardas Modern, *Secularism in Antebellum America* (Chicago: University of Chicago Press, 2011), especially 239–78.

35. Reed may have known about Seward's role in the controversial trial of William Freeman, an ex-slave and former Auburn inmate who murdered a local family, apparently without motive, in 1846. Arguing for the defense, Seward claimed that the severe beatings that Freeman had received at Auburn had rendered him insane. See Andrew W. Arpey, *The William Freeman Murder Trial: Insanity, Politics, and Race* (Syracuse, NY: Syracuse University Press, 2004). At one point, according to the prison's ledger of punishments, Freeman had been whipped for the offense of "dancing Jim Crow"—a detail (not cited by Arpey) that reveals much about how popular culture and the racist fantasies of the minstrel stage had penetrated even the austere silence of the Auburn system.

36. Clinton Prison, Record Book of Prison Inspectors, 1848–1864, New York State Archives.

37. "Robert Reed *alias* Austin Reed" of Monroe County was discharged from Auburn Prison on December 14, 1867. Inspectors of State Prisons of the State of New York, *Twentieth Annual Report* (Albany: C. Van Benthuysen, 1868), 213.

Editor's Note on the Text

1. The first testing on the ink and paper was conducted by Marie-France Lemay, a special collections conservator in the Yale University Library system; further examinations were made by Cathleen A. Baker, conservation librarian at the University of Michigan and author of *From the Hand to the Machine. Nineteenth-Century American Paper and Mediums: Technologies, Materials, and Conservation* (Ann Arbor, MI: Legacy Press, 2012), the authoritative study of the topic. Comparisons to other nineteenth-century bound books were made with the help of Beinecke Rare Book Library curators Nancy Kuhl, Melissa Barton, and George Miles. For Herman Melville's ficitonalized account of his visit to Carson's Mill, see "The Paradise of Bachelors and the Tartarus of

Maids," in *Billy Budd and Other Stories* (New York: Penguin Classics, 1986). On Melville's complicated relationship to paper, see Jonathan Senchyne, "Our Paper Allegories: Intimacy, Publicity, and Material Textuality in Colonial and Antebellum American Literature," PhD diss., Cornell University, 2012.

2. An analysis of Reed's handwriting on the indenture agreement, the manuscript of the "Life and Adventures," and the letters to the superintendent was performed by Diane Ducharme, an archivist and paleographer at the Beinecke Rare Book Library. On the gendering of scripts in the nineteenth century, see Tamara Plakins Thornton, *Handwriting in America: A Cultural History* (New Haven, CT: Yale University Press, 1996), especially chap. 2.

3. Caleb Smith, "Harry Hawser's Fate: Eastern State Penitentiary and the Birth of Prison Literature," in *Buried Lives: Voices from the Early American Prison*, ed. Michele Tarter and Richard Bell (Athens: University of Georgia Press, 2011); Caleb Smith, "Harriet Jacobs Among the Militants: Transformations in Abolition's Public Sphere, 1859–61," *American Literature* 84, no. 4 (December 2012); A. D. Eddy, *"Black Jacob."*

4. Beinecke Rare Book and Manuscript Library, http://beinecke.library.yale .edu.

5. *The Bondwoman's Narrative*, attributed to Hannah Crafts (or Hannah Bond), is one of a very few book-length manuscripts, composed by an African American author before the Civil War but not published during her lifetime, that we might compare to Reed's. See Hannah Crafts, *The Bondwoman's Narrative*, ed. Henry Louis Gates, Jr. (New York: Grand Central, 2002). The original manuscript is held in the Beinecke Rare Book Library and makes for fascinating comparisons to Reed's "Life and Adventures."

The Life and the Adventures of a Haunted Convict

1. Austin Reed's father, Burrell Reed, died on February 4, 1828, so this line indicates that he may have written the first part of his memoir as early as 1846 or 1847. For more on Burrell Reed, see the Introduction, pp. xx–xxi.

2. Census records indicate that Austin Reed had two brothers, Edward and Charles Reed. Charles appears periodically in Rochester city directories throughout the middle of the nineteenth century, sometimes living with Maria Reed on Hunter Street, and he is listed as an inmate of the Monroe County Poor House in 1891. The name of Austin Reed's sister (or sisters) has not been discovered.

3. Herman Ladd (1770–1848), of a distinguished New England family, moved to Livingston County, New York, and built a house there in about 1806. His daughters Martha (b. 1801), Fanny (b. 1804), and Marie (b. 1809) were in their twenties and thirties in 1832–33, when Austin Reed was indentured. See

Warren Ladd, *The Ladd Family: A Genealogical and Biographical Memoir* (New Bedford, MA: Edmund Anthony, 1890). Herman's son Warren (b. 1790) had established a large household of his own nearby, and an 1840 census record lists two "free colored persons" living with the family, probably as indentured servants or laborers. On the system of indentured servitude in nineteenth-century New York, see the Introduction, p. xxxv.

4. Probably a reference to Dr. Frederick Fanning Backus (1794–1860), a Yale graduate (class of 1813) who established a medical practice in Rochester (then Rochesterville) in 1817. Backus, a Presbyterian and a reformer, would go on to serve in the New York State Senate, where he sought government support to establish an asylum for the intellectually disabled and the Western House of Refuge for juvenile delinquents, which opened in Rochester in 1849. See "Biographical Note of Frederick Fanning Backus, M.D.," *Documents of the Assembly of the State of New York*, 83rd session (1860), 4:176–80.

5. The last numbered chapter break in the manuscript.

6. *Hart* changed for consistency with Reed's more frequent spelling, *Heart*, in the subsequent pages. The reference is to Nathaniel Hart, superintendent of the New York House of Refuge when Reed arrived in 1833. A former school-teacher and a member of the Methodist Church, Hart had taken office on July 2, 1826, succeeding the first superintendent, Joseph Curtis (elected 1824) and would serve until 1838. Hart's system of juvenile reformation, which combined labor, education, and religious instruction, would govern life in the House of Refuge for many years beyond his own administration. Although Reed's narrative draws a sharp contrast between Hart and his successor, David Terry, Jr., historians have stressed the continuities between their administrations, including the frequent use of corporal punishment under both superintendents. In an 1869 account of Hart's tenure, the House of Refuge's acting chaplain, B. K. Peirce, wrote, "It is remarkable how few changes have been made in [the regulations] from that day to this." Peirce, *A Half Century with Juvenile Delinquents*, 125. The French authors Gustave de Beaumont and Alexis de Tocqueville, who visited the House of Refuge in June 1831, praised Hart in the highest terms: "If a model of a superintendent of a house of refuge were required, a better one, perhaps, it would be impossible to find." Beaumont and Tocqueville, *On the Penitentiary System in the United States*, trans. Francis Lieber (1833; reprint, Carbondale: Southern Illinois University Press, 1979), 148. Hart prepared his own history of the institution's early years in the form of a collection of speeches, reports, statutes, and sermons. See Nathaniel C. Hart, ed., *Documents Relative to the House of Refuge, Instituted by the Society for the Reformation of Juvenile Delinquents in the City of New York in 1824* (New York: Mahlon Day, 1832). For more on Hart, see also Pickett, *House of Refuge*.

7. A reference to Samuel S. Wood, who would go on to serve as superintendent

of the House of Refuge from 1844 to 1849. Wood later served as superintendent at the Western House of Refuge in Rochester.

8. House of Refuge records include no case file for "Jack Kimbell."

9. *The English Reader* was a textbook compiled by the English editor Lindley Murray and first published in 1799. Many English and American versions were published in the subsequent decades. See the Introduction, p. xxxiii.

10. House of Refuge records include no case file for "Mike Flinn."

11. Albert Williams was the schoolteacher at the House of Refuge in the mid-1830s.

12. House of Refuge records include no case file for "Joe Long." There is a file for Joseph Lang, inmate number 406, but he was indentured in 1828, five years before Reed arrived. Lang was originally from Canada and does not seem to fit Reed's description of Joe Long, an "English boy."

13. Probably a reference to Jacob Hays (1772–1850), the legendary high constable of New York City from 1802 to 1844. Hays is credited with developing modern forms of police record-keeping, cultivating networks of informers, and solving some notorious mysteries, and he became the subject of a nostalgic biography, "Old Hays—There Was a Cop!," *New York World-Telegram*, March 1–6, 1937. See Jonathan Nash, "Hays, Jacob," in *The Social History of Crime and Punishment in America: An Encyclopedia*, ed. Wilbur R. Miller (Los Angeles: Sage, 2012), 747–48.

14. Reed's description of Joe Long borrows heavily from the description of a character in the Irish author Jemima von Tautphoeus's *The Initials: A Novel* (London: Richard Bentley, 1850): "most interesting person you ever saw; brilliant dark eyes with long eye-lashes; magnificent teeth, beautiful mouth, refined manners, and ever so much more! Now, I think him a most effeminate looking, supercilious boy" (15).

15. Reed takes this passage, almost word for word, from Jemima von Tautphoeus's *The Initials*: "She who seemed to be the mother of the children, a tall gaunt person, had her head and chin bound up with a large pocket-handkerchief, and seemed to be suffering from toothache, which rather puzzled Hamilton, when he had discovered that she had apparently lost all her teeth, though by no means old, as appeared from her fresh coloured features and hair untinged with grey. The other two were very young and perfect personifications of German beauty—blue eyes, blooming cheeks, red lips, and a profusion of brown hair most classically braided and platted. That they were sisters scarcely admitted of a doubt, so remarkable was their resemblance to each other—a nearer inspection made it equally evident that one was much handsomer than the other. They were both tall and very slightly formed, and their dark cotton dresses were made and put on with an exactness that proved they were not indifferent to the advantages bestowed on them by Nature" (12–13).

16. By the 1830s, the American Temperance Society and other reform groups had begun to promote the cause of "Temperance ships," which, according to one observer, "have done wonders" for the cause. American Temperance Society, *Annual Report* (1835), 35.

17. See Revelation 10:1–2.

18. According to at least one nineteenth-century minister, the sailor's tale in Reed's memoir reproduces a parable commonly told to children: "There is a story familiar in the nursery, but it so exactly illustrates a Christian's confidence that the repetition of it may be perhaps permitted. There was a storm at sea. The lightning leaped, the thunder cracked and bellowed; the screaming of the tempest through the cordage was outscreamed by the terrified passengers, for the ship was given over for lost. But in the midst of the confusion and dismay, the pilot's son was observed to hold on by some casual stay with undisturbed self-possession; and when after all, the vessel righted, and all on board were saved, the child was asked how it was that he had not shared the general consternation. His answer stands recorded in the story, 'I had no cause to be afraid; my Father was at the helm.' This is almost a perfect picture of a Christian's confidence." Jane Octavia Brookfield, ed., *Sermons by the Late Rev. W. H. Brookfield* (London: Smith, Elder, & Co., 1875), 54.

19. House of Refuge records include a case file for a William McCullough from New York City, first admitted to the reformatory on October 22, 1836, when he was thirteen years old. After being indentured to a master in Rochester and returning to the Refuge in 1838, he escaped from the institution on September 7, 1839.

20. House of Refuge records include a case file for William Teeling, inmate number 2103, admitted to the reformatory on April 4, 1838, when he was thirteen years old. Teeling had lived with his mother and stepfather on Pearl Street in Albany, New York. He was bound out of the Refuge in 1840 but soon left his master.

21. The "Indian play" is probably John Augustus Stone's *Metamora: or, The Last of the Wampanoags* (1829) or one of the several imitations and parodies produced to capitalize on its popular success. Loosely based on the historical Metacomet (or King Philip), the melodrama is set during the wars between the Puritans and the Wampanoag tribe. Metamora's infant child is killed by the English, and he murders his own wife, Nahmeokee, so that she will not be captured and sold into slavery. Professors Joseph Roach, Marc Robinson, and Don Wilmeth read this passage from Reed's memoir and made the connection to Stone's play. For more on *Metamora*, see Scott C. Martin, "Interpreting *Metamora*: Nationalism, Theater, and Jacksonian Indian Policy," *Journal of the Early Republic* 19, no. 1 (Spring 1999): 73–101.

22. These opening phrases of this sentence appear to have been adapted from a description of the landscape of western New York in an anonymous story, "A

Queer Case," which appeared in *Harper's Magazine* in July 1856: "One fine spring morning—and how glorious are our spring mornings, bursting on the sober face of nature like the coquettish laugh of a beautiful woman, short but delicious—one fine spring morning he made a remarkable discovery in natural history; to wit, that the birds went in pairs" (212).

23. House of Refuge records include a case file for Squire Miller, inmate number 1757, from South Salem, New York. Miller was twelve years old when the police delivered him to the reformatory on May 25, 1836. A year later, on April 6, 1837, he was bound out as an apprentice to Benjamin Fuller, a farmer in South Salem. Reed calls Miller an "English boy," but the superintendent's note indicates that he was "of American parents."

24. Probably a reference to the Scottish physician John Brown's *Elementa Medicinae* (1780), a popular medical treatise that circulated widely in English translations.

25. Probably a reference to Peter McEvoy, inmate number 1686, who was admitted to the House of Refuge on January 20, 1836, when he was fourteen years old. Within a week of being confined to the reformatory, McEvoy was punished for attempting to escape. In 1837 he was bound out as an apprentice to a baker in Rockland County and, according to the superintendent's notes, eventually entered the printing trade.

26. Possibly a reference to William H. Teele of Troy, New York, who was admitted to the Refuge on June 15, 1831, when he was twelve years old. A "very trying" case, according to the superintendent's notes, Teele was bound out to a painter and upholsterer in New York City on April 1, 1833, a few weeks before Reed arrived.

27. Reed was released from Auburn State Prison in April 1853 and was at large until March 1854.

28. As he wrote his "Life and Adventures," Reed seems not to have known that his House of Refuge file had in fact survived the fire. His 1895 letter to the superintendent suggests that he had only recently learned that such records still existed. See Appendix B for transcriptions of these documents.

29. On this incident, see the Introduction, p. xxviii.

30. The manuscript uses two spellings, *Thom* and *Tom*, to refer to McGollin. There does not appear to be any existing case history for a boy by this name in the Refuge during the years 1833–39.

31. Joseph B. Roe, assistant superintendent at the House of Refuge in 1831. Roe was replaced by W. Sampson in 1832, the year before Reed was admitted to the Refuge.

32. House of Refuge records include a case file for William Burris of Albany, New York, inmate number 1701, admitted on February 17, 1836, when he was fifteen years old. He escaped from the reformatory in June 1838 and went to sea.

33. House of Refuge records include a case file for Thomas King of New York City, inmate number 1149, admitted to the Refuge on May 20, 1833, when he was sixteen years old. King died in custody a year later, on May 2, 1834. For more on this episode, see the Introduction, p. xxxix.

34. House of Refuge records include a file for Henry Strongman of Schenectady, New York, inmate number 1091, admitted in 1833, when he was thirteen years old. (Austin Reed arrived in the same year.) According to his case history, Strongman was born in England and emigrated (with his sister, Jane) first to Quebec and then to the United States. After working for brief periods as a laborer and apprentice in Albany and Schenectady, he was arrested for stealing a horse and sent to the House of Refuge. Officials described him as a "hard boy" and a "natural thief" who "frequently gets into difficulties in consequence of his ugly temper." "Henry has been locked up much of time," the superintendent recorded in 1837, "that we might not be obliged to punish him every day in some other way—for the mischief he would be constantly making." Strongman was finally indentured to a Cyrus Curtis for a three-year whaling voyage aboard the ship *Helvetia*, which sailed out from Hudson, New York, under Captain Shubael Cottle. According to Reed's memoir, Strongman eventually enlisted in the U.S. Navy under a false name and was put to death for a crime committed at sea.

35. The House of Refuge was destroyed by fire in May 1839. Newspapers reported that the inmates had burned it down. See the Introduction, p. xxxvii.

36. The line "All was still and silent as death" appears in Sir Walter Scott's popular romance *The Pirate* (1821).

37. Jack Sheppard was an eighteenth-century thief who became the hero of William Harrison Ainsworth's *Jack Sheppard: A Romance*, published serially in 1839–40. Dick Turpin was a legendary highwayman who was executed in York, England, in 1739. See James Sharpe, *Dick Turpin: The Myth of the English Highwayman* (London: Profile, 2004).

38. This is the first of Reed's two polemics against novels and novel reading. Their placement in the narrative may be significant: each appears during an episode that departs substantially from the history of Reed's life that can be reconstructed from other records. In other words, Reed may preach most vehemently against novels in the passages where his own narrative is most fictionalized.

39. House of Refuge records include a case file for Nicholas Miller, inmate number 1872, who was admitted in 1837, when he was about sixteen years old. After emigrating from France, Miller's family had settled in Hamburgh, New York. He was arrested for stealing three watches from a watchmaker's shop in Buffalo. According to the case file, Miller was bound out to work for a Mr. D. Van Dike, a farmer in New Jersey, in 1838.

40. Reed later identifies the captain as "Captain Smith," probably a reference to

Isaac P. Smith (1802–69), who operated a steamboat line on the Hudson. His boats included the *Orange* and the *Arrow*. See Frank Bertangue Green, *History of Rockland County* (New York: A. S. Barnes, 1886), 213.

41. House of Refuge records and Reed's 1895 letters indicate that Reed did not escape but was indentured to Abraham Haring in the nearby village of Ramapo. However, Reed's descriptions of Haverstraw, New York ("Harvest Straw"), are accurate enough to suggest that he spent some time in the port town, perhaps after he left his apprenticeship. On the American Hotel and an inn called "Johnson's Tavern," see Amasa Freeman, "Haverstraw," in *History of Rockland County, New York, with Biographical Sketches of Its Prominent Men*, ed. David Cole (New York: A. S. Barnes & Co., 1886), 170–200.

42. Probably a reference to Samuel G. Johnson (c. 1791–1850) of Haverstraw, a businessman and founder of a hotel called Johnson's Tavern.

43. The lines are adapted from the crime ballad "Jack Williams," about a thief who is betrayed by a "false woman" and escapes from London's Newgate Prison: "As the heavens proved kind to me / As you shall plainly see, / I broke the chains and scal'd the walls, / And gained my sweet liberty." Cited as reprinted in the popular anthology *Songs of the Sea* (Philadelphia: Fisher & Brother, 1851), 81–83.

44. See Daniel 4:33.

45. Perhaps a reference to John P. Smith, who served as a district attorney in Rockland County from 1820 to 1833.

46. *Annias and sophire* changed to *Ananias and Sophira*. The biblical Ananias and Sophira are struck dead by God, apparently as punishment for lying to the apostles about the money they received from the sale of their lands. Acts 5: 1–11.

47. Reed inserts a version of "The Morning Dream" (1788) by the British poet and abolitionist William Cowper. Although many verses in Reed's text match Cowper's published text, there are also substantial changes in the phrasing and the ordering of lines. It is possible that Reed wrote his version from memory, rather than copying it from a printed text. Interestingly, Reed omits the concluding lines of Cowper's poem, which imagine "BRITANNIA" (Great Britain) resolving to abolish the slave trade and the practice of slavery in its colonies. Reed may have edited the poem for an American audience (or memorized a version that had been edited by someone else). Cowper's poems, which appeared in some editions of *The English Reader*, were well known to American antislavery writers in the nineteenth century. The term *loophole of retreat*, taken from another Cowper poem, "The Task," figures prominently in Harriet Jacobs's *Incidents in the Life of a Slave Girl*.

48. Austin Reed's family was connected to the African Methodist Episcopal Church in Rochester, founded by Austin Steward. See the Editor's Introduction, p. xxi.

49. William (or Willie) Riley is the outlaw-hero of a popular crime ballad.

50. What follows is a temperance tale, drawing from the biblical story of Legion. If Reed is referring to a literal "manuscript," he may have in mind a temperance tract such as the Reverend Stephen Higginson Tyng's *My Name Is Legion* (New York: National Temperance Society and Publication House, 1873).

51. Johann David Wyss's novel *The Swiss Family Robinson* was first published in German in 1812. Using the story of a shipwrecked family to deliver moral and practical lessons, the book shows the influence of another of Reed's favorite books, Daniel Defoe's *Robinson Crusoe*.

52. See Proverbs 2:16–19.

53. See Matthew 8:20.

54. The lines are adapted from "The Watchman," a ballad by the Irish poet Thomas Moore (1779–1852): "Good night, good night, my dearest / How fast those moments fly! / 'Tis time to part, thou hearest / That hateful watchman's cry."

55. The second of Reed's polemics against novels and novel-reading. For the first, see p. 65.

56. Perhaps a reference to Susan Mutimer, the wife of Jarvis Mutimer, of Rochester, who died of "intoxication and exposure to cold" in late November 1841. A local newspaper reported that Mutimer was "found dead . . . in a field . . . with a bottle of whiskey nearly emptied of its contents, lying by her side" (*Rochester Daily Democrat*, December 9, 1841, p. 2). Reed uses both *Mrs.* and *Miss* to refer to the woman he calls Ann (or Annie) Mutermer.

57. The Eagle Hotel had a reputation as "Rochester's leading hotel for a full three decades" in the mid-nineteenth century. Blake McKelvey, "From Stagecoach Taverns to Airline Motels," *Rochester History* 31, no. 4 (October 1969): 8.

58. Probably a reference to the Rochester attorney Orlando Hastings (1789–1861). Born in Litchfield, Connecticut, Hastings grew up in Clinton, New York, studied law under Judge Ebeneezer Griffin in Oneida, and moved his practice to Rochester in 1830. Hastings was one of the first attorneys in the city, and over the next thirty years he became one of the most prominent in the state. He was active in the Presbyterian Church and in reform. When New York expanded its juvenile detention system, Hastings joined the board of managers of the Western House of Refuge (opened 1849), serving on the discharging committee and, for the last ten years of his life, teaching Sabbath school. He probably would have known the superintendent, Samuel S. Wood. Hastings had a reputation as a political and religious conservative but also as a sympathetic attorney who often took cases on behalf of poor clients. According to the sermon preached at his funeral in 1861, "Thousands, who had nothing to pay, have gone to him." The minister paused to note that Hastings was a "chief friend" to Rochester's "coloured people." Frank Ellinwood, *A*

Discourse Delivered at the Funeral of Orlando Hastings (Rochester, NY: Printed for the Family, 1861), 11. Hastings is also mentioned in William Farley Peck, *History of Rochester and Monroe County, New York* (New York: Pioneer Press, 1908), which describes him as an "albino" (355).

59. According to House of Refuge and prison records, Austin Reed was born in 1833 and was about seventeen years old in 1840, when he was sent to Auburn State Prison for the first time. If he was actually thirteen (born in 1827), as he claims in the memoir, then he would have been just an infant at the time of Burrell Reed's death in 1828.

60. Reed probably adapts the phrase *bound down in iron strong* from the crime ballad "Jack Williams," which is quoted earlier in the memoir. See note 43.

61. Probably a reference to the Rochester insurance agent Henry A. Brewster, whose family was involved in charity and education reforms.

62. The lines are from the popular hymn "O tell me no more of this world's vain store," attributed to John Gambold and published in the English *Moravian Hymn Book* in 1742.

63. Here Reed comes to the end of the last page in his bound notebook. The memoir continues on hand-sewn gatherings of loose folio paper. Pasted onto the back cover of the notebook is an excerpt from the Book of Lamentations. See p. lv.

64. Montezuma, Cayuga County, New York, a river and canal port near Auburn.

65. Robert Cook served as principal keeper, or warden, at Auburn State Prison from 1840 to 1843.

66. John D. Cray, who served as the assistant keeper at Auburn under the legendary Elam Lynds in the 1820s, is a mysterious figure, rumored to have served and deserted the British side during the War of 1812. Cray has been credited both with inventing some of the distinctively harsh features of the Auburn "system" and with introducing education and other reform measures. See Lewis, *From Newgate to Dannemora*, 84–87. Cray left Auburn in 1823, reportedly for Detroit, so it is not clear how Reed could have become "acquainted" with him. What follows is a description of Copper John, the statue of a soldier that was mounted over Auburn's gates.

67. The lines are adapted from Psalm 115.

68. Reed's description of the condition of the workshops matches the one published by Auburn's board of inspectors in 1843: "The main building, including the north and south wings, were erected upwards of twenty-five years since, and they now are in need of extensive repairs. The roofs are in a leaky and bad condition, the hall floor requires relaying, and the cabinet shop, spin shop, comb shop, machine shop, and silk shop are all worn out and leaky. They were but temporary erections in their day, and are at best contracted and inconvenient. They are now, notwithstanding some temporary repairs, in no respect fit for permanent use, and cannot be repaired so as to be fit for the

present increased business of the prison." Board of Inspectors of the Auburn State Prison, *Annual Report* (1843), 4–5.

69. Probably a reference to James E. Tyler, an officer at Auburn in the 1840s. It is unclear how Tyler might have become "acquainted" with Reed's father.

70. House of Refuge records include case files for some names close to the ones Reed lists here: Alanson Mills ("a bad boy, inclined to steal," admitted June 23, 1832); John Williams (July 13, 1832); James H. Williams ("color'd," June 6, 1837); and James Edwards ("*colord*," June 24, 1837).

71. Daniel Hewson was an Auburn, New York, businessman and one half of the furniture company Parsons and Hewson, contractors who ran the cabinet shop at Auburn State Prison in the 1840s. He was also a deacon in the Presbyterian Church, a director of the Auburn City Bank, and mayor of Auburn in 1849.

72. Adapted from Romans 10:15.

73. It seems likely that "Iverson" (rather than Thomas) was the "fictitious name" of Reed's fellow inmate. Halsey Thomas was twice arrested for theft as a juvenile in Rochester and sent to the House of Refuge on October 31, 1836 (inmate number 1850, fourteen years old). The superintendent's notes describe him as "a boy of very little life or sprightliness of appearance." In April 1838 Thomas was bound out as a cooper's apprentice, but he continued his career as a thief. Reed seems to have known him from Rochester, and their paths crossed on a few occasions. In December 1842, Halsey Thomas and Austin Reed were among the several defendants to be indicted by the same grand jury (for separate offenses) in Monroe County; their names are listed together in a local newspaper article ("Monroe General Sessions," *Rochester Daily Democrat*, December 14, 1842). Thomas arrived at Auburn on December 19, 1842. He died less than two years later. According to the prison physician's report, "Thomas was a man of very vicious habits. Grossly intemperate, and laboring under lues veneria [syphilis] at the time of his coming to prison. Died July 11th, 1844." The official cause of death was "chronic rheumatism and pneumonia." Board of Inspectors of the Auburn State Prison, *Annual Report* (1845), 81, 83.

74. Reed includes this poem in his 1895 letter to the House of Refuge as "a few verses I composed myself." See Appendix B. Some of the lines bear strong similarities to "Moan of the Prisoner," attributed to Oliver Johnson and printed in *The Prisoner's Friend*, December 30, 1846, 205. Here are the first two stanzas of "The Moan of the Prisoner": "The convict immured in the prison's cold cell, / Away from the friends who have loved him so well, / In silence sits musing on the scenes of the past, / His heart full of grief, his tears falling fast. How piercing his groans! how plaintive his moans— / 'I'm only a Prisoner whom nobody owns.' O sad was the hour when he turned from the way, / And yielded his heart to the tempter a prey! / The waves of despair how

wildly they roll, / As the darkness of night settles down on his soul! / How piercing his groans! how plaintive his moans— / 'I'm only a Prisoner, whom nobody owns.'"

75. Halsey Thomas died in Auburn State Prison on July 11, 1844. See note 73, above.

76. Spencer Parsons was a businessman and one half of the furniture company Parsons and Hewson, contractors who ran the cabinet shop at Auburn State Prison in the 1840s. Parsons also worked with Hewson and other investors to establish a local bank. His son, Jesse Ives Parsons, continued in the family business as a contractor at Auburn in the 1850s.

77. On Daniel Hewson, see note 71, above.

78. See Genesis 4:13.

79. Two other convicts, Joseph Quincy and Luman Palmer, were discharged with Austin Reed in 1842. *Report of the Agent to the Board of Inspectors of the State Prison at Auburn* (1842), 42.

80. Austin Reed received three dollars to cover the cost of his travel from Auburn to Rochester. *Report of the Agent to the Board of Inspectors of the State Prison at Auburn* (1842), 42.

81. *Mastabation* changed to *Masturbation*. In the passages that follow, Reed adopts the official view that masturbation among prison inmates leads to high rates of disease and insanity. See, for example, the Physician's Report for 1840, describing a "strongly marked" case of insanity at Auburn that, in the opinion of Dr. Erastus Humphreys, had been "produced by masturbation." State Prison at Auburn, *Annual Report* (1841), 16. Two years earlier, the physician at Philadelphia's Eastern State Penitentiary reported that "the cases of mental disorder occurring in this Penitentiary are, with a few exceptions, of short duration, curable, and caused by masturbation, and are mostly among the colored prisoners." Massachusetts Prison Discipline Society, *Fourteenth Annual Report* (1839), 349.

82. Probably a reference to Dr. Lansing(h) Briggs, the head physician and surgeon at Auburn State Prison in 1839–40.

83. The preceding lines are adapted from a hymn, "Death Has Been Here," which appeared in anthologies such as *The Chapel Hymn Book* (Boston: Simpkins, 1842) 229–30. A version was also quoted in John Eliot Howard, *The Island of Saints, or Ireland in 1855* (London: Seeley's, 1855), 132.

84. Reed appears to have adapted this stanza from a popular temperance song, "I Saw a Little Girl," where the "demon" is a "drunkard": "I saw an unfrequented mound, / Where weeds and brambles wave:— / On which had fallen no mourning tear,— / It was a drunkard's grave." Lidya Howard Sigourney, *Water-Drops* (New York: Robert Carter, 1848), 129.

85. The crimes in Reed's dream bear some similarities to the famous murders committed by William Freeman in Auburn, New York, in 1846. Freeman,

who had been an inmate at Auburn with Austin Reed, was defended at trial by William H. Seward, who argued that abusive treatment in the prison had rendered Freeman insane. See note 35 to the Editor's Introduction, above.

86. A reference to the biblical figure whose story is told in the Book of Esther.

87. Here Reed seems to confuse two different escapes from the Refuge—one with Mike Flinn and Joe Long, the other with Nicholas Miller and Henry Strongman.

88. See Luke 15:16: "And he would fain have filled his belly with the husks that the swine did eat." Here Mike Flinn draws from the Bible to tell the parable of the boy who strays from home but eventually returns, chastened and reformed. This "story of a bad boy and a good father," according to one nineteenth-century anthology of sermons for children, "has been told thousands of times, and has done a great deal of good; for the boy represents sinful men, and the father represents our loving Father in heaven." William Armstrong, *Five-Minute Sermons to Children* (New York: Hunt & Eaton, 1887), 119.

89. Perhaps a reference to a relative of Mark H. Sibley (1796–1852), a prominent Canandaigua attorney, judge, and Whig politician who served in the federal Congress in 1837–39.

90. On the establishment of prison libraries, reading instruction, and new regulations for punishment at Auburn, see the Introduction, p. lii.

91. Auburn's (incomplete) ledger of punishments indicates that Austin Reed was punished for "insolence" on at least two occasions, August 28, 1843, and January 27, 1844.

92. From Auburn's ledger of punishments, December 31, 1845: "Eli Gallup punished Austin Reed six blows with the cat for insulting the relief Keeper by being saucy &c."

93. According to the ledger of punishments, Reed was punished in the showering bath on June 14, 1843, "for showing temper in presence of the Keeper."

94. The officers who punished Reed in the 1840s, according to Auburn's daily punishment report, included J. Newbury, C. L. Wheaton, and Eli Gallup.

95. According to Auburn's ledger of punishments, Reed was punished on at least two occasions for talking: February 12, 1844, and September 16, 1844.

96. Perhaps a reference to Levi Lewis, who served as warden at Auburn from 1834 to 1836 (while Reed was still in the House of Refuge) and continued to play a role in New York prisons through the 1850s, serving as principal agent at Auburn in 1857 and 1858.

97. Probably a reference to Colonel John Richardson (1780–1849), a War of 1812 veteran who became a prominent furniture-maker in the town of Auburn in the first half of the nineteenth century. An early history of the region identifies Richardson as "a close friend and admirer of Secretary [William H.] Seward." Joel H. Monroe, *Historical Records of a Hundred and Twenty Years, Auburn, New York* (Geneva, NY: W. F. Humphrey, 1913), 51–53.

98. Compare to Reed's description of Christ in "A Sequel to the Dream," page 188: "Casting his eyes down towards his feet, me thought he showed me the marks where the murderers drove the rough spikes through his feet."

99. Probably a reference to Horace T. Cook (1822–97), a prominent Auburn citizen who studied law with William H. Seward before being elected city treasurer, an office he held for many decades. Cook was also active in the Presbyterian Church, a founder of the Cayuga County Savings Bank and the Fort Hill Cemetery Association, and a reformer and philanthropist. See Monroe, *Historical Records*, 178–80.

Appendix B: Austin Reed House of Refuge Case File, Indenture Agreement, and Letters from Austin Reed to the Superintendent

1. Reed includes a version of the same poem in his "Life and Adventures." See pp. 163–64. On its similarities to another poem, "The Moan of the Prisoner" (1846) by Oliver Johnson, see note 74.

ABOUT THE AUTHOR

Austin Reed was born in Rochester, New York, in 1823. He wrote this memoir around 1858–59, during his incarceration in Auburn State Prison. The date of his death is unknown.

ABOUT THE EDITOR

Caleb Smith is a professor of English at Yale University and the author of *The Prison and the American Imagination* and *The Oracle and the Curse*.

ABOUT THE FOREWORD AUTHORS

David W. Blight is Class of 1954 Professor of American History and director of the Gilder Lehrman Center for the Study of Slavery, Resistance, and Abolition at Yale University. He is the author of *Race and Reunion: The Civil War in American Memory*, *A Slave No More: Two Men Who Escaped to Freedom, Including Their Own Narratives of Emancipation*, and a biography of Frederick Douglass.

Robert B. Stepto is a professor of African American studies, American studies, and English at Yale University. His publications include *From Behind the Veil: A Study of Afro-American Narrative*, *Blue as the Lake: A Personal Geography*, and *A Home Elsewhere: Reading African-American Classics in the Age of Obama*.

ABOUT THE TYPE

The text of this book was set in Janson, a typeface designed about 1690 by Nicholas Kis (1650–1702), a Hungarian living in Amsterdam, and for many years mistakenly attributed to the Dutch printer Anton Janson. In 1919, the matrices became the property of the Stempel Foundry in Frankfurt. It is an old-style book face of excellent clarity and sharpness. Janson serifs are concave and splayed; the contrast between thick and thin strokes is marked.